NAVIGATING
HUMAN SERVICE
ORGANIZATIONS

Third Edition

Also available from Lyceum Books, Inc.

Advisory Editor: Thomas M. Meenaghan, *New York University*

An Experiential Approach to Group Work
by Rich Furman, Diana Rowan, and Kim Bender

Social Work Practice with Latinos: Key Issues and Emerging Themes
edited by Rich Furman and Nalini Negi

Practical Tips for Publishing Scholarly Articles: Writing and Publishing in the Helping Professions, Second Edition
by Rich Furman and Julie T. Kinn

Strategic Leadership and Management in Nonprofit Organizations: Theory and Practice
by Martha Golensky

Pracademics and Community Change: A True Story of Nonprofit Development and Social Entrepreneurship During Welfare Reform
by Odell Cleveland and Robert Wineburg

Caught in the Storm: Navigating Policy and Practice in the Welfare Reform Era
by Miguel Ferguson, Heather Neuroth-Gatlin, and Stacey Borasky

Improving Performance in Service Organizations: How to Implement a Lean Transformation
by Joyce A. Miller, Tania Bogatova, and Bruce Carnohan

Social Work with HIV and AIDS: A Case-Based Guide
by Diana Rowan and Contributors

Advocacy Practice for Social Justice, Second Edition
by Richard Hoefer

Case Management: An Introduction to Concepts and Skills, Third Edition
by Arthur J. Frankel and Sheldon R. Gelman

Citizenship Social Work with Older People
by Malcolm Payne

Rich Furman
University of Washington Tacoma
&
Margaret Gibelman

NAVIGATING HUMAN SERVICE ORGANIZATIONS

Third Edition

LYCEUM
BOOKS, INC.
Chicago, Illinois

© Lyceum Books, Inc., 2013

Published by

LYCEUM BOOKS, INC.
5758 S. Blackstone Ave.
Chicago, Illinois 60637
773+643-1903 (Fax)
773+643-1902 (Phone)
lyceum@lyceumbooks.com
http://www.lyceumbooks.com

7 6   16 17

ISBN 978-1-935871-24-8

Cover image: © Mauro Bighin | Dreamstime.com | Title: Wind Rose

Library of Congress Cataloging-in-Publication Data

Furman, Rich.
   Navigating human service organizations / Rich Furman & Margaret Gibelman.—3rd ed.
      p. cm.
   Margaret Gibelman appeared as first named author in the previous edition.
   ISBN 978-1-935871-24-8 (pbk. : alk. paper)
  1. Human services. 2. Organizational behavior. 3. Social work administration.
I. Gibelman, Margaret. II. Title.
   HV40.G53   2013
   361.0068—dc23
                                                                              2012020224

Contents

Preface to the Third Edition

Since the publication of the second edition of this book, the context of human services has changed greatly. The country has gone through the worst economic downturn since the Great Depression. Even today, it is unclear how long it will take to recover. At the beginning of the recession, unemployment was around 3 percent; it now hovers just below 10 percent, and this is not expected to improve dramatically for the foreseeable future. This is a huge, too rarely discussed transformation of American life—millions of people who were once able to provide support for their families are no longer able to do so. This recession has also been referred to as the "man-session"; employed men, specifically poor men of color in both urban and rural areas, were disproportionally affected. As employers struggle to survive, they are often compelled to cut health insurance and other benefits. Pensions and other employer contributions to retirement funds are declining. Workplace wellness programs in some of the most challenging and dangerous jobs are being slashed. Aspects of the social welfare system that in the past have been covered by employers are now less supported in struggling industries.

It is clear that with such a huge increase in unemployment, the stresses and strains on human service organizations will be increasing. This, of course, comes at a time of drastically shrinking local and state budgets. In the state of Washington, for example, state agencies have taken nearly 30 percent in cuts in funding over the last several years. At the beginning of 2011, the governor was compelled to reduce many state agency budgets by an additional 20 percent, cuts that are unprecedented. The pain is being felt throughout state health, child welfare, and other social service programs. For instance, drastic cuts have been proposed in English as second languange programs for resident immigrants. This is not good news for the rapidly growing Latino population, which needs increased English proficiency during times of increased competition for employment and social services.

What is clear is that these new fiscal realities will have a significant impact on the lives of human service agencies, their clients, and their workers. Increased caseload, declining resources, and more-complex social problems mean that human service organizations are becoming increasingly difficult to navigate; new and experienced practitioners alike must find new ways of surviving and thriving in their roles as professional helpers. Managers are being called upon to find ways to help their workers handle increased stress in their own lives and in their clients' lives. Human service workers are increasingly finding themselves going through periods of unemployment or finding only part-time positions, which make it difficult to provide for their families. As caseworkers confront clients whose lives are becoming increasingly complex, we all find ourselves grasping for how to respond to the challenges of an ever-globalizing, post-recession America.

This new edition seeks to take into account these and other social and economic realities. But the task in any revision is to make needed changes without compromising what has worked for readers in the past. Toward this aim, I have contacted teachers and practitioners who have used this book previously and sought their feedback on how to improve the book. The changes, while not overarching, correct some of the weaknesses that readers have identified. For example, some instructors have asked for more discussion of classic and modern theories of organizational behavior. I have added content in this area, but in a manner that does not change what many readers have stated is a key strength of the book—a practical, hands-on guide that can be used in the classroom and by more seasoned practitioners no longer in school. Where theory has been added, I have made it as practice-oriented and user friendly as possible. Indeed, there is nothing more practical than a good theory when its utility is demonstrated. Readers will also find examples and materials that address the new realities of the key transformations of our time: a world economic recession, globalization, and uncertainty about the economic and global position of the United States.

Preface

Surviving and thriving in the workplace is a universal concern that transcends professions, industries, and sectors. The need to adjust to the culture and demands of the workplace confronts most new human services workers. Even for the more experienced practitioner, the organizational environment poses challenges that are often perceived as frustrating and beyond the realm of strategic intervention. This book seeks to provide information and resources for social workers and social work students to feel more empowered in their agencies. We seek to help students and workers overcome the sometimes overwhelming complexities of working in an agency by exploring many of the realities of organizational life. We hope to show that social workers are both affected by and have an impact on the organizations in which they work. At times, some of the organizational power structures of social service agencies feel very top down; that is, much of what is required is dictated to social workers. This book attempts to address such realities in a straightforward manner, while exploring the responsibilities of social workers toward organizational, community, and social change.

This book is intended as a text for foundation practice courses at the BSW and MSW levels and focuses on issues related to the organizational context of practice. Since understanding and becoming competent in navigating organizations is at the heart of social work practice, this book can be used as a primary or supplemental text in many courses. For instance, we know of colleagues who use this book as the primary text in BSW foundation practice and in MSW advanced concentration organizational practice courses. The book has been utilized in social work, human service, and even in counseling programs. Successful adjustment to and work within human service organizations requires knowledge about how they operate and what role the human services worker can play within them. New professionals entering practice are likely to face a host of organizational issues that bear directly on practice but for which they have had little concrete preparation. Even more seasoned social workers who take on new roles or begin employment in a different agency may find the adjustment to a new organizational setting challenging.

Themes related to values and ethics, social justice, human behavior and the social environment, and social welfare policy and services are woven throughout this book, as each influences the nature of practice within the organizational setting. Specific chapters of this book may also be used as supplemental readings for courses that specifically focus on these interrelated curriculum areas. Public and private human service managers and human service practitioners will also find it useful in conducting in-service training and orienting new staff to the agency setting. This book attempts to help both new and more experienced workers develop the skills and strategies needed to thrive in agencies. As such, it may be useful in field placement seminars and to field liaisons and agency supervisors in their work with students and supervisors.

The Workplace

One might think that human service organizations, whose mission it is to assist in the growth and development of individuals, families, and communities, would provide a people-oriented workplace, different from that of business. This is not necessarily the case, because human service organizations are businesses too. Common sense might also hold that the people skills possessed by social workers, who constitute the majority of the workforce of human service organizations, would positively influence the work environment. Furthermore, one might assume that these people skills could be applied to address workplace issues.

The fact is that human services workers are seldom fully prepared for the realities of the workplace. This is especially true in the second decade of the twenty-first century, given the enormous challenges that the current recession and global economic crisis have compelled human service programs to face. They are often disappointed and disillusioned. No empirical data exist to support an argument that human services workers encounter more disillusionment within their work settings than do professionals in other disciplines. However, three differences are readily apparent. First, human service organizations are committed to furthering, in some specific way, human well-being. The missions of these organizations are anchored in a set of principles and values that have as their core the promotion of the public welfare. Second, social work is a profession that has traditionally been organizationally based. The values and ethics of the profession are expected to be mirrored in and consistent with those of the organization. Finally, the professional staff of human service organizations—predominantly social workers—are held to a *Code of Ethics* (National Association of Social Workers, 1999) that acknowledges the organizational base of practice and sets forth obligations to the employing organization.

Learning about Organizations

There is substantial literature about organizational processes, most of which has been prepared for use in the political, social, and behavioral sciences. Thus, the focus is frequently on the theoretical understanding of organizational dynamics, often without attention to the practical application of theory to everyday organizational life. There are also a substantial number of works on management practice, to which social work has made a significant contribution (see, for example, Edwards, Yankey, & Altpeter, 1998; Gummer, 1990; Hasenfeld, 1992; Lawler & Bilson, 2010; Netting, Kettner, & McMurtry, 2008; Patti, 2000; Slavin, 1985). In general, this literature has focused on the knowledge and skills necessary for management, or macro practice. Such works tend to view organizations through the lens of management rather than from the practitioner's perspective. This book, however, is also focused on the organizational issues and concerns of the professionals working within the organizations, not just of those at the top.

The organization can and should be approached as a dynamic in the equation of effective practice that needs to be analyzed and understood. How social workers practice, what they do, the resources available to them, the technologies they use, and the barriers they face in providing quality services are all influenced by the organizational setting in which they work. To practice effectively, social workers must understand their organizations. They must be able to intervene through systematic problem solving to address impediments to the delivery of services and to enhance the quality of the services that are provided.

This book is oriented to the practical aspects of work within human service organizations. It seeks to inform new practitioners about the dynamics of the agencies in which they work. It also seeks to help them intervene within the organization itself to bring about change. The basic premise—and challenge—is that social workers can and must influence their work environments in positive ways. The issues discussed range from the larger sociopolitical context in which organizations function to the day-to-day annoyances that characterize every workplace. Issues both large and small have an impact on the climate and culture of all organizations and, ultimately, on the ability of human services workers to carry out their work effectively.

Case Study Approach

Case studies are used throughout the book to highlight how the organizational setting influences practice in concrete ways. Case studies bring material to life; they illustrate the principles and facts under discussion, add vitality to the presentation, and help students and practitioners to identify with the material. The case materials lend real voices to the types of situations and problems encountered on a day-to-day basis.

The case studies are drawn from a number of sources. Daily newspapers such as the *Washington Post* and *New York Times,* for example, offer columns about workplace issues; some of the themes addressed in these columns have been used to illustrate situations that confront employees across a variety of settings. Margaret Gibelman also drew from her own experience as a manager, board member, and practitioner to construct the case studies. Colleagues and doctoral students, primarily but not exclusively at Yeshiva University,

Wurzweiler School of Social Work, were generous in providing materials and case situations from their work settings. This assistance also resulted in a disproportionate use of case illustrations from the Northeast and, especially, metropolitan New York. The adage "Write what you know about" applies here. However, the social services field has been subject to the same nationalization and globalization as have other spheres of our economic and social environment. Agencies in the northeastern corridor often belong to the same alliances or national networks as agencies in other parts of the United States. The social problems addressed by human service agencies also cut across geography and regional distinctions.

Although the materials provided by individuals and obtained through public sources form the basis for the case studies, editorial license was exercised throughout to ensure confidentiality and adapt the cases to exemplify typical situations that arise in the organizational setting of social work practice. Thus, none of the cases illustrates, per se, real occurrences in any one agency. Similarly, samples of agency policies and procedures are drawn from actual documents but have been modified to ensure their broadest applicability. On the other hand, when mission statements are provided and attributed to a specific agency by name, no editorial changes have been made.

The chapters are sequenced in an inductive manner. The reader is first introduced to human service organizations as the historic and current base of most social work practice. The different types of human service organizations and their distinguishing characteristics are highlighted in these early chapters, along with the roles and responsibilities of key players within and external to the organizations. Once the reader has become more familiar with the purposes and operating modes of human service organizations as the setting in which social work practice is carried out, attention then turns to the less tangible environments of organizations and how the formal and informal climate affects attitudes and work.

The *Code of Ethics* (National Association of Social Workers, 1999) is used throughout this book as a frame of reference. The *Code of Ethics* both acknowledges that social work is an organizationally based profession and, in its specific provisions, highlights some of the potential ethical conflicts that can arise between professional practice and the organizational context in which such practice is carried out. Some of the case vignettes point to the ethical dilemmas that can emerge when the interests or ways of doing business of the organization are in opposition to the dictates of good practice and the best interests of the clients served.

Building on this foundation about organizations and how they work, social work principles and practices are used as a base to guide professional interventions oriented to the agency itself. As an open system, the organization is typically receptive to the input of key players in its environment. Such key players go beyond funding bodies and consumer groups. Social workers, too, are key players, as it is their work that promotes or inhibits achievement of the organization's goals and objectives.

To facilitate the learning process from a pedagogical framework, each chapter concludes with a summary of key points covered, followed by discussion questions. Due to the complexity of organizations and how they work, this book does not purport to provide an in-depth exploration of organizational dynamics. A list of additional readings on each subject covered is provided, and readers are encouraged to use these resources in areas of individual interest.

Acknowledgments

A special thank you goes to the students of Wurzweiler School of Social Work for their contributions of ideas and their questioning of why things are as they are. Writing is sometimes characterized as a lonely endeavor. The ongoing exchange with students and academic and agency colleagues made the preparation of this book feel like an open exchange.

My appreciation is also extended to Professor Sheldon R. Gelman, dean of the Wurzweiler School of Social Work, who read every word of the first draft of this book and offered concrete suggestions as well as gentle prodding to get it done and out. A thank you also goes to Professor Tom Meenaghan, who also read an earlier version of the book and offered a different perspective about how it might be made more useful to both social work students and to new practitioners. Finally, this book is dedicated to my father, William Gibelman, who throughout his eighty-eight-year life consistently valued learning, thinking, and writing. He taught me these values, which have played a significant role in defining who I am and what I do.

Margaret Gibelman

First and foremost, I would like to thank Professor Gibelman, who served as the director of the doctoral program at Wurzweiler while I was a doctoral student. A prolific scholar, she was a demanding teacher who settled for nothing but the best. I hope my work on this revision is worthy of her fine example. The profession of social work education has been diminished by her loss. I would also like to thank Tom Meenaghan, whose counsel and advice about the previous revision were invaluable. Special thanks go to David Follmer of Lyceum Books, who has believed in me more, perhaps, that I have myself. I want to thank all the colleagues who have shared with me their feedback about the strengths and weaknesses of the second edition. I have listened to your feedback carefully and have integrated it into this third edition. I want to thank my students at the University of Washington Tacoma, who have been a pleasure and an honor to teach.

Rich Furman

References

Edwards, R. L., Yankey, J. A., & Altpeter, M. A. (1998). *Skills for effective management of nonprofit organizations.* Washington, DC: NASW Press.

Gummer, B. (1990). *The politics of social administration: Managing organizational politics in social agencies.* Englewood Cliffs, NJ: Prentice Hall.

Hasenfeld, Y. (Ed.). (1992). *Human services as complex organizations.* Newbury Park, CA: Sage Publications.

Lawler, J., & Bilson, A. (2010). *Social work management and leadership: Managing complexity with creativity.* Oxford, UK: Routledge.

National Association of Social Workers. (1999). *Code of ethics.* Washington, DC: Author.

Netting, F. E., Kettner, P. M., & McMurtry, S. L. (2008). *Social work macro practice* (4th ed.). New York: Pearson.

Patti, R. J. (Ed.). (2000). *The handbook of social welfare management.* Thousand Oaks, CA: Sage Publications.

Slavin, S. (Ed.). (1985). *Social administration: The management of the social services.* New York: Haworth Press.

Chapter 1

Getting to Know the Human Service Organization

The vast majority of social workers are employed in organizations. The organizational base of social work practice is rooted in the history of the profession. Social policies, in the form of legislation at the federal, state, and local levels, funding patterns, and societal sanctions help explain why so much of the practice of social work is carried out through organizations.

Each organization is different. Differences relate to varying missions, demographics, location, physical environment, management style, levels of funding and financial conditions, staff size, informal culture, and whether the organization is public, nonprofit, or for-profit, among other factors. This first chapter introduces the organization as a work setting for social workers and other human service professionals. There are many types and sources of information that can help you get to know an organization and determine whether you want to work there and, once there, how you can work effectively within it. Applicable sections of the National Association of Social Workers *Code of Ethics* (1999) are highlighted as they pertain to practice within the organizational setting.

The Work Setting

Most work in our society is carried out through organizations. There are many different types of organizations, ranging from big-business concerns that produce products and goods we need and want to service-oriented organizations that offer specialty services to meet individual, community, and societal needs.

Newspapers contain numerous reports of the work of organizations, and how what has happened in these organizations has impacted the lives of many. Problems in the financial and banking sector triggered a collapse in real estate prices, which in turn has led to our current recession. Policy makers and business leaders alike are trying to understand how changes in these organizations can help lead our country out of the recession and prevent this from happening again. The cost of these organizational problems has been enormous; unemployment stands at just under 10 percent, and many Americans are suffering. Clearly, business and organizational life have had a huge impact on us all.

Human service organizations are business concerns, too, only their business is to address the human condition rather than produce a product; they are in the business of providing programs of service to address the needs of individuals, groups, and communities. They do this through the planning, provision, and evaluation of a wide range of services to prevent or ameliorate personal, interpersonal, community, and social problems. Human service organizations take their purpose from societal needs and priorities as defined by the larger social environment at any given time. In many ways social work practice is defined, facilitated, and at the same time constrained by the purposes and operating modes of human service organizations. For this reason, they are of great importance and concern to the social welfare community.

The majority of social workers are employed by human service organizations, and the profession of social work is unique among the helping professions in its historic and traditional organizational base of practice. Some social workers work independently as private practitioners who provide therapeutic services independent of any organization. Other helping professionals, such as psychologists and psychiatrists, tend to work independently in larger proportion than do social workers. Social workers practice, for example, in hospitals, clinics, and schools—all of which are organizations.

Within these varied organizational settings, the practice of social work is approached in different ways. Some organizations focus on a specific set of services, such as mental health or child and family services. Others, such as schools, courts, and hospitals, have primary purposes other than the provision of human services yet nevertheless provide a human service because it is consistent with or facilitates the achievement of their major missions.

Human service organizations also operate under different auspices (nonprofit, for-profit, government) and, depending on their mission, address different types of problems (e.g., marital discord, depression, poverty, unemployment), provide different services (e.g., marital therapy, case management, discharge planning) oriented to different treatment goals (e.g., prevention, problem resolution, symptom alleviation), and serve different client populations (e.g., the homeless, children with learning disabilities, people with chronic mental illness). They may also employ different modalities (e.g., social group work, case work, community organizing). What human service organizations share, however, is their orientation to the prevention, amelioration, or resolution of health, mental health, social, or environmental problems that afflict individuals, families, specific groups, or communities (Gibelman, 2004). Barker (1999) defines human services as those "programs and activities designed to enhance people's development and well-being, including providing economic and social assistance for those unable to provide for their own needs" (p. 224).

Agency Roles for Social Workers

Direct service workers, including managers, clinicians, and other line-level social workers, are the core workforce of human service organizations. These levels of practice are typically distinguished by skill and experiential requirements.

For example, those holding management positions tend to have several years of direct service or supervisory experience. Within administration, there may be middle managers who occupy program management positions and upper-level managers who carry overall responsibility for the operations of the agency.

Direct service workers are the core workforce of human service organizations. They are responsible for carrying out the range of professional activities with and on behalf of clients in which the specified goals of the people served are reached through personal contact with and the immediate influence of the social worker.

The role of the direct human service worker depends on many factors, including the organizational setting and context and the needs of the clients and communities being served. Social workers carry out functions that are defined by the organization, often in a job description. Each of these functions is composed of a set of distinctive tasks that relates to the position occupied (Gibelman, 2004). The function of the social worker is defined by a confluence of factors—his or her role and job description; the training, values, and skills of the social worker; and the evolving needs of the community.

Why Do We Need to Know about Organizations?

People interact with organizations in all aspects of their lives. As children, we attend school; many of us go to a mosque, church, synagogue, or other religious institution; we go to the supermarket; our health care needs are met by a team of medical specialists who work for hospitals, clinics, or health maintenance organizations. The HMO may be a part of a nationwide network or a locally based medical group. Schools, religious institutions, supermarket chains, and hospitals are all forms of organizations. In April, we file our annual income tax returns with the federal, state, and local governments. These, too, are organizations, but under public auspices.

The fundamental interrelationship between people and organizations was summed up by Etzioni (1964) in his classic work on modern organizations:

> Our society is an organizational society. We are born in organizations, educated by organizations, and most of us spend much of our lives working for organizations. We spend much of our leisure time paying, playing, and praying in organizations. Most of us will die in an organization, and when the time comes for burial, the largest organization of all—the state—must grant official permission. (P. 1)

Social work knowledge, skills, and values, along with organizational needs, norms, and culture, are dynamic forces that shape social work practice. Organizational contexts may be a particularly powerful shaping force and can have both positive and negative influences on social work practice. Positive attributes include the authority and mandate to provide services in the public interest. Negative attributes include sometimes burdensome paperwork and operating rules that may run counter to the provision of timely or effective service to clients. Organizations also are the funnel through which government and philanthropic dollars flow. The receipt of these dollars, in turn, obligates the organization to do certain things—serve particular groups rather than others, provide specific types of services for designated periods of time, prepare reports, and account for the outcomes of services. These attributes suggest the multidimensional environment of the organization. All human service organizations interact with the larger sociopolitical environment. Many of the policies and procedures of an organization are actually the byproducts of requirements imposed by funding bodies, legal authorities, regulatory agencies, community groups, and professional interest groups.

The organization is thus afforded both opportunities and constraints by its larger environment, a subject more fully explored in later chapters. The organization processes these opportunities and constraints into a mode of operating on a day-to-day basis. Understanding the larger context in which the organization operates and how the organization translates its mission and goals into roles and functions carried out by its employees also helps social workers understand why things are as they are. This understanding helps clarify what areas of organizational functioning can be changed to make them more responsive to the people served, those potentially in need of services, and the employees who provide the services. The more you know about how organizations work, the more possible it becomes for you to identify creative possibilities for programs, services, and practice that meet professional standards and are consistent with the best interests of the people served.

Human service organizations exert a powerful influence in shaping the nature of social work practice. The agency provides the legitimation and sanction for carrying out society's mandates in regard to the health and well-being of our citizens and controls the resources necessary to accomplish this work (Hanson, 1998; Netting, Kettner, & McMurtry, 2008). The organization defines and establishes the boundaries of social work practice.

It is common to hear social workers voice dissatisfaction with their employing organization, and typical career development patterns suggest that social workers switch jobs several times, particularly in the early days of their practice (Gibelman, 2004). There are practical reasons for this trend; social workers often earn promotions and raises when they move from one agency to another. This trend is probably also rooted in the conflict between what practitioners learn in their professional education and what they experience on the job. Organizations are dynamic and exciting, frustrating and challenging, and the way they function has enormous implications for what services are provided, to whom, for how long, and how well.

Most social workers practicing within an organization can describe in detail the organizational problems that influence their practice. These include lack of time, large caseloads, poor communication, lack of supervision, burdensome administrative requirements, too much paperwork and not enough attention to client needs, and seemingly arbitrary rules that are subject to frequent change through new directives. Such workplace issues affect workers' attitudes toward their jobs, their clients, and their profession.

Although it is relatively easy to list the downside of organizationally based practice, it is more difficult for social workers to explain or even understand the organizational dynamics that are the basis for these problems (Resnick & Patti, 1980). Similarly, the benefits of organizationally based practice are often overlooked or not well considered. Each of the chapters in this book is intended to help human service professionals understand and work effectively within the employing organization.

Clarifying Terminology

All professions have their own language, and it is important to clarify how terms are used, particularly when more than one term is used to describe the same phenomenon.

Organizations have been defined as "formally structured arrangements of people, tools, and resources brought together to achieve predetermined objectives through institutionalized strategies" (Barker, 1999, p. 341). Within the human services, *organizations* are frequently referred to as *agencies*. These terms are used interchangeably in this book. Following are other commonly used terms:

- *Public agencies* are often referred to as *governmental agencies*.
- *Not-for-profit organizations* are also known as *nonprofit organizations* or *voluntary agencies*.
- *For-profit organizations* are also known as *proprietary organizations*. (In chapter 2, the distinctions between organizational types are discussed.)
- *Social workers* who perform direct service roles are sometimes called *workers, therapists, case managers,* or *clinicians*, depending on the nature of the job and traditions within particular organizations.
- The term *administrator* is often used synonymously with *manager*.
- The paid senior manager of the organization is called the *executive director, executive vice president,* or *chief executive officer (CEO)*.
- Paid employees of human service organizations are also referred to as *staff, personnel,* or *worker*.
- The term *human services* has been used synonymously with *social services* and *welfare services* but is considered to be more neutral and without the negative connotation associated with the term *welfare*. *Human services* became part of the professional vocabulary in 1979, when the former U.S. Department of Health, Education, and Welfare was renamed and replaced by the U.S. Department of Health and Human Services (Barker, 1999).

Ethical Guidelines

The practice of social work within an organizational setting is acknowledged in the profession's *Code of Ethics*. Many of the sections of the *Code* imply an organizational base of practice and address worker-supervisor relationships, maintenance of client records, staff development and training, conflicts of interest, relationships with colleagues, and workplace issues such as sexual harassment and labor-management disputes. One section of the *Code* deals specifically with the range of commitments to the employing organization. Section 3.09 of the *Code* (National Association of Social Workers, 2008) specifies that:

(a) Social workers generally should adhere to commitments to employers and employing organizations.

(b) Social workers should work to improve employing agencies' policies and procedures and the efficiency and effectiveness of their services.

(c) Social workers should take reasonable steps to ensure that employers are aware of social workers' ethical obligations as set forth in the NASW *Code of Ethics* and of the implications of these obligations for social work practice.

(d) Social workers should not allow an employing organization's policies, procedures, regulations, or administrative orders to interfere with their ethical practice of social work. Social workers should take reasonable steps to ensure that their employing organizations' practices are consistent with the NASW *Code of Ethics*.

(e) Social workers should act to prevent and eliminate discrimination in the employing organization's work assignments and in its employment policies and practices.

(f) Social workers should accept employment or arrange student field placements only in organizations that exercise fair personnel practices.

(g) Social workers should be diligent stewards of the resources of their employing organizations, wisely conserving funds where appropriate and never misappropriating funds or using them for unintended purposes. (Pp. 21–22)

Several sections of the *Code* recognize that the organizational base of social work practice may produce conflicts between the professional and the agency. These points of conflict have long been recognized by the profession and continue to pose challenges to the conditions and nature of practice. These sections of the *Code* also recognize certain obligations on the part of social workers to the organizations that employ them, one of which is loyalty. The professional has a responsibility to ensure the organization's compliance with laws, professional standards, and ethical conduct. Finally, the professional is an agent of change, with responsibility to improve the organization in a manner consistent with the highest levels of professionalism and in the best interests of the people served.

However, ethical decision making is not always so easy. While the *Code of Ethics* does provide excellent guidance, ethical behavior is not nearly as simple as following principle x or principle y. This is because ethics are contextual. In his discussion of managed mental health care, Furman (2003) explores the contextual nature of ethics:

The ethics of an action cannot be decided outside of explicating the nature of the relationship between the two parties involved in a particular action. For example, an action that is ethical between two friends may not be ethical between a social work professional and her client. Therefore, we can say that ethical actions are the result of social work values in action within the context of the social worker-client relationship. (P. 40)

This is because different ethical mandates often clash. This is what is referred to as an ethical dilemma. According to Beckerman (1997), an ethical dilemma "is that situation in which an action is required that reflects only one of two values or principles that are in opposition to one another" (p. 6). Recognizing the competition that lies at the heart of ethical dilemmas is imperative. In consultation with their supervisors and with other social workers, social workers must often make difficult decisions to elevate one value over another. In this book, we will explore several situations in which social workers must make difficult choices between conflicting values. As you encounter these situations, ask yourself what you would do, and why. Developing the ability to reflect upon ethical dilemmas and make good, rational decisions is essential for all social workers and other human service professionals. Doing so is not easy; at times, you may feel overwhelmed and as if there is no correct decision. This is natural and is a part of what makes ethical dilemmas challenging. When you feel conflicted about your choices, it may be helpful, in addition to discussing your options with your supervisor, to contact your professional organization, such as the National Association of Social Workers. State licensure boards may also be of help in resolving these issues.

Social Work and Organizations: Historic Roots

An understanding of the dynamics of today's human service organizations requires an appreciation of the context in which they developed (Shafritz, Ott, & Jang, 2010). Since its inception, social work has been considered an organizationally based profession, with the majority of its workforce employed within formal organizations. At the end of the nineteenth century, social workers provided community-based services as part of the settlement house movement (Linn, 2000). Settlement houses were a way of serving the poor in urban areas; workers lived in the communities they sought to serve. Hull-House, founded by social work pioneer Jane Addams, was an early and influential settlement house in Chicago. Settlement houses provided direct services and political action, representing a true generalist practice (Payne, 2006). During the Great Depression, social workers further developed their institutional base as human service workers in New Deal programs, and later through child and family guidance clinics (Axinn & Stern, 2007). Lubove (1965) described this phenomenon: "Unlike other professions, social work was almost exclusively a corporate activity, with little opportunity for independent practice. To carve out a niche, the social worker had to attain hegemony within the agency"

(p. 159). This interdependence between practitioners and organizations is in contrast to many other professions, such as law and medicine, in which a large proportion of practitioners work independently or in small groups.

The considerable literature about professionals and organizations, whether pertaining specifically to social work or to other helping professions, includes exploration of the conflicts and/or points of congruence between professionals and bureaucracies (see, for example, Blau & Scott, 1962; Etzioni, 1964, 1969; Hasenfeld & English, 1974; Scott, 1969; Simon, 1957; Weber, 1922/1994). A bureaucracy is a type of formal organization characterized by hierarchy predicated on firmly established patterns of superior-subordinate relationships, formal and rigid operating rules and regulations, specialization and expertise, and formal operations and communications (Simon, 1957).

This classic model of bureaucracy helps us understand some aspects of organizations, but pure types of bureaucracies are more myth than fact in the human services. The automobile assembly line is more likely to display the classic bureaucratic characteristics than is the neighborhood social service agency (Weber, 1922/1994). On the other hand, huge public agencies, such as public welfare departments and child welfare agencies, have historically been linked with the bureaucratic form of organization. These organizations have been criticized for their cumbersome processes and inefficient and ineffective services. In addition, bureaucratic organizations can often feel impersonal and dehumanizing to both clients and workers. Social workers should always remember to guard against treating clients in an overly impersonal manner. It is important for workers to continually remind themselves of the reasons why they chose the profession in the first place and to do their part in humanizing their workplace. For instance, developing an appreciation for the strengths of colleagues and clients can be a way of guarding against impersonal treatment. Also, continually striving to provide culturally competent services helps to individualize social work services and meet the needs of diverse groups of clients (Harper & Lantz, 2007).

Conflicts between Professionals and Organizations

Despite modern innovations in how organizations are managed, the fact remains that professional practice within an organizational context contains some anomalies that produce strain. Organizational theories, particularly the classic theory of bureaucracy (see Weber, 1922/1994), suggest that employees will identify with, and have unconditional loyalty to, the organization. They will show a high level of acceptance of the goals and activities of the organization, and their values and norms will be consistent with and accepting of those of the organization (Scott, 1969). However, professionals, by virtue of their training and ability to perform specialized tasks autonomously, could have different priorities and work styles than those demanded by the employing organization.

Professionals are socialized to look to the profession, rather than the employing organization, as their point of reference. The worker, on the other hand, is an "agent of the agency," receives sanction and authority from the agency, and in turn is constrained by its limitations. On the other hand, the worker's career aspirations are professional, not organizational. These differing orientations are outlined in box 1.1.

BOX 1.1
Major Points of Conflict between Professionals and Their Employing Organizations

Distinguishing Characteristics	Organizations	Professionals
Ideological commitment	Organizational loyalty	Professional norms
Primary Frame of Reference	Internal— organization based	External— professional body
Knowledge base	Organizational training	Professional education
Status base	Internal—promotion	External—credential
Legitimacy	Rules	Knowledge
Context of practice	Organizational procedures	Professional standards
Role	Employee	Practitioner
Tasks	Technical	Skill based
Performance measures	Efficiency	Effectiveness
Autonomy	Prescribed	Open ended
Accountability—to whom	Structure	Clients
Accountability—for what	Process	Outcome
Decision making	Autocratic	Democratic
Relationships among staff	Hierarchical	Collegial
Attitude toward authority	Compliant	Intractable
Management of conflict	Avoidance	Advocacy
Orientation to change	Reactive	Proactive
Orientation to future	Long-term commitment	Open-ended commitment
Orientation to organization	Career	Instrumental
Orientation to organizational goals	Ends	Means
Orientation to management	Subservient	Facilitative
Orientation to clients	People processing	People serving

One of the components of efficiency relates to the collection of the fees that help to maintain the organization and allow it to operate smoothly. Because of the division of labor between the business and professional activities of the organization, conflicts may arise about whose job it is to collect fees from clients and what procedures should govern nonpayment situations. The vignette in box 1.2 illustrates how the differing orientations may clash.

BOX 1.2
A Clash in Orientation and Attitudes

Rosemarie was new to her position as chief financial officer for a mental health clinic. She was highly experienced in financial operations, but her work in the past had been in for-profit organizations. When she assumed her new position, Rosemarie was told that one of the important components of her job was to ensure that billing for clinical services was handled appropriately. The clinic had been losing a lot of revenue because the prior finance person was not vigilant about collecting outstanding payables.

Rosemarie took this charge seriously. In her past jobs, she learned the importance of adhering to the specifics of her job description and to performing the tasks expected of her. She was efficient and ran a "tight ship." If collecting outstanding payments from clients was her charge, this is what she would do.

Rosemarie first set out to learn why clients were not paying their bills. She identified the receptionist, who collected fees, as part of the problem. June, the receptionist, had a big heart, and when clients indicated that they couldn't pay or forgot to bring a checkbook, June let it go. The other problem Rosemarie identified was that the social workers didn't deal with clients about financial issues. In informal discussions with a few of the staff social workers, Rosemarie learned that they were reluctant to bring up financial issues, particularly when a client had no insurance. The social workers knew that most of the clients served by the agency had marginal incomes and that pressing the issue of payment might either scare them away or create some tension in the client-worker relationship. They left it, by default, to the untrained receptionist.

Rosemarie asked June to notify her when a client with a "balance due" showed up for an appointment. Although reluctant, June saw no other option. It did not take long before a situation that June decided should be brought to Rosemarie's attention arose.

Eric had been seen by his social worker for over six months and had a balance due with the agency of over $500.00. With the payment schedule in hand, Rosemarie went to the reception area and asked Eric if she could speak with him for a minute. Rosemarie did not introduce herself until they were in her office, and she shut the door. She knew nothing about Eric other than his name, the length of time he had been a client, and his outstanding balance. Rosemarie waved the payment schedule at him as she said, "We have a serious problem, Eric. Your social worker will not be able to continue to see you until you take care of this outstanding bill. We don't give away services here."

Eric became visibly flustered and began to explain that he and his social worker had an understanding about paying this balance. Rosemarie interrupted and said that the social worker had been remiss about following the clinic's rules; payment for services was to be made each time Eric was seen. Eric turned bright red, and instead of returning to the reception area to wait for his social worker, he left the clinic.

Rosemarie understood that part of her job was to make sure that payments for billable hours were received and that the backlog of outstanding accounts was cleared up as soon as possible. When Rosemarie was given this directive by the clinic director, she took her assignment seriously. She quickly got the impression that the clinic staff, particularly the social workers, were not acting responsibly when they failed to discuss payments with their clients.

From Rosemarie's point of view, there was nothing wrong with her actions. However, she took action based on incomplete information. She acted as if the collection of fees was immutable law and of singular importance (Ezell, 2000). She knew nothing about Eric, his problems, or his financial situation. She did not first speak to the social worker to discuss how Eric might best be approached and by whom. She violated Eric's confidentiality, embarrassed him, and threatened his status as a client of the agency. The trust built up between Eric and his social worker was also jeopardized in this encounter. Due to her inability to understand the culture of the organization and adapt business practices to this culture, she may also have lost a client. And since reputation and the community's belief in the organization's friendliness are often human service programs' strongest marketing strategies, Rosemarie might have hurt the program from a business perspective.

In this instance, administrative goals took precedence over service goals. To the social worker, skill, knowledge, and service commitments are the primary principles in working with clients; for the organization, represented in this case by a fiscal administrator, organizational maintenance is the operating principle. The collection of fees was construed by Rosemarie as the most important goal; she viewed the aggressive pursuit of late payers as ensuring the organization's solvency. However, in this process she not only stepped on the toes of the social worker but may have caused emotional harm to the client.

Accommodations in Conflicting Orientations

The *Code of Ethics* (National Association of Social Workers, 2008) clearly states the professional's central point of reference: "Social workers' primary responsibility is to promote the well-being of clients" (p. 4). Certain limitations to this core responsibility are noted in the *Code,* such as social workers' responsibility to the larger society or to specific legal obligations. Performance criteria, decision-making prerogatives, and the exercise of discretionary judgment are, for the social worker, based on the special knowledge and skills of the profession. From the organization's point of view, such prerogatives may conflict with rules, regulations, and operating procedures in which individuality is deliberately overshadowed by standardized role prescriptions. There may be sanctions exercised against the social worker who fails to conform to the agency's ways of doing business. The result may be a high level of frustration, culminating in burnout.

Although the literature has emphasized the conflicts between organizations and professional practice, the relationship is not always dysfunctional. Blau and Scott (1962) and Vinter (1974), for example, noted several points of congruence, including ideology and standards related to affective neutrality or impersonality, derivation of agency goals and professional service aims from the same humanitarian value system, and discharging professional functions through circumscribed roles that complement the organization's assignment of official duties.

Accommodation between professional practice and organizational operations is possible. This accommodation allows the professional to exercise functional autonomy within his or her area of specialization. The organization is dependent on its workforce to achieve its objectives and, accordingly, there must be some attention to the "human element" to motivate and maintain that workforce (Argyris, 1962; McGregor, 1960). The worker receives compensation in the form of wages, insurance, vacation, and sick leave. The organization also offers position, experience, and security. The worker, on the other hand, offers skill, energy, work, and commitment.

Human service organizations must constantly adapt to their larger environment—to changes in laws, budget allocations, contractual arrangements, and societal attitudes about people in need and the appropriate responses to such needs. The functions of the organization are thus not constant, and who gets served, with what kinds of services, and for what length of time are influenced by legal mandates and fiscal allotments decided by authorities outside the organization. On the other hand, the professionals working within these same organizations are consistent in their allegiance to professional norms and a commitment to service. The consistency of purpose of the professional workforce is a mediating factor in the cycles of organizational change.

Changing Conceptions of Organizations

Today, attitudes toward how organizations should be run differ substantially from the classic bureaucracy described by earlier theorists. Efficiency has ceased to have its appeal as the most important goal or characteristic of organizations. The work environment itself is seen as a critical variable in how much and how well organizations function to achieve their purposes.

New schools of thought emphasize the importance of the human element in organizational dynamics, as well as noneconomic social rewards and informal communication and leadership structures (Etzioni, 1964). Conceptualizations of the modern organization also include attention to values, norms, beliefs, symbols, and rituals that provide meaning and direction for individual and collective behavior within the context of the work environment (Bolman & Deal, 2008). Organizations are now perceived to be open systems, linked integrally to their environments (Hanson, 1998).

In today's view, organizations are dynamic, evolving and changing in interaction with external stimuli. Alliances within and between organizations form and re-form among employees, key stakeholders, and interest groups as each seeks to enhance its own interests. Within this context, each organization develops a unique culture that affects how it operates and how well (Hanson, 1998).

As social work has become increasingly legitimized and respected as a profession, social workers have been able to exert more influence on the climate and operating modes of human service organizations. They have done this, in part, by becoming the managers of these organizations. Social work managers are likely to evidence an openness to community, professional, and client input, to adopt a more collaborative management style, to respect and encourage a substantial degree of autonomy in regard to professional practice, and to focus on the outcomes achieved rather than just the process of the work conducted by the organization.

Social workers in management positions have found alternative ways of viewing organizations. It is important to remember that the purpose of human service organizations is to serve clients. Toward this end, organizations should never forget the needs of those who work directly with clients—human service workers (Rapp & Poertner, 1992). Saleebey (2002) describes the strengths perspective in the following way:

> Practicing from a strength orientation means that everything you do as a social worker will be predicated, in some way, on helping to discover and embellish, explore and exploit clients' strengths and resources in assisting them to achieve their goals, realize their dreams, and shed the irons of their own inhibitions and misgivings. (P. 3)

Leaders who operate from the strengths perspective seek to point out the strengths of those they supervise. They understand that drawing attention to and helping staff maximize their strengths facilitates the achievement of organizational goals (Netting, Kettner, & McMurtry, 2008). They seek to promote organizational structures and practices that encourage workers to develop their skills as workers and as human beings while providing services to clients. This approach is congruent with new collaborative and participatory styles of management that have become increasingly important in the business and health care arenas (Nissan, Merrigan, & Kraft, 2005).

Sources of Information about Organizations

There are times in a social worker's career when learning about an organization is critical. One obvious time is during the job search process, when one must make decisions about the fit between oneself and a job. The newly employed social worker will need to learn quickly about how the organization functions. A thorough look at the organization may also be useful to the more seasoned employee, particularly at such times when he or she wants to change certain aspects of the organization's operations that are seen as having a negative impact on work performance and/or client services.

Like people, organizations are complex. Each, for example, has a personality, a style, and strengths and weaknesses. We make decisions about the features we like about organizations based on our own personal preferences and styles.

We do this as part of the job search process. We also do this once on the job, when we evaluate for ourselves the fit between what we want to be doing as professionals and the opportunities afforded by the agency. We do this, too, when we engage in a process of deciding to change jobs.

Individuals have their own criteria when judging what a good working environment is. Factors in personal decision making include the nature of the job itself—the problem situations presented by clients, the program of services designed to meet client needs, the types of intervention used, and so on. In addition, every organization has its own climate and unique environmental features. It is important to learn as much about the agency's culture as possible and to assess how compatible this environment is with one's own preferences and work style. Two agencies may have positions with a similar title involving the same client population, but the work may be quite different depending on the agency context. The critical difference, in fact, may lie within the organization—its type, its management, and its culture.

There's a lot more involved in getting to know an organization than can be found in a job description, a position title, or a salary figure. It's important for social workers to look at the culture of the organization and determine whether they would really enjoy doing that job in that particular environment (Joyce, 2000).

Your thoughts when you interview for a job or begin to wonder if where you work is a good match with what you want to be doing may be similar to those expressed in box 1.3.

BOX 1.3
The Right Fit

You've just received your BA, BSW, or MSW. It's spring, and there are many job listings. You send out ten resumes on the first round to test the water. You are called in for four interviews. All involve work with people with chronic mental illness. Two are neighborhood centers that provide day treatment. One is large, the other much smaller. One interview is with a residential facility in the suburbs. It's a rather lengthy commute, but the place is beautiful. The final interview is with the city's Department of Mental Health.

It's not so simple to decide which job may be best for you. You need to ask more questions, look things over more carefully, even analyze your own personality before you say yes to a job.

You need to ask yourself: Do I want to work in a small agency or a large one? Do I want a formal environment where I wear a suit or a more relaxed atmosphere? Do I want to be surrounded by low-sided cubicles that give me easy access to conversation, or do I work better alone? Will I get along with my supervisor? With my colleagues? What's most important to me—how much I get paid or how large my caseload will be? These issues can ultimately determine your level of job satisfaction.

(*continued on next page*)

We all know that the people interviewing us are sizing us up. Do we have the necessary qualifications? How good are our skills? Will we get along with coworkers? We wonder about whether we made the proper impression. It's human nature to feel as though the job interview is the test of our attractiveness as a prospective employee. However, interviews should be two sided. This is the time to ask questions.

Many people don't interview very well, because they interview for the job but not for the organization or career. Selecting a job—and being selected by the agency— is about a mutual fit.

You probably have some idea of what you want from a job, a career, and a workplace. Looking for that right fit involves forethought about what these personal and professional wants are. As you interview, as you walk around the agency and talk to staff, are you seeing the type of environment in which you want to work?

The City Department of Mental Health offers a lot more money than the other three agencies with which you interviewed. It is a huge agency, employing hundreds of people. The atmosphere gives modern-day credence to Max Weber's (1922) description of a classic bureaucracy: large, impersonal, rule-oriented, and procedurally rigid. You think back to those textbook descriptions. You need to know more. And you need different perspectives—not just those of the supervisor or manager with whom you are interviewing but also those of the staff. Ask staff members about what a typical workday is like. What are the real work hours as opposed to those posted?

There is no perfect agency size; it depends on individual preference. It's worthwhile to visit and experience agencies of different types and sizes. You can learn a lot about an agency by observing what's going on. How do people interact? What's the feel of the place? Most important, how does the agency feel to you? How did you feel about your potential supervisor and new colleagues? If you are offered a position and did not spend enough time with them to form an opinion, you may certainly ask to come back and meet with them again (or for the first time, if you did not meet with some key people). You can explain that you are extremely interested in the position and want to make sure that it is a good fit for both you and the agency. They will respect your thoroughness, and you will be able to make a more informed assessment.

A substantial amount of homework is required in advance of a job interview. The first consideration is knowing what background information you need. A review of written materials before the interview will help you to ask the right questions.

What to Request

For students whose first introduction to human service organizations is their field placement, the foundation practice class provides the opportunity to learn about what questions to ask and what documents to request. The field instructor, in conjunction with the classroom teacher, will assist you in obtaining the documents and responding to questions. Prior to asking for these documents, check the website to see if you can find some of them yourself. Many agency websites now have a great deal of material online.

For the graduating student who is job hunting and cannot find the needed resources online, how to access such documents that describe the organization may be less clear. Some people may be concerned that asking for too much information will be viewed negatively by the potential employer. This is seldom the case. Managers tend to view it as a plus when potential employees do their homework in advance and can speak knowledgeably about the organization and their fit within it. The same holds true for the more experienced practitioner who is interested in exploring new job opportunities.

Box 1.4 provides examples of the broad range of questions you can ask about specific human service organizations. Because social workers spend a large proportion, if not all, of their careers in the organizational setting, picking the right agency in which to work is as important as decisions about the functions they want to perform and the populations with whom they wish to work. In other instances, colleagues may be able to provide important information about actual experiences in working with the organization. The informal network works well in providing the real scoop about a workplace.

BOX 1.4
What You Want to Know about an Organization

- Under what auspices does the organization operate (for-profit, nonprofit, or public)?
- What are the stated purposes of the organization?
- If it is a voluntary organization, who serves on the board of directors?
- How are the programs and services financed?
- Who's the boss?
- How many professional employees are there?
- What is the organization's orientation to service?
- What type of supervision is available and how often?
- Does the organization have a clearly delineated target population?
- What's the atmosphere like?
- How long do professional-employees, on average, stay on the job?
- Are there promotional opportunities from within the organization?
- Has the agency been experiencing any financial challenges? If so, can you describe them?
- What do people in the community know and think about the organization?
- What do employees say about the organization?
- What kinds of continuing education opportunities are available through the organization?
- Does the organization pay for and provide time off from work for participation in continuing professional education programs offered outside the organization?
- Are professional employees unionized?
- Has the agency ever laid off employees? If so, when and how was this accomplished?

Most organizations have information sheets or pamphlets available to the public about their services. These public information documents typically define the services the organization provides, eligibility requirements for service, and specific target groups or populations for which the organization's services are designed. Sometimes these documents include information about fees. In bilingual communities, such information is often available in the languages spoken.

Many organizations prepare an annual report. Public agencies are often required by law to issue a yearly statement about their progress toward achievement of their goals. Nonprofit agencies may prepare an attractive annual report to help in their fund-raising and public education efforts. This report usually includes statements by the president of the board of directors and the executive director in the form of a review of the past year's accomplishments, a description of the programs offered, demographics of the client population, financial reports, and future plans.

Other documents helpful to understanding the organization are the bylaws and the constitution. Although these documents may be written in legalistic terms, they provide information about the governance structure, mission, and goals of the organization.

It is essential that social workers understand the philosophical base of their organization. Although this information is sometimes available in written form, as illustrated in box 1.5, it may best be gleaned from conversations with staff. Such conversations also allow the social worker to judge the extent to which a written philosophical statement is consistent with actual practice. How committed is the agency to serving underserved populations? What happens if the client can't pay? Is there a sliding fee scale? Will fees be waived? How does the

---

BOX 1.5
One Organization's Philosophy

Our services are guided by a philosophy that emphasizes understanding the unique qualities and experience of each child as influenced by the complex interaction of personality, emotional and cognitive development, family situation, and social environment.

We view psychotherapy with children as a dynamic, interactive assessment and treatment process that examines problems while building on strengths, and believe our intervention is most effective when parenting figures are actively involved.

We are committed to making our services accessible to all children and families in the community who can safely and productively participate in outpatient mental health treatment, while offering referral and advocacy for those who may require a more restrictive and structured environment.

Source: Adapted from Child Guidance Center of Southern Connecticut (1999) p. 1.

agency feel about the use of staff time for case-and-cause advocacy? Is this part of the expectations or are social workers expected to advocate on their own time? How receptive is the organization to program expansion to meet the changing needs of the community? In this same vein, what does the organization do to tap the pulse of the community to determine service needs?

You will want to know the auspices of the organization. Is it for-profit? If so, what does this mean in terms of the types of clients served and eligibility for service? If the organization is nonprofit, who are the members of the board of directors? How involved is the board? From where does the agency raise its money? Does the agency have assets? Does the organization routinely monitor and evaluate the services it provides? Are there systems for involving consumers and staff in planning, designing, modifying, and making other important decisions about its operations that affect the quality of care?

The remaining chapters of this book focus on the distinguishing characteristics of human service organizations and how their features and operating modes affect the day-to-day practice of social work within them. Because organizations are so diverse, it is not possible to touch on all the factors that influence the organizational base of practice. The areas selected for discussion in the following chapters show the range of factors that influence the organization, both internally and externally. Internal factors have to do with decisions largely (but not exclusively) made within the organization about how it will carry out its business, for example, organizational structure and management style. External factors include social welfare laws and regulations, judicial decisions, funding allocations, and the level of competition among similar agencies in the community. These and other factors establish the parameters in which the organization functions and set the boundaries for social work practice within them.

Key Points

- ◆ Organizations affect every aspect of our personal and professional lives.
- ◆ Human service organizations are one type of organization; their specific focus is the broad arena of human well-being.
- ◆ The NASW *Code of Ethics* acknowledges the reciprocal relationship between the social worker and the organization.
- ◆ The mission statement, program goals, objectives, and operating modes define the nature of professional practice within the organization.
- ◆ Since its inception, social work has been considered an organizationally based profession, with the majority of its workforce employed within formal organizations.
- ◆ Conflicts between organizations and their professional workforce are rooted in differing orientations, including those of work style, priorities, and loyalties.

◆ Ethical dilemmas are a fundamental reality in social service organizations. How workers approach these dilemmas is key to effective practice.

◆ Despite the emphasis on conflict between organizations and professionals, there are points of congruence, including objectivity, neutrality, and humanitarian values.

◆ Today's organization is seen as an open system, dynamic, evolving, and changing in interaction with its employees, key stakeholders, interest groups, and the larger community.

◆ The organizational context has both positive and negative influences on professional practice.

◆ Much of the information a social worker wants to know about an organization is a matter of public record. Knowing what to ask for is the key.

Suggested Learning Activities and Discussion Questions

1. Section 3.09 of the NASW *Code of Ethics* points out the ethical obligations of the social worker within his or her employing agency. Is the obligation one sided? Read over the *Code* to see whether there are provisions that apply to the obligations of the agency to its employees. Is there anything missing from the *Code* that you think should be there in regard to the obligations of the agency?

2. Identify two points of conflict between professionals and organizations that seem particularly applicable to your field placement agency or current work environment. Provide specific examples of these conflicts and discuss how they play out in day-to-day work. How have these conflicts been addressed?

3. Put yourself in the role of Eric's social worker. Eric was the client whom Rosemarie, the chief financial officer, confronted about fees he owed to the agency. How would you address this situation in regard to your supervisor, Rosemarie, Eric, and perhaps others in the agency?

4. Make a list of the five most important things you would want to know about an organization before you would consider working for it. Then devise a plan for how you would get answers to these questions before an interview.

5. Suppose that you have your pick of jobs. How would you make a decision? What would be most important to you in deciding between two or three different agencies?

Recommended Readings

Cryer, S. (2008). *The nonprofit career guide: How to land a job that makes a difference.* Minneapolis, MN: Fieldstone Alliance.

Gibelman, M. (1995). *What social workers do.* Washington, DC: NASW Press.

Hall, R. H. (1996). *Organizations: Structures, processes, and outcomes.* Englewood Cliffs, NJ: Prentice Hall.

Krannich, R. L., & Krannich, C. R. (1998). *Jobs and careers with nonprofit organizations: Profitable opportunities with nonprofits.* New York: Impact Publishers.

National Association of Social Workers. (2008). *Code of ethics.* Washington, DC: Author.

Ritter, J. A., Vakalahi, H. F. O., & Kiernan-Stern, M. (2009). *101 careers in social work.* New York: Springer.

Segal, E. A., Gerdes, K. E., & Steiner, S. (2010). *An introduction to the profession of social work: Becoming an agent of change* (3rd ed.). Belmont, CA: Brooks Cole.

Shafritz, J., Ott, S., & Jang, Y. S. (2005). *Classics of organization theory* (6th ed.). Belmont, CA: Thomson/Wadsworth.

Wells, C. C. (1999). *Social work day to day* (3rd ed.). New York: Longman.

References

Argyris, C. (1962). *Interpersonal competence and organizational effectiveness.* Homewood, IL: Dorsey Press.

Axinn, J., & Stern, M. (2007). *Social welfare: A history of the American response to need* (7th ed.). Boston: Allyn & Bacon.

Barker, R. L. (1999). *Social work dictionary* (4th ed.). Washington, DC: NASW Press.

Beckerman, N. (1997). Advanced medical technology: The ethical implications for social work practice with the dying. *Practice, 8*(3), 5–18.

Blau, P. M., & Scott, R. (1962). *Formal organizations: A comparative approach.* San Francisco: Chandler.

Bolman, L. G., & Deal, T. E. (2008). *Reframing organizations* (4th ed.). San Francisco: Jossey-Bass.

Child Guidance Center of Southern Connecticut. (1999). *About the child guidance center.* Stamford, CT: Author.

Etzioni, A. (1964). *Modern organizations.* Englewood Cliffs, NJ: Prentice Hall.

Etzioni, A. (Ed.). (1969). *The semi-professions and their organization.* New York: Free Press.

Ezell, M. (2000). Financial management. In R. J. Patti (Ed.), *The handbook of social welfare management* (pp. 377–393). Thousand Oaks, CA: Sage Publications.

Furman, R. (2003). Frameworks for understanding value discrepancies and ethical dilemmas in managed mental health for social work in the United States. *International Social Work, 46*(1), 37–52.

Gibelman, M. (2004). *What social workers do* (2nd ed.). Washington, DC: NASW Press.

Hanson, M. (1998). Practice in organizations. In M. A. Mattaini, C. T. Lowery, & C. H. Meyer (Eds.), *The foundations of social work practice* (2nd ed., pp. 240–264). Washington, DC: NASW Press.

Harper, K. V., & Lantz, J. (2007). *Cross-cultural practice: Social work with diverse populations* (2nd ed.). Chicago: Lyceum Books.

Hasenfeld, Y., & English, R. A. (1974). *Human service organizations.* Ann Arbor: University of Michigan Press.

Joyce, A. (2000, March 6). Career track: Make sure the job works for you. *Washington Post,* p. F35.

Linn, J. (2000). *Jane Addams. A biography.* Urbana: University of Illinois Press.

Lubove, R. (1965). *The professional altruist: The emergence of social work as a career, 1880–1930.* New York: Atheneum.

McGregor, D. (1960). *The human side of enterprise.* New York: McGraw-Hill.

National Association of Social Workers. (2008). *Code of ethics.* Washington, DC: Author.

Netting, F. E., Kettner, P. M., & McMurtry, S. (2008). *Social work macro practice* (4th ed.). Boston: Allyn & Bacon.

Nissan, L. B., Merrigan D. M., & Kraft, M. K. (2005). Moving mountains together: Strategic community leadership and systems change. *Child Welfare, 84*(2), 123–140.

Payne, M. (2006). *What is professional social work?* Chicago: Lyceum Books.

Rapp, C. A., & Poertner, J. (1992). *Social administration: A client-centered approach.* New York: Longman.

Resnick, H., & Patti, R. J. (Eds.). (1980). *Change from within: Humanizing social welfare organizations.* Philadelphia: Temple University Press.

Saleebey, D. (2002). *The strengths perspective in social work.* Boston: Allyn & Bacon.

Scott, R. (1969). Professional employees in a bureaucratic structure. In A. Etzioni (Ed.), *The semi-professions and their organization: Teachers, nurses, social workers* (pp. 83–131). New York: Free Press.

Shafritz, J., Ott, S., & Jang, Y. S. (2010). *Classics of organization theory* (7th ed.). Belmont, CA: Thomson/Wadsworth.

Simon, H. A. (1957). *Administrative behavior* (2nd ed.). New York: Free Press.

Vinter, R. D. (1974). The social structure of service. In P. E. Weinberger (Ed.), *Perspectives on social welfare* (2nd ed., pp. 453–471). New York: Macmillan.

Weber, M. (1994). Bureaucracy. In F. Fischer & C. Sirianni (Eds.), *Critical studies in organization and bureaucracy* (2nd ed., pp. 4–19). Philadelphia: Temple University Press. (Originally published 1922).

Chapter 2

Distinguishing Features of Organizations

In this chapter, the characteristics of human service agencies are explored. Organizations that seek to respond to and meet human needs are represented by several different organizational types, including public, nonprofit, proprietary, and self-help. Each type has been traditionally associated with certain funding bases. However, the boundaries between organizational types have become increasingly blurred, in large part due to the availability of the same or similar funding sources and to the accountability requirements that each must meet. Discussion then turns to some of the distinguishing features of organizations that influence how they function, including mission, size, and structure. Each of these characteristics influences organizational behavior and, in turn, affects how social workers and other helping professionals perform their jobs.

Defining Human Service Organizations

Holland (1995) refers to organizations as "formalized groups of people who make coordinated use of resources and skills to accomplish given goals or purposes" (p. 1788). However, Holland (1995) notes, human service organizations (also referred to as social service organizations) are distinguished from other types, especially in their focus on "promoting and enhancing the well-being of the people they serve" (p. 1787).

The practice of social work has traditionally been carried out in organizational settings. Within the human services, typologies have been developed on the basis of the operating authority under which such organizations were created and their mission was established. Throughout the history of American social welfare, these settings have been of two types: public and private. "Public" and "private" are broad categories, encompassing different types of organizations. Private organizations include both for-profit and nonprofit, distinctions that are clarified in box 2.1. Nonprofits may also be under religious (sectarian) auspices. They operate at different levels, ranging from the local community to umbrella, or affiliated, organizations.

Putting Theory to Practice

Before we explore the types of organizations that you will find, we will briefly explore organizational theory. We want you to become familiar with some of the theories that have influenced the development of human service organizations and that may serve to influence your thinking if you ever are called upon to develop new programs or agencies. Often, practitioners and students in various human service disciplines distrust theory; theories are viewed as being disconnected from real-life practice situations. You will find the theories presented here embedded in many of the practices and principles that we take for granted in organizations. Theory is presented not only here, but in chapters where it helps illuminate important organizational issues. An intensive discussion of theory is not the purpose of this book, but we want to at least help you become more theory friendly and encourage you to learn more about theory over time.

A good theory is extremely practical. Theories are not merely hypothetical concoctions of abstract ideas. Good theories connect different real-world factors; they show the relationships between real events, real people, and real social forces. A good theory allows us to explain, and often predict, how people and institutions respond. One of my favorite ways of thinking about theories is to think of them as travel guides. In truth, you don't always need a travel guide. If you are in familiar territory, going somewhere very close by, you might wish to be adventurous and "wing it." But what if you are traveling to a faraway land where they do not speak your language and all the signs and symbols are incomprehensible? Yes, you could probably handle the basics, a place to stay and things to eat, but think of how much harder that might be. A good travel guide will not only help you find a place to stay and a place to eat, but it will help you choose places to visit based upon your needs and desires. There are many different guidebooks, and each has its strengths and will be geared toward a different type of traveler.

Theories are like guidebooks in that while they may not be 100 percent necessary (at least some seem to feel this way), they help you make good choices for the activities that you will engage in. Learning a theory or multiple theories provides you with different ways of approaching and thinking about different situations. They help you be more efficient and avoid certain mistakes. Theories can help you see situations in new lights, learn the rules, and determine why you may wish to follow some "rules" sometimes and break some rules at other times.

Max Weber, the father of organizational theory, died in 1920, and although he lived in an earlier century, his ideas are still important because they have influenced a good deal of modern organizational theory. In fact, you will find much of what we assume to be inevitable in organizations within Weber's ideas.

Weber was the first to focus on the nature of bureaucracies. He was concerned with the way that power and authority existed within organizations. He made a distinction between the two, noting that power relies upon force to compel individuals to adhere to organizational rules, while legitimate authority creates the conditions whereby individuals comply with organizational dictates willingly. Weber (1997) noted that the most appropriate metaphor for an organization was the machine. He presented a description of what an organization should look like in his articulation of the "rational legal bureaucracies." This idealized organization consisted of the following, smoothly running, machinelike attributes: authority based on clearly delineated rules, which trump informal social relationships; clearly defined hierarchies; well-developed and highly specific lines of responsibility; formalized rules and regulations; a high degree of specialization and technical competence; and promotion based on performance. In Weber's mechanistic organization, all rules and regulations should be written down, and all members of the organization should understand these rules.

Weber stressed the importance of uniformity and stability in terms of work performance and expectations. To Weber, smooth-running bureaucracies are ones in which clear lines of authority are presented, and roles and responsibilities are logical and clear.

Many large human service organizations are based on this rationalist, bureaucratic model. In fact, many human service organizations are actually more typical of Weber's ideal than are many modern businesses. There are several consequences of this adherence to this model. First, many large, intensely bureaucratic human service organizations often feel rigid and lifeless and do not encourage innovation and creativity. During times of change and transformation, when community needs are affected by rapid changes in a world greatly influenced by global factors, this can be highly problematic. For example, a large child welfare organization was having a difficult time serving a new immigrant population. The group of immigrants did not fit easily into the model of delivery—office visits—and did not relate to the services provided. Given the bureaucracy's tendency to be self-perpetuating, many in the agency seemed to find fault in their new clients and not in their own highly restricted manner of functioning.

Understanding classic organizational theory provides us with an important sense of where the study of organizations and management originated. Based on these early studies, scholars and practitioners from various fields representing many different perspectives have continued the development of research and theory. In reaction to this classic approach to organizations, more progressive models began to be developed in the 1960s in human service organizations.

The use of the terms *progressive* and *radical* have become increasingly controversial over the last several decades. In general, the human services, mirroring society in general, have become increasingly conservative. Evidence-based practice, the medicalization of human services, and other forces have led us to view individuals as the primary focus of change, not institutions. Progressive approaches to macro practice focus on the structural and social factors that inhibit the growth and development of individuals, families, and small groups in the context of organizatioins. In general, one can say that the progressive viewpoint is that people are not the problem, but that systems are problems or, perhaps more correctly, structural dynamics embedded within systems are the problem. As such, radical perspectives or organizational theories are ones that highlight the oppressive nature of social institutions and encourage the transformation of organizations to remove barriers of oppression.

One progressive perspective that has had significant influence over organizational theory is feminist theory. According to feminist organizational theorists, the fundamental problem within most human service organizations, and with organizational theory, is the centrality of hierarchy (Iannello, 1992). Feminist organizational theorists and practitioners seem to be somewhat split on whether or not any hierarchy in organizations is necessary, but what is clear is that they believe that an overemphasis on hierarchy and authority have deleterious effects on organizations. Feminist theorists have tried to develop various models as alternatives. Feminist managers tend to work toward a flat organizational structure where decisions are based upon collaborative and consensus models of decision making (Balka, 1997).

Evidence-based practice is a movement that started in the medical field. It evolved from the recognition that only a small percentage of actual medical decisions that doctors made were based on current available research and fact. Doctors instead relied on what they learned in school many years ago, unproven traditions, their own experience, and generally preferred methods.

Over the last decade evidenced-based practices (EBP) have become increasingly important in human services practices. In EBP, practitioners select, if available, interventions that have been validated by systematic research and evaluation. More recently, various researchers, theorists, and practitioners have turned their attention toward the application of EBP principles to leadership and organizational management. An article in the *Harvard Business Review* by Pfeffer and Sutton (2006) noted that managers are even less likely to use research and evidence than are physicians. Therefore, the movement to get managers and leaders to use evidence has led to the development of an evidence-based practice connected to organizational leadership, management, and development. The authors present several key behaviors that EBP leaders should engage in: demanding evidence, examining logic, encouraging experimentation, and engaging in continuous learning. They do not believe that wisdom and experience should not count, but rather that appropriate quality evidence should be privileged over these important leadership skills.

There are many other theories that have strong influence over organizational life. We encourage you to explore these and other theories in depth, as the internalization of theory and knowledge, combined with your real-life experience, is what helps you develop practice wisdom (which even evidence-based leadership theories find of value).

Types of Organizations

Types of human service organizations (i.e., how they are classified) include a spectrum of options, ranging from auspice or legal basis, characteristics of the clients served, and services rendered. Blau and Scott (1962) identified four types of organizations under which human services are carried out:

1. Mutual benefit organizations, created by groups wishing to provide services for their own membership (e.g., churches, labor unions, and civil clubs)
2. Governmental or public organizations, established and funded by the general public to perform services that benefit all people
3. Service organizations, established as nongovernmental, nonprofit, voluntary social agencies
4. Business or entrepreneurial organizations, including for-profit organizations and private, non–agency-based practice

Each of the four types delineated by Blau and Scott (1962) can also be defined in terms of their operating authority—their legal standing—as illustrated in box 2.1.

BOX 2.1
Operating Authority of Human Service Organizations

Type of Organization	*Operating Authority*
Nonprofit	Incorporation in the state or locality in which it operates, with a charter, constitution, and bylaws. Has its own governing body and/or is organized as an identified organization of a religious body with legal status or is an identified organization of another legal entity that is recognized under the laws of the jurisdiction
Public	Authorized and established by statute or is a subunit of a public organization with which a clear administrative relationship exists
For-profit (proprietary)	Organized as a legal entity as a corporation, partnership, sole proprietorship, or association and has a charter, partnership agreement, or articles of association and a constitution and bylaws

Source: Adapted from Council on Accreditation of Services to Families and Children (1997).

The operating authority sets the parameters within which the organization functions. Organizations are allowed to do certain things—raise money in particular ways, devise a governance structure, recruit and use volunteers and/or staff, provide certain types of services—based largely on their operating authority. For example, a for-profit organization cannot solicit charitable contributions from individuals, corporations, or foundations; tax-exempt nonprofit organizations, as determined by the Internal Revenue Service, can solicit charitable contributions. Public agencies are authorized by statute to provide certain types of services that nonprofit and for-profit organizations may not provide; these include, primarily, services in which the organization acts as an agent of the state, such as in child or adult protective services.

Public versus Private Organizations

Public Organizations

Public organizations—those concerned with social welfare and other agencies under government auspices, such as the Immigration and Customs Enforcement, the Department of Housing, and the Department of Public Health—are created by legislative bodies at the local, state, and/or federal level.

Federal departments often have their counterparts in state agencies. For example, all states have a Department of Education. However, because education is primarily under local jurisdiction and control, counties or other defined geographic areas such as communities may similarly have their own education department (commonly known as the Board of Education). Large cities may have a set of public agencies or departments that correspond to those of the state department structure.

Public human service organizations are also known as governmental agencies. Within the human services, some public organizations are federally operated but have decentralized structures within local communities. For example, the network of Veterans Administration hospitals is under federal auspices even though the hospitals themselves are locally based. Public child welfare programs and programs for older adults are typically under the jurisdiction of state or local public agencies, although a sizable portion of their budgets comes from the federal government. Social workers who work for the government typically work under civil service rules and regulations. Each state has substantial leeway in how it organizes its service delivery system; thus, there is no one structural format that applies to all states (Gibelman, 2000).

The missions of public agencies are described in legal codes and government regulations (Garthwait, 2011). They are funded by tax dollars. This funding base is sometimes offset to some degree by fees-for-service or co-payments that clients/consumers may be required to pay to be eligible for public services. An example might be a fee for health inoculations. The fee generally does not cover the full cost of the service.

The majority of public social service agencies no longer directly provide most social services under their jurisdiction but rather contract with other agencies to deliver the services (Gibelman, 1998). Examples of public services that are contracted out include foster care, day care, residential treatment, family preservation services, and group homes.

Private Organizations

The private sector includes both nonprofit and for-profit agencies. Nonprofits have the longest tradition in providing human services in the United States. For-profits are relative newcomers to the human services market. Although both nonprofits and for-profits receive government funds and other benefits, they are considered to be independent of government control.

Nonprofit Organizations   Nonprofit organizations, based in philanthropic support of the arts, education, and human services, have a distinctly American flavor. The formation of voluntary associations to solve community problems predates the industrial era and grew exponentially with the social dislocation associated with industrialization, urbanization, and immigration (Karger & Stoesz, 2009). The origins of professional social work are rooted in the nonprofit charity organization societies and settlement house movements of the late nineteenth and early twentieth centuries. Government was a latecomer in the development and delivery of human services in the United States; it was only with the Great Depression that an ongoing public commitment to human welfare became manifest.

Within the not-for-profit sector (or nonprofit sector, as it is also called) there are two types of agencies: sectarian and nonsectarian. Sectarian agencies are those that operate under the auspices of or with the financial support of religious organizations or that are oriented toward providing services primarily to members of a specific religious group. Examples include Catholic Charities USA and its affiliates across the country, Jewish Family Services, Lutheran Social Services, and the Methodist Board of Child Care (Barker, 2003). Although less known in traditional social work circles, Muslim social service agencies are also an important part of U.S. and international social welfare. For instance, Islamic Relief USA has provided economic and social supports to people of all faiths who were victims of Hurricane Katrina. Nonsectarian social welfare agencies may be under a national rubric, such as the Child Welfare League of America or Family Service America, but are also located within communities and attempt to respond to community needs. Nonprofit organizations share the characteristics shown in box 2.2.

Most traditional social service and social change organizations are nonprofit. A nonprofit agency is accountable to its board of directors, which sets

---

BOX 2.2
Attributes of Nonprofit Organizations

- ◆ They are created or chartered to serve some facet of the common good.
- ◆ As corporations, they are legally under the control of a board of directors whose members are empowered to act on behalf of the organization.
- ◆ The board of directors represents the interests of the community or group that the agency seeks to serve and supports the agency's work.
- ◆ Revenues raised must be used to support their programs of service.
- ◆ They are restricted by IRS and many state statutes from participating in partisan political activities, including lobbying and promoting political candidates.
- ◆ They are publicly accountable for their activities.
- ◆ They are specifically empowered to hire employees to carry out their mission and engage in fund-raising to support their programs of service.

Source: Holland (1995); Garthwait (2011).

overall policy. The bylaws of the agency define the clients, the problems to be addressed, and what services are to be provided (Barker, 2003).

Nonprofit organizations maintain a special, privileged position among American organizations. They are distinguishable from public and for-profit organizations in a number of important ways. For example, nonprofit human service organizations provide important public benefits by offering services that, due to the nature of the marketplace, the for-profit community cannot provide in adequate quantity or quality and by ensuring that the entire community, not just those who can afford to pay, has access to needed services. In addition, because service, not profit, is their primary motive, nonprofits have earned the trust of their communities.

Faith-Based Groups Sectarian, or nonprofit organizations or groups under religious auspices, deserve special mention because of their place on the recent political agenda. Religion has played a critical role in the evolution of social services in the United States, and a primary goal of such services has been the promulgation of particular faiths (Canda, 2009; O'Connor, 2001). Most forms of organized social welfare have religious origins. Many of the earliest organizations established to serve the needs of the poor were under the auspices of evangelical Protestant and Catholic groups (Smith & Lipsky, 1993). Catholic social welfare systems grew in response to the increasing tide of Catholic immigration that began in the mid-nineteenth century.

Soon after taking office in January 2001, President Bush announced a "faith-based initiative" designed to promote the use of religious groups in the delivery of social services. This initiative was based on several assumptions about the organizations that were responsible for service delivery, such as:

◆ Private charities, including those under religious auspices, should have the fullest opportunity to compete for funds on a level playing field.
◆ Regulations barring such a level playing field should be revised or eliminated.
◆ Faith-based and grassroots groups will enlist and rely upon volunteers.
◆ An "outpouring" of private giving will be stimulated.
◆ Faith-based services offer "love as well as services, guidance and friendship as well as a meal or training" (Bush, 2001, p. 4).

Responses to the Bush plan ranged from applause among those who believed that faith had been the missing element in government social service programs to outrage by those who predicted that government would be enabled to play favorites with religions, that this would result in discriminatory hiring and firing practices, and that government would be reticent to monitor potential abuses among religious organizations (Farnsley, 2001; Goodstein, 2001; Hruby & Lipman, 2001).

Politicians and some clergy, notable among them evangelical Christians, Muslims, and other religious groups that had heretofore been excluded from government contracts, argued that faith-based groups offered high levels of community trust, a potential pool of volunteers, and a spiritual message that appeared to be associated with the success of some sectarian services providers (Lobdell & Watanabe, 2001). Opponents of the initiative came from more mainstream church groups. Their objections focused on the possibility that religious efforts might be corrupted by the receipt of government funds that were tied to government regulation and oversight (Edsall & Milbank, 2001).

When Congress did not act as fast or as favorably as the administration would have liked, the president initiated administrative changes that accomplished many of his faith-based goals (Milbank, 2001), such as giving preference to faith groups in the competition for federal grants and contracts. Through these contracts, government support for faith-based services expanded. For instance, the Office of Drug Free and Safe Schools, along with other federal grant-funding programs, focused considerable energy on faith-based initiatives. The Substance Abuse and Mental Health Services Administration (2007) of the U.S. Department of Health and Human Services renamed its community programs initiatives "faith-based community initiatives." While President Obama has largely continued to administer these programs with little deviation from the Bush policies (Biebricher, 2010), beginning in 2009, federal support for some of these faith-based initiatives has declined due to the reduction in overall grant funding for several of the federal agencies that focus on human service–related grants. While many programs give what is competitive preference for faith-based initiatives, the number of applications seems to have increased, while the recession has caused a decrease in the overall support of many initiatives.

For-profit Organizations   In recent years, for-profit organizations, also known as proprietary organizations, have increasingly entered the human services market, particularly in such settings as nursing homes, home health, residential treatment centers, and adult and child day care. Although these organizations employ social workers and other mental health professionals, they are privately owned and operated (Gibelman & Demone, 2002; Morales, Sheafor, & Scott, 2011). Their purpose is to sell services, and their operations reflect the goal of yielding a profit for investors and stockholders (Garthwait, 2011). Many such businesses are part of supercorporations, such as Psychiatric Institute, which owns and operates inpatient and outpatient psychiatric facilities across the country, and nursing home chains such as Golden Living. These types of franchises are similar to those of McDonald's or Walmart, but their only product is a human service.

The entrance of for-profits as providers of human services can largely be explained by changes in federal funding regulations that, in the late 1960s, began to allow for-profit organizations to apply for and receive contract funds (Gibelman, 1998). Such changes in federal regulations reflect a growing preference for privatization, based on the largely unproven premise that the free market and heightened competition will increase efficiency and reduce costs (Ingraham, Thompson, & Sanders, 1995). For over two decades, the health and mental health professions have been arguing about the various benefits and liabilities of for-profit services. Concerns have been expressed about the money-making motivation and its impact on the quality of care (Strom, 1992; Welte, 1993); the impact on the consumers of service (Culhane & Hadley, 1992; Rosenheck et al., 1998; Weigand, 1995); the cost of services (Kirwin & Kaye, 1993); and the ability of nonprofits to compete (Hirth, 1997; Litos, 1996; Tokarski, 1996). Despite concerns about the incompatibility of human services and profiteering, for-profits represent a growing force among human service organizations.

Boundary Blurring: Justifiable Confusion

The distinction between organizational types may be confusing, and with good reason. Today, no sector has exclusive jurisdiction over a service area. The substantial and growing amount of overlap in the characteristics of all human service organizations is largely the byproduct of boundary blurring brought about by the public financing of many privately delivered human services. The result is the creation of hybrid human service agencies. The term *hybrid* refers to a blending of two different entities, traditions, or cultures.

Because nonprofits and for-profits are now engaged in the same enterprise, it is not surprising that their distinctive features would become unclear in the public mind. The financial records of a nonprofit organization may indicate that the organization has a positive balance (an excess of revenues over expenses). Furthermore, a nonprofit may receive a large proportion of its annual revenues from government, including Medicaid and Medicare reimbursements and contracts. Nonprofits may have for-profit subsidiaries, and for-profits can have nonprofit subsidiaries. Examples include the nonprofit YMCA/YWCAs and Jewish Community Centers' fitness programs that compete in virtually all respects with for-profit sports facilities, except that the latter do not have any on-site human services. They compete for the same customers and the same dollars (Gibelman & Demone, 2002). These boundary issues may be confusing not just to the public but also to the professionals working within human service organizations, as exemplified in the vignette in box 2.3.

BOX 2.3
Hey, Isn't This a Nonprofit Agency?

This was Cynthia's second job after she obtained her MSW. Prior to entering the MSW program, she had been employed by the city's Department of Human Services and was awarded a scholarship to attend graduate school. As a condition of this scholarship, she was to work for the department for a period of two years. Although she had willingly accepted this obligation, Cynthia did not feel that the two years had been professionally rewarding. She had been placed in the child protective services unit in which she worked prior to beginning her MSW studies; the caseload was the same, and the conditions of work were the same; the frustrations, however, were even

(*continued on next page*)

worse, because she was not able to use her newly acquired knowledge and skills in a way that benefited the clients or the agency.

As the end of her commitment to the agency drew near, Cynthia sent out a large number of applications for jobs to nonprofit agencies in the city. She still wanted to work in child welfare services, only for an agency in which professionalism was expected and innovation and initiative were possible and rewarded. After interviewing with several agencies and asking what she perceived to be the right questions—caseload size, agency supports, availability of supervision—she accepted a job with a community-based multiservice center. She was assigned to the family preservation unit as a social worker II.

In the first few weeks on her new job, Cynthia was thrilled. The agency provided an in-depth orientation, and she was introduced to her caseload gradually. She carried fifteen cases and was expected to work intensively with the families assigned to her. Things were going well!

After a month on the job, Cynthia participated in a staff meeting in which the program director announced that the city had just issued new requirements for contracted agencies, which would mean more frequent and more intensive reporting. For each case served by the agency under contract with the city, a monthly report would now need to be submitted. Previously, reports had been submitted quarterly. Unlike previous reporting requirements, the social worker was now being asked to include clinical assessments and clinical benchmarks toward achievement of the service plan. Cynthia, as well as the other social workers present, immediately responded by saying that this would violate clients' confidentiality and adversely affect the worker-client relationship. The program director acknowledged the legitimacy of the concerns but said that the city could pretty much "call the tune" on what was to be reported and how often.

A secondary concern to Cynthia and her colleagues was the workload implications. It seemed that more and more time would need to be devoted to producing written reports that had dubious value. Cynthia began to wonder how different work in the nonprofit agency would really be. If the city was able to set the conditions of the worker-client relationship and, in essence, impose its own bureaucratic procedures on the contracted agency, maybe there were fewer advantages in the nonprofit work environment than she had thought. In fact, Cynthia had not realized that there was an interrelationship between the family preservation program offered by the community service center and the city agency for which she had previously worked.

Although Cynthia was employed by a nonprofit organization and her salary check was issued by the multiservice community center, the funds to pay her salary came from a city contract. As a recipient of public funds, the nonprofit agency was obligated to meet the reporting requirements of the city agency. Cynthia failed to understand the implications of contracting on the day-to-day operations and service programs of her new agency. This impact was substantial, and the nonprofit agency had little recourse but to do what was required.

Since the mid-1970s, the practice of privatization has been widespread in all sectors of the economy, including the human services. Privatization refers to divesting government of the responsibility for the funding and provision of products or services (Gibelman, 1998). The political ideology favoring the reduction of the size and power of government is centered on antigovernment sentiment and the belief that the private sector can do a better job (Gibelman, 1998; Morin, 1995; Passell, 1998).

It was some of the negative structural features of public agencies, such as rigid rules and their negative consequences on client services, the anti-professionalism associated with the public sector, and the slow, cumbersome, user-unfriendly systems, that led to the desire to seek alternative means to deliver services. However, as contractual arrangements with nonprofits mushroomed, the public sector began to impose its own bureaucratic rules and regulations on its contracted providers. Thus, nonprofit and for-profit agencies that contract with government have taken on some of the bureaucratic features typically associated with the public sector. In this case, privatization has many unintended consequences, some of which offset the perceived advantages of using the expertise of private agencies. Small community-based agencies serving diverse populations, which value community needs and client empowerment over efficiency, have been particularly hard hit by privatization and managed care.

Many have noted that the values of privatization may be incompatible with those of the social work profession and may indeed lead to ethical dilemmas (Dumont, 1996; Furman & Langer, 2006). For instance, the primary goal of for-profit corporations is to maximize profits for shareholders in each fiscal quarter. Furman (2003) observes that social workers have reported conflicts between the goals of for-profit managed care organizations and the social work values of confidentiality, autonomy, client empowerment, and self-determination and describes why it is essential for social workers to recognize these discrepancies as ethical dilemmas, not merely as workplace conflicts:

> The dilemmas social workers face in managed care contexts are often related to conflicting values, because the values of social workers and the profession as a whole differ markedly from [those of managed mental health organizations]. By understanding the nature of such dilemmas, social workers can help reframe them in a manner that allows for their successful resolution. (P. 50)

Self-Help Organizations

Self-help organizations do not often employ social workers. In fact, "pure" types of self-help organizations may not have any employees at all. Nevertheless, it is important to include them, as they offer a parallel system of human service delivery. In addition, social workers need to know about these alternative service systems, as they provide low-cost interventions that can augment, if not replace, some of the traditional roles of mainstream organizations.

We are probably all familiar with "anonymous" self-help organizations (twelve-step groups), the most notable of which is Alcoholics Anonymous. There are also "anonymous" groups associated with substance abuse, battering, overeating, a variety of compulsive behaviors, such as gambling, and mental disorders, for example, depression and neurosis. In addition to these widely known organizations, there are a large number of informal groups that deal with issues of common concern, such as loss of a loved one or the special issues of parental or marital status (single, widowed) or sexual orientation (gay, lesbian). Examples include Mothers Without Custody, Parents of Premature and High-Risk Infants, and Parents Without Partners.

Barker (2003) defines self-help organizations as "formally structured organizations that provide mutual support assistance for participants who share a common problem with which one or more of the participants has coped successfully" (p. 433). Self-help groups are characterized by cost-free or low-cost membership or services that are directed toward a common concern or situation, a helping process characterized as mutual support among members, and an absence of time limitations (Wituk, Shepherd, Slavich, Warren, & Meissen, 2000). Participation is sometimes seen as a lifelong process.

Distinct from the twelve-step programs are organizations concerned with public education, emotional support, and referral networks for people suffering from chronic ailments and their families. The best known of these organizations, including the American Cancer Society and the American Lung Association, would not be considered within the self-help category, given their degree of formalization, level of staffing, financial resources, and diversity of activities. However, the local chapters of these organizations often follow a self-help model. Smaller and lesser-known groups, such as the Lupus Foundation of America and its affiliate chapters, have their origins in grassroots self-help efforts and maintain their identity with mutual support networks rather than professionally driven services. These local units operate as self-help groups, with organizational support and resources coming from the well-structured, formalized national organizations.

Thus, self-help groups vary significantly in their level of formal organization, resources, use of professional staff, and identification. Their commonality lies in the coming together of individuals who share the same problem or concern and their focus on members providing emotional support to one another with the goal of improving their condition and that of others similarly affected (Wituk et al., 2000).

Indigenous helping resources found within many ethnically diverse communities also constitute a form of self-help (Foster, Phillips, Hamel, & Eisenburg, 2000). Indigenous or transitional helpers provide psychosocial and physical health support within the context of the historical beliefs and traditions of a particular ethnic group. While not typically seen as self-help by the world of social services, many communities possess helpers who are not professional in nature but provide community members with valuable support. Some of these, such as *curanderas*, may be considered faith based. *Curanderas* are usually older women in Latino communities who lend physical, emotional, and social support through the provision of advice, massage, candles, and prayer. It is important for social workers to ask their clients about the use of traditional helpers and healers and to find ways of incorporating these helpers into treatment plans. The ability to do so is a key aspect of culturally competent practice (Ayala, Vaz, Earp, Elder, & Cherrington, 2010; Seipel & Way, 2007).

It is estimated that more than 25 million Americans have been associated with self-help groups at some point in their lives (Kessler, Mickelson, & Zhao, 1997). Despite these groups' level of activity and use by the public to meet a variety of human needs, professionals do not, in general, make use of these networks as referral sources (Gartner, 1997). There are several explanations. First, professionals may see certain problems, such as mental illness or substance abuse, to be outside the purview of self-help, believing instead that professional services are both appropriate and necessary (Meissen, Mason, & Gleason, 1991). Second, professionals may simply be unaware of these groups. However, one study of self-help groups in one state revealed that a sizable proportion of them were peer led with some professional involvement; a lesser proportion were peer led with no professional involvement (Wituk et al., 2000). Professionals were involved with these groups in a variety of ways, including providing consulting services, serving as referral sources, and sponsoring participants. These data suggest that human service professionals do work with self-help groups, though not typically on a full-time basis.

Mission

All organizations have purposes. In the case of human service agencies, these purposes are usually articulated in a mission statement. Some organizations may have implicit rather than explicit purposes, but all come into existence to achieve specific ends. All organizations acquire and allocate resources needed to accomplish their goals. Some structural form is created and used to organize and coordinate activities. Organizations also rely on staff, members, volunteers, or constituents to carry out their activities. One or more persons are delegated to lead or manage others (Shafritz, Ott, & Jang, 2011).

Within each area of commonality among organizations lies the potential for variations. These variations have to do with the combination of purpose, structure, staffing, resources, leadership, and the like, within each organization. An additional influencing factor is the place of the organization within the community and the impact of external forces on it. Although the essential elements of organizations may be similar, how these elements are configured makes each organization unique.

Organizational Mission

The mission of the organization refers to why it exists and what it seeks to accomplish. Virtually all human service organizations have a defined purpose that, in general, is responsive to the needs of individuals, families, and groups in the community it serves. The community may be defined as a specific locality, such as Chicago; a population, such as children and youth; a problem affecting some members of the community, such as chronic mental illness or homelessness; or a characteristic of a group, such as gender (shelters for battered women) or religion (Catholicism, Judaism, Lutheranism).

The mission of a nonprofit organization can be found in its articles of incorporation and/or its bylaws. While defining the mission is part of the responsibility of the board of directors, the impetus for doing so and the work of defining the mission often emanates from organizational leaders and executives. The mission statement is not a static document. Most boards periodically reexamine the mission to determine whether it needs to be reaffirmed, updated, or revised (Axelrod, 1994).

The mission of a public agency is codified in statute and is spelled out in documents of incorporation or partnership, or in association with other documents authorizing the organization to operate as a subunit of another legal entity. For example, a statute might specify that an administrative structure be established to implement the program components of a law, such as the Older Americans Act (P.L. 89–73) and its subsequent amendments. A state government may assign implementation of the law to an existing agency, such as the Department of Human Services. This department will already have several divisions or subunits, such as child welfare, mental health, and mental retardation and developmental disabilities. A new unit may be created to plan, implement, and oversee programs for older Americans.

The mission of the for-profit organization is quite straightforward; the purpose or reason for being is to make a profit (Weinbach, 2008). Even though the commodity offered—human services—furthers a public interest, the product can be conceptualized as no different from the manufacturing of widgets or canned fruit (Gibelman, 2000).

Mission Statements

For many human service organizations, the mission statement concerns the provision of services to meet and respond to the expressed needs of persons in a community, toward the goal of strengthening individuals and families and their social and psychological functioning (Council on Accreditation, 1997). An organization's mission statement answers the questions, Who are we? What is supposed to happen for whom because of what we do? Several examples of mission statements appear in box 2.4.

BOX 2.4
Examples of Mission Statements

The Child Guidance Center of Southern Connecticut is a professionally-staffed outpatient mental health center for children and adolescents who experience psychological, behavioral, developmental, social or family problems. We are dedicated to reducing emotional suffering and dysfunctional behavior and to helping each individual achieve optimal potential. (Child Guidance Center of Southern Connecticut, 1999, p. 1)

* * *

(continued on next page)

Based upon Jewish tradition and values, the mission of Jewish Family Service of Bergen County is to strengthen and preserve the well-being of individuals and families; to help them effectively meet the challenges throughout life by providing quality human services and professional counseling to all who call upon its services. (Jewish Family Service of Bergen County, 2000)

* * *

Neighborhood Self Help by Older Persons Project's (SHOPP) mission is based on the philosophy of self-help and mutual assistance. We believe that older people are capable of helping themselves and helping others improve their capacity to deal with the physical, emotional, social and financial challenges they face as they age. SHOPP's philosophy of self and mutual assistance is translated into programs which empower older persons through knowledge, support, stimulation, and motivation. With SHOPP's involvement, older persons are provided with opportunities to achieve their potential by strengthening their social support systems, improving their quality of life, and becoming stakeholders in their own communities. (Neighborhood Self Help by Older Persons Project, 2000)

* * *

Steinway Child and Family Services, Inc. is a voluntary, non-sectarian and non-profit human services agency dedicated to reducing the incidence of mental health breakdown among children, families and adults, thereby restoring clients to their optimal level of functioning. To counter the effects of poverty, family breakdown and many other social pathologies experienced by many community residents, we provide a wide range of human services throughout the geographic area. (Steinway Child and Family Services, 1999)

* * *

Our aims are:
◆ To promote for the benefit of the Somali community the advancement of education and the provisions of the facilities in the areas of social welfare recreation and leisure.
◆ To provide services and activities which are designated to meet particular needs of Somali families.
◆ To assist people, in particular refugees in condition of hardship, sickness or distress by the provision of advice, information and other social welfare allied services.
◆ To promote effective strategies which will assure the equal provision of services to members of the Somali community. (Somali Women's Refugee Centre, 2007)

* * *

Congreso's mission is to strengthen Latino communities through social, economic, education, and health services; leadership development; and advocacy. (Congreso de Latinos Unidos, 2007)

How the Mission Is Carried Out

By definition, the mission statement is broad. Most organizations go beyond a statement of purpose to delineate their specific program goals and objectives and describe the subset of the communities they seek to serve. The goals and objectives may be articulated in a separate statement or as part of the mission statement. The organization's goals are statements that describe the condition or attributes the organization seeks to obtain (Tecker, 1991). Objectives flow from these goals; they are more concrete than goals and describe how the goals will be achieved. The mission is carried out through the programs of the organization. Box 2.5 describes how the missions of three nonprofit organizations are implemented.

BOX 2.5
Implementing the Mission Statement

The mission of Jewish Family Services is carried out in a number of ways, including:

◆ Making available the services of trained mental health professionals to furnish counseling or other appropriate assistance to develop the capacities to handle their problems;

◆ Identifying the causes of family disorganization and educating the community in practices of good family living through family education;

◆ Providing leadership and participating in community planning for the improvement of those social conditions essential to wholesome family life and promoting social legislation toward these ends;

◆ Contributing to professional education through providing field work training for students in accredited schools of social work; and

◆ Conducting such other activities as the board of trustees deems necessary to effectuate the mission. (Jewish Family Service of Bergen County, 2000)

* Our programs provide a full range of mental health and social services including psychiatric examinations, ongoing treatment and referrals—all designed to meet client needs which include acute situational disorder, chronic mental illness, family breakup, domestic violence prevention, substance abuse, and AIDS/HIV services and prevention. It is our abiding goal to meet these needs regardless of ability to pay. To deliver comprehensive, quality human services, Steinway's board of directors, executive staff, clinicians, and support staff are committed to active collaboration between our agency and the clients we serve. (Steinway Child and Family Services, 1999)

* Through the support and efforts of our senior citizens, community groups, and leaders, local political representatives, and staff, the Ridgewood Senior Citizens Council, Inc. has been able to obtain funding and to provide and make available a wide variety of social service programs to the residents of Bushwick, Williamsburg, Greenpoint, Ridgewood, Glendale, and surrounding communities. We sponsor services that range from direct social services,

(continued on next page)

counseling, and home care to training, employment, building rehabilitation, and construction. Founded in 1976 as a senior-oriented Council, the Ridgewood Bushwick Senior Citizens Council has extended its mission beyond its original scope and has evolved into a full-service community-based organization providing services to people of all ages. (Ridgewood Bushwick Senior Citizens Council, n.d.)

Jewish Family Services, Steinway Child and Family Services, and Ridgewood Bushwick Senior Citizens Council are all nonprofit organizations governed by boards of directors. The job of the board includes periodic reexamination of the purpose or mission to ensure that it is responsive to and reflective of changing community needs. The board and the administration are also responsible for defining the programs that will ensure that the mission is achieved. Good boards and administrations take into account the feedback of their various constituents as they undertake these tasks.

Range of Program Offerings

Human service organizations may offer only one or two types of specialized programs, or they may offer a large range of programs. The Child Guidance Center of Southern Connecticut (1999), for example, offers a large range of programs including child, adolescent, and family therapy, crisis intervention services, a child sexual-abuse response team, school-based health clinics, a therapeutic nursery, mental health services for HIV-affected children, a child and adolescent crime victims assistance program, a parent consultation service, a community emergency response program, consultation services, and community education. VIP Community Services in the Bronx, New York, focuses on different social needs and client populations and offers a range of programs, including transitional housing for women, day treatment for drug addictions, housing development, a men's residence, a methadone maintenance treatment program, health services and HIV prevention and education, vocational and educational services, and a women's residence (VIP Community Services, 1999).

On the other hand, a homeless shelter may provide lodging and meals only, or it may offer a program of information and referral. Because the clients are generally served for a short period of time and for a specified reason, a full range of programs would not typically be available through the shelter. Somewhere between the multiservice organization and a single program agency is the agency that provides several programs but to one specific population. A case in point is a child development center serving young children who are experiencing a range of emotional and/or developmental difficulties and their families. A child development center may offer a therapeutic nursery school, an early intervention program, an outpatient clinic, and an early childhood group therapy program.

It is useful to distinguish between a program and a service. Barker (2003) defines a program as "a relatively permanent organization and procedure designed to meet ongoing client needs" and "a plan and guideline about what is to be done" (p. 381). A program has structural dimensions; there may be a manager and workers charged with planning, implementing, and evaluating the program, a specified budget, and a targeted clientele. A service is an activity—what is done to carry out the program. It is the actual deployment of the organization's resources in a planned and systematic manner (Council on Accreditation, 1997). Social workers working within an organization are assigned to specific programs. They use their knowledge and skills to provide a service—psychotherapy, case management, crisis intervention, child placement, and the like—to their clients. In some instances, the program and the service may have the same name. For example, Meals on Wheels is a program—it has a defined purpose, structure, budget, and staff. It is also a service involving the actual delivery of meals to people who need them.

Each program of the organization usually has a defined purpose. For example, the purpose of the Youth Services Program of the Ridgewood Bushwick Senior Citizens Council (n.d.) is to offer youth "a means of using their free time constructively to better themselves personally, academically, and culturally" (p. 14). Within this one program are several distinct subprograms. One is the Youth Awareness Prevention Program, which offers individual and group counseling to young people between the ages of twelve and nineteen who display at-risk behavior (e.g., violence, gang activity, truancy, drug abuse). Another component of Youth Services is the Teen Network Project, the objective of which is to assist youth who are parenting, pregnant, or at risk of becoming pregnant. The program seeks to realize its objective through high school equivalency classes, basic education and tutoring, and workshops aimed at defining personal goals. Each program and each subprogram has its own target population (clients). Revenues and expenditures associated with each component are calculated separately.

The agency mission, then, represents the broad purposes for which the organization was formed. The programs of the organization are the means to realize the mission. Each program area has its own set of goals and objectives. The overarching program area may have several components or subprograms that further clarify how the organization is to achieve its purposes. Finally, each program goal is operationalized into a series of objectives. Because goals are timeless, broad statements that describe desired ends, they cannot be operationalized directly. Instead, another step is needed—the formulation of objectives.

Formulating Objectives

Objectives are measurable, attainable milestones that articulate time frames for successfully achieving a goal. An example of a goal is to serve all children at risk of teen pregnancy in a specified community. This goal is not measurable;

there are no indicators of how the organization will know when it is achieved, nor are there time frames for its achievement. There are likely to be several objectives that relate to this goal. Two examples are:

1. To conduct, between the years 2008 and 2011, a demographic survey of the thirteen- to eighteen-year-old age group residing in Corona, California, and to analyze the results for use in program planning
2. To initiate, by September 2010, an after-school program in three different schools, serving twenty teens per site, which offers recreational activities, instruction regarding birth control and family planning, and counseling services, as appropriate and indicated

These objectives specify what will happen, within what time frame, and where. They can be further refined to include the parties responsible for implementation. Attainment of these objectives can be observed and measured. However, such measurement will not tell us about the quality of the survey or the after-school program. Measuring the outcome of services is explored in later chapters.

Although the organization has primary responsibility for defining its mission and the program goals and objectives by which the mission will be carried out, many external forces affect the exact way in which programs and services are articulated and operationalized. The precise nature of programs, for example, may be influenced by the demands of political groups, funders, and community members (Hanson, 1998). Ideally, a broadly stated organizational mission allows for some adaptability and flexibility in regard to how it is achieved. However, the demands made on the organization by external sources may stretch the boundaries of the original mission and thus impede the capacity of the agency to achieve its purposes.

Direct service social workers, in their interactions with administrators, influence the mission as well as the implementation of the mission into goals and objectives. For instance, social workers working in an agency in Texas that served primarily African Americans noted that the values and the culture of the community were not well integrated into the structure of the programs. Agency administrators responded to this critique by holding community forums, which enabled them to incrementally change the mission and objectives of the agency. As this example illustrates, agency norms and structures may be created in a reciprocal and collaborative fashion by various stakeholders.

Organizational Structure

All organizations have formal structures through which to carry out their work and achieve their purposes. Skidmore (1990) defines structures as the "actual arrangements and levels of an organization in regard to power, authority, responsibilities, and mechanisms for carrying out [organizational] functions and practices" (p. 97).

An organizational chart is the best descriptor of the structure of an organization and shows its lines of authority, relationships, and substructures (which
may be called departments, units, or divisions). Each organization structures itself somewhat differently, a reflection of the particular programs it sponsors, its
financial resources, its system of governance, management philosophy, and
agency traditions. An example of an organizational chart is provided in box 2.6.

The organizational diagram tells us many things about the organization.
First, the chain of command—who reports to whom—is specified. Second, it
provides some idea of the size and complexity of the organization. The programs are delineated. The number and type of staff assigned to each program
may be featured. In short, the organizational chart is a blueprint of the agency's
structural relationships.

Substructures

Organizations, once created, seek to establish systems to carry out their
work and, further, to ensure their own survival and growth. The development of
formal substructures affects how and how well the work is carried out. Formal
substructures include the divisions, departments, or units needed to do the
agency's work, staffing patterns, the pattern of governance, including the appointment or election of board and committee members, and board-adminis-
tration-staff arrangements.

The structure of the organization includes its physical location and space.
Some organizations occupy one location; others may have a main headquarters
and one or more satellite offices. The Legal Aid Society of New York, for example, is headquartered in Manhattan, and its eight distinct divisions are located in
thirty-nine or more sites across the five boroughs of New York City (Legal Aid
Society, 1999).

The Jewish Board of Family and Children's Services (1998), centrally located in Manhattan, offers its programs in the five boroughs of New York and
on Long Island and in Westchester County—suburbs of the city. Its scope of
program offerings is vast and includes AIDS services, day treatment programs,
early childhood programs, and family violence programs. Some programs are
residential, others are day treatment, and still others provide periodic services.
Each program has its own administrator, such as the director of services for the
developmentally disabled or the director of group treatment. Not all programs
are available in all locations. For example, the Russian Outreach Program is located in an area in which many Russian immigrants live. Counseling services,
on the other hand, may be housed in many locations. The dispersion of the target population served may require multiservice sites to provide accessibility to
clients. These satellite service centers constitute a decentralized subsystem for
the local implementation of services. Given the breadth of the population
served by the organization, the use of multiple sites is essential to accomplish
program goals.

BOX 2.6
Example of an Organizational Chart

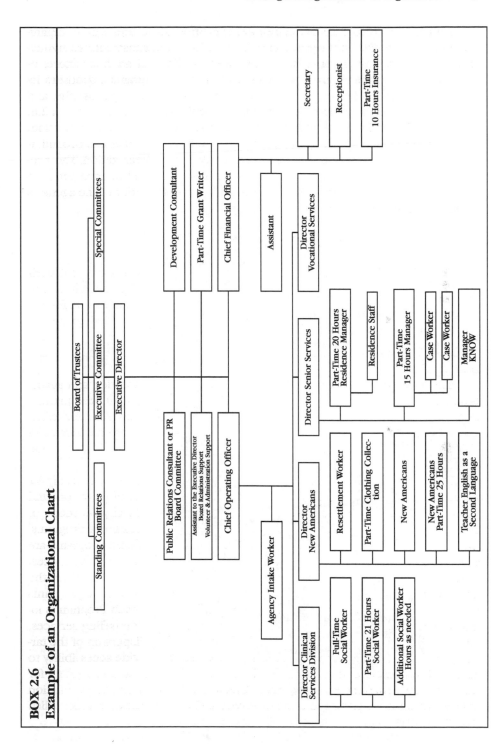

Public human service agencies, too, are often structured on a county-by-county basis, with varying degrees of control from the umbrella state organization. The size of the organization, number of clients served, and range of programs offered are also important variables in determining the need for decentralized sites.

Size is an important determinant of the overall structure of an organization and the nature and breadth of its substructures. Large public bureaucracies, for example, are characterized by centralization of decision making and formalization of work procedures through guidelines and a clear division of labor to allocate responsibility for the organization's work.

The range of potential subsubstructures is large. How the organization is structured, however, is subject to change.

Structural Change

That structures are not static can be observed in the frequency with which organizations reorganize. In New York City, the Administration for Children's Services was formerly known as the Bureau of Child Welfare. This was not simply a change in name. This agency has gone back and forth between being a highly centralized structure to being a highly decentralized, community-based structure, a phenomenon that has also occurred in similar agencies in other major cities throughout the United States as part of an ongoing attempt to fix the system.

These changes in structure reflect philosophical changes in how the goals and objectives of the organization can best be carried out. For example, a community-based, decentralized structure is predicated on a model of service delivery that emphasizes proximity to and accessibility for consumers.

Finally, structural change may be an immediate and relatively easily implemented response to crisis. For example, when a particularly gruesome case of child abuse is exposed and the press places the blame on the child protective services agency (typically for knowing about but not acting on the situation), an initial organizational response may be structural change. Reorganization can be accomplished. Intractable social problems are less easily addressed.

Structural change may also be promoted by changes in federal or state legislation. For example, during the 1960s, the separation of income maintenance and social services actuated in the Social Security Amendments of 1962 led to the creation of two service delivery structures where there had previously been one. The complexity of structural arrangements has also been affected by the increase in the number of clients served and the range of services offered. Technology has also made decentralized structures possible, with heightened coordination available through the use of computers.

The Future

As we look toward the future, we are likely to see increased competition between nonprofit and for-profit organizations, as well as the continued decline in the public sector's role in the direct delivery of services. One of the hallmarks of the last decade has been the proliferation of for-profit companies offering services previously provided primarily by nonprofit and government agencies (Moore, 1998). Conversion of organizations from one type to another—profit to nonprofit or nonprofit to profit—also has the effect of blurring the traditional distinctions between the sectors.

The long-term effects of boundary blurring remain within the realm of speculation. What is clear is that the traditional distinctions between organizational types no longer represent an accurate picture of modern human service agencies (Kramer, 1998).

Self-help organizations remain largely immune from the permutations experienced by traditional human service organizations. Their place within the spectrum of organizational types, however, may become more important as traditional service providers look for cost-effective partnerships to serve their clientele.

Globalization: Another Consideration for the Future

It is difficult to open the newspaper without reading about globalization and seeing evidence of the increasing interconnectedness of economic and social institutions. The integration of world economic structures, the policies of neoliberalism, the advances of increasingly sophisticated hypertechnology, and the complex and extensive patterns of international migration are but a few of the factors that contribute to the creation of social needs that are global in nature. Social work too is becoming increasingly globalized (Estes, 1992; Ramanathan & Link, 1999). International social work is being increasingly recognized as an important area of practice (Furman, Puig, Szto, & Langer, 2003; Healy, 2001).

An even newer development is the notion of transnational social work. Transnational social work is a practice that works with transnational migrants (people who move back and forth across and between nation-states) and that transcends international borders. While few social work services are currently transnational in nature, it is inevitable that as the world's populations become increasingly transnational, social work practice will follow. Furman and Negi (2007) offer a glimpse into transnational social work:

> Another important service need is to establish multi-service social welfare agencies that are capable of responding to transnational populations. This may entail fostering transnational alliances with social workers from Latin American countries. Such social work transnational alliances could assist social workers of both receiving and sending communities to develop effective interventions that cut across nation state boundaries. Social workers from both receiving and sending communities can then benefit from each others' expertise and collaboratively develop intervention strategies that maintain the well-being of transnational Latino migrants across boundaries. These alliances can be built through active involvement in international conferences and other international social work networking opportunities. (P. 110)

Key Points

- ◆ Agencies are "typed" on the basis of several dimensions, including legal basis, clients served, services offered, and technology or interventions used.
- ◆ The mission of public agencies is described in legal codes and government regulations.
- ◆ The private sector is multifaceted and includes for-profit and nonprofit organizations, both nonsecular and secular.
- ◆ Although nonprofit organizations are independent, they are authorized by government through their tax-exempt status and are subject to government oversight.
- ◆ For-profit organizations have recently become major players in the delivery of human services, in large part because of changes in federal funding regulations.
- ◆ For-profit organizations seek to yield a profit for their investors and stockholders; this raises questions about the quality and cost of services, as well as the impact on the ability of nonprofits to compete.
- ◆ There is substantial overlap in the types of services provided by for-profits, nonprofits, and public agencies, resulting in boundary blurring.
- ◆ Self-help organizations offer a parallel system of human services delivery.
- ◆ The purpose of an organization can be found in its mission statement.
- ◆ The programs of an organization flow from and relate directly to its mission.
- ◆ An organization's mission, goals, and objectives evolve and change in response to both internal and external influences.
- ◆ Agencies create structures to organize and carry out their work.
- ◆ The organizational diagram depicts an agency's structure.
- ◆ The future of human service organizations suggests increased competition between for-profits and nonprofits and even more boundary blurring between the different types of organizations.

Suggested Learning Activities and Discussion Questions

1. Locate and read your organization's articles of incorporation or bylaws. Summarize what you discover about the legal authority of the organization. What are the major phrases or words that inform you about the organizational type?
2. If your agency is a public agency, trace the specific legislation or statute that created the agency. What is the scope of the agency's authority and responsibility?
3. If your agency is for-profit, who are the owners? How are profits invested and used? Is the agency part of a larger corporation? How are policy decisions made?

4. Does your agency refer clients to self-help groups? If yes, under what circumstances are such referrals made? Are such referrals instead of or in addition to continued agency services to the client?

5. Obtain a copy of your organization's mission statement. Analyze the fit between the stated mission and the programs the organization now runs.

6. Write a mission statement for a new agency that will provide services to an underserved community.

Recommended Readings

Cnaan, R. A., Wineburg, R. J., & Boddie, S. C. (1999). *The newer deal: Social work and religion in partnership*. New York: Columbia University Press.

Gibelman, M., & Demone, H. W., Jr. (Eds.). (1998). *The privatization of human services: Policy and practice issues*. New York: Springer.

Hasenfeld, Y. (1994). *Human services as complex organizations*. Newbury Park, CA: Sage Publications.

Kurtz, L. F. (1997). *Self-help and support groups: A handbook for practitioners*. Thousand Oaks, CA: Sage Publications.

Salamon, L. M. (1999). *America's nonprofit sector: A primer*. Washington, DC: Foundation Center.

Wagner, D. (2000). *What's love got to do with it? A critical look at American charity*. New York: W. W. Norton.

References

Axelrod, N. R. (1994). Board leadership and board development. In R. D. Herman & Associates (Eds.), *The Jossey-Bass handbook of nonprofit leadership and management* (pp. 119–136). San Francisco: Jossey-Bass.

Ayala, G. X., Vaz, L., Earp, J. A., Elder, J. P., & Cherrington, A. (2010). Outcome effectiveness of the lay heath advisor model among Latinos in the United States: An examination by role. *Health Education Research, 25*(5), 815–840.

Balka, E. (1997). Participatory design in women's organizations: The social world of organizational structure and the gendered nature of expertise. *Gender, Work & Organization, 4*(2), 99–115.

Barker, R. L. (2003). *Social work dictionary* (5th ed.). Washington, DC: NASW Press.

Biebricher, T. (2010). Faith-based initiatives and the challenge of governance. *Public Administration, 89*(3), 1001–114.

Blau, P. M., & Scott, R. (1962). *Formal organizations: A comparative approach*. San Francisco: Chandler.

Bush, G. W. (2001, May 26). *Rallying the armies of compassion*. Available: http://www.whitehouse.gov/news/reports/text/faith-based.html

Canda, E. R. (2009). *Spiritual diversity in social work practice: The heart of helping* (2nd ed.). New York: Oxford University Press.

Child Guidance Center of Southern Connecticut. (1999). *About the Child Guidance Center*. Stamford, CT: Author.

Congreso de Latinos Unidos. (2007). *Mission statement*. Available: http://congresso.net.mission.php

Council on Accreditation of Services to Families and Children. (1997). *1997 standards for behavioral health care services and community support and education services* (U.S. ed.). New York: Author.

Culhane, D. P., & Hadley, T. R. (1992). The discriminating characteristics of for-profit versus not-for-profit freestanding psychiatric inpatient facilities. *Health Services Research, 27*(2), 177–194.

Dumont, M. P. (1996). Privatization and mental health in Massachusetts. *Smith College Studies in Social Work, 66*(3), 293–303.

Edsall, T. B., & Milbank, D. (2001, March 8). Blunt defense of "faith-based" aid. *Washington Post*, p. A8.

Estes, R. J. (1992). *Internationalizing social work education*. Philadelphia: University of Pennsylvania.

Farnsley, A. E., II. (2001). Can faith-based organizations compete? *Nonprofit and Voluntary Sector Quarterly, 30*(1), 99–111.

Foster, D. F., Phillips, R. S., Hamel, M. B., & Eisenburg, D. M. (2000). Alternative medicine use in older Americans. *JAGS, 48*, 1560–1565.

Furman, R. (2003). Frameworks for understanding value discrepancies and ethical dilemmas in managed mental health for social work in the United States. *International Social Work, 46*(1), 37–52.

Furman, R., & Langer, C. L. (2006). Managed care and the care of the soul. *Journal of Social Work Values and Ethics, 3*(2). Available: http://www.socialworker.com/jswve/content/view/39/46

Furman, R., & Negi, N. J. (2007). Social work practice with transnational Latino populations. *International Social Work, 50*(1), 107–112.

Furman, R., Puig, M., Szto, P., & Langer, C. (2003). Infusing international content in the social work curriculum. *Currents: New Scholarship in Human Services, 2*(2). Available: http://fsw.ucalgary.ca/currents/articles/furman_v2_n2.htm

Garthwait, C. (2011). *The social work practicum: A guide and workbook for students* (5th ed.). Boston, MA: Allyn and Bacon.

Gartner, A. J. (1997). Professionals and self-help: Can they get along? *Social Policy, 27*, 47–52.

Gibelman, M. (1998). Theory, practice, and experience in the purchase of services. In M. Gibelman & H. W. Demone, Jr. (Eds.), *The privatization of human services: Policy and practice issues* (Vol. 1, pp. 1–51). New York: Springer.

Gibelman, M. (2000). Structural and fiscal characteristics of social service agencies. In R. J. Patti (Ed.), *The handbook on social welfare administration* (pp. 113–131). Newbury Park, CA: Sage Publications.

Gibelman, M., & Demone, H. W., Jr. (2002). The commercialization of health and human services: Neutral phenomenon or cause for concern? *Families in Society, 83*(4), 387–397.

Goodstein, L. (2001, January 30). Nudging church-state line, Bush invites religious groups to seek federal aid. *New York Times*, p. A18.

Hanson, M. (1998). Practice in organizations. In M. A. Mattaini, C. T. Lowery, & C. H. Meyer (Eds.), *The foundations of social work practice* (2nd ed., pp. 240–264). Washington, DC: NASW Press.

Healy, L. M. (2001). *International social work: Professional action in an interdependent world*. New York: Oxford University Press.

Hirth, R. A. (1997). Competition between for-profit and nonprofit health care providers: Can it help achieve social goals? *Medicare Care Research and Review, 54*(4), 414–438.

Holland, T. P. (1995). Organizations: Context for social service delivery. In R. L. Edwards (Ed.-in-chief), *Encyclopedia of social work* (19th ed., pp. 1787–1794). Washington, DC: NASW Press.

Hruby, L., & Lipman, H. (2001, May 3). Religious leaders assail plan to aid faith groups. *Chronicle of Philanthropy*, pp. 43–44.

Iannello, K. P. (1992). *Decisions without hierarchy: Feminist interventions in organization theory.* New York: Routledge.

Ingraham, P. W., Thompson, J. R., & Sanders, R. P. (Eds.). (1995). *Transforming government.* San Francisco: Jossey-Bass.

Jewish Board of Family and Children's Services. (1999). *Directory of programs and services: 1999–2000.* New York: Author.

Jewish Family Service of Bergen County. (2000). *Personnel policies and practices.* Teaneck, NJ: Author.

Karger, H. J., & Stoesz, D. (2009). *American social welfare policy: A pluralist approach* (6th ed.). New York: Longman.

Kessler, R. C., Mickelson, K. D., & Zhao, S. (1997). Patterns and correlates of self-help group members in the United States. *Social Policy, 27,* 27–46.

Kirwin, P. M., & Kaye, L. W. (1993). A comparative cost analysis of alternative models of adult day care. *Administration in Social Work, 17*(2), 105–122.

Kramer, R. M. (1998). *Nonprofit organizations in the 21st century: Will sector matter?* Washington, DC: Aspen Institute, Nonprofit Sector Research Fund, Working Paper Series.

Legal Aid Society. (1998). *Annual report.* Available: http://www.legal-aid.org/ar99/crimd.htm

Litos, D. (1996). Partnerships with for-profits. *Michigan Health Hospital, 32*(5), 26–27.

Lobdell, W., & Watanabe, T. (2001, January 30). Shelter may get presidential seal; Supporters of a homeless lodging planned on Tustin Marine base land take heart in Bush's promise to help faith-based groups. *Los Angeles Times*, p. B1.

Meissen, G., Mason, W. C., & Gleason, D. F. (1991). Understanding the attitudes and intentions of future professionals toward self-help. *American Journal of Community Psychology, 19,* 699–714.

Milbank, D. (2001, August 19). Bush urges senators to act on faith bill. *Washington Post*, p. A4.

Moore, J. (1998, August 13). A corporate challenge for charities. *Chronicle of Philanthropy*, pp. 1, 34–36.

Morales, A. T., Sheafor, B. R., & Scott, M. E. (2011). *Social work: A profession of many faces* (12th ed.). Boston: Allyn & Bacon.

Morin, R. (1995, October 11). A united opinion: Government doesn't do a good job. *Washington Post*, p. A12.

Neighborhood Self Help by Older Persons Project. (2000). *Annual report, 1999–2000.* Bronx, NY: Author.

O'Connor, S. (2001, May 26). When children relied on faith-based agencies [Op-ed]. *New York Times*, p. A24.

Passell, P. (1998, January 5). Doing the American-opposition-to-big-government 2-step. *New York Times*, p. D10.

Pfeffer, J., & Sutton, R. I. (2006). Evidenced-based management. *Harvard Business Review* (On-Point Article). Retrieved January 14, 2012, from http://jeffreypfeffer.com/wp-content/uploads/2011/10/HBR-Jan2006.pdf.

Ramanathan, C. S., & Link, R. J. (1999). *All our futures: Principles and resources for social work practice in a global era.* Pacific Grove, CA: Brooks/Cole.

Ridgewood Bushwick Senior Citizens Council. (n.d.). *Description of programs.* Brooklyn, NY: Author.

Rosenheck, R., Armstrong, M., Callahan, D., Dea, R., Del Vecchio, P., Flynn, L., Fox, R. C., Goldman, H. H., Horvath, T., & Munoz, R. (1998). Obligation to the least well off in setting mental health service priorities: A consensus statement. *Psychiatric Services, 49*(10), 1273-1274, 1290.

Seipel, A., & Way, I. (2007). Culturally competent social work practice with Latin clients. *The New Social Worker, 12*(4), 4-7.

Shafritz, J. M., Ott, J. S., & Jang, Y. S. (2011). *Classics of organization theory* (7th ed.). Belmont, CA: Thomson/Wadsworth.

Skidmore, R. A. (1990). *Social work administration* (2nd ed.). Englewood Cliffs, NJ: Prentice Hall.

Smith, S. R., & Lipsky, M. (1993). *Nonprofits for hire: The welfare state in the age of contracting*. Cambridge, MA: Harvard University Press.

Somali Women's Refugee Centre. (2007). *Aims*. Available: http://www.swrc1.org.uk/pages/aims.htm

Steinway Child and Family Services. (1999). *Mission statement and agency background*. Available: http://www.steinway.org

Strom, K. (1992). Reimbursement demands and treatment decisions: A growing dilemma for social workers. *Social Work, 37*, 398-403.

Substance Abuse and Mental Health Services Administration. (2007). *Faith-based and community initiatives*. Available: http://samhsa.gov/FBCI/fbci.aspx

Tecker, G. H. (1991). *Strategic program assessment*. Silver Spring, MD: National Association of School Psychologists.

Tokarski, C. (1996). Joint ventures between for-profits and not-for-profits: Do they work and how? *Health System Leadership, 3*(3), 4-13.

VIP Community Services. (1999). *Changing lives, transforming the community*. Bronx, NY: Author.

Weber, M. (1997). *The theory of social and economic organization* (edited and with an introduction by Talcott Parsons). New York: Simon & Schuster.

Weigand, N., Jr. (1995). For profits: No less focused on communities. *Hospital Health Network, 69*(11), 8.

Weinbach, R. W. (2008). *The social worker as manager: A practical guide to success* (5th ed.). Boston: Allyn & Bacon.

Welte, T. (1993). Mental health and managed care for the elderly: Issues and options. *Generations, 17*, 69-72.

Wituk, S., Shepherd, M. D., Slavich, S., Warren, M. L., & Meissen, G. (2000). A topography of self-help groups: An empirical analysis. *Social Work, 45*(2), 157-165.

Chapter 3

How Organizations Are Financed

> "Dad," the eight-year-old said to his father, "can I have $75 for a new pair of Nike sneakers?" The father looked up from his newspaper and said, "Do you think money grows on trees in the backyard? You've already spent all of the money set aside for your new school clothes this year."

As adults, we are familiar with the need to balance our personal checkbooks. When the balance gets close to zero, we stop writing checks. Otherwise, the checks would bounce, there would be service charges, and the store or company to which the bounced check was written would send delinquent notices.

Throughout our lives, we all have experience with budgets and finances. The same financial principles that govern our personal lives apply to organizations. They, too, have financial concerns, and there is a direct relationship between the amount of money that comes in (income or revenues) and what can go out (expenditures). In this chapter, the sources of income for different types of human service organizations are reviewed. The emphasis is on where the money comes from, how sources of funds relate to agency programs and services, how such money may be spent and how it is managed, and the impact of organizational finances on the work of the agency and practitioners. The use of mergers as a strategy to conserve and efficiently use resources is also discussed.

The *Code of Ethics* (National Association of Social Workers, 1999) specifies that "social workers should be diligent stewards of the resources of their employing organizations, wisely conserving funds where appropriate and never misappropriating funds or using them for unintended purposes" (p. 22). To comply with this ethical mandate, every practitioner must have some familiarity with how the employing agency is financed and what constraints, as well as enabling features, the sources of funds have on programs and operations.

The sources of money, the dependability of these funds year after year, and the financial viability of the organization have an immediate, ongoing, and significant impact on all staff. The finances of the organization influence both the context in which the agency functions and the parameters in which change strategies may be considered. This chapter serves as an introduction to the ways in which money enhances and constrains the work environment, as well as organizational growth and change.

In common to all types of human service organizations is the demand for financial accountability. Accountability is rooted in concerns about how organizations spend the money entrusted to them. The financial management systems of human service organizations are thus developed, implemented, and evaluated within the context of meeting internal and external accountability requirements.

Sources of Funds

Financial Bases by Sector

Historically, the three sectors described in the previous chapter—nonprofit, for-profit, and public—have been identified with different and noncompeting financial bases, as illustrated in box 3.1. The public sector, of course, has its financial base in public allocations that come from tax dollars. The nonprofit sector receives a large proportion of its financing from charitable contributions, including monies earmarked to specific types of organizations through the United Way of America and other combined campaigns. For-profit organizations are associated with fee-for-service financing, in which individuals or groups pay for the services rendered according to fees established by the organization, which are based, in turn, on what the market will bear. However, reality is more complex as borders get blurred and overlap occurs.

BOX 3.1 Traditional Sources of Funding: Pure Types	
Organizational Type	*Primary Source of Funding*
Public	Legislative allocations
Nonprofit (voluntary)	Charitable contributions
Private (proprietary)	Fee-for-service

Nonprofit organizations, since the very beginning of public financing of social services, have received government funds to implement specific programs of service. Traditionally, state and local governments have chosen to meet part of their responsibilities by financing the provision of care and services by local nongovernmental organizations. The relationship between nonprofits and governments thus has a long history, the nature of which has varied over time depending on changing conceptions of the role and functions of each sector.

Purchase of Services

Purchasing services from the private sector is a favored means of delivering social services. Many of the services offered by nonprofit human service agencies are financed by government through grants and contracts, and billions of dollars are spent annually on health and human services through Medicaid and Medicare, in which consumers select their own service providers.

The old adage "He who pays the piper calls the tune" is an apt description of the end result of these contracting arrangements. On the positive side, as a condition of government funding, nonprofits have developed new management competencies, including negotiating skills and financial accountability systems. Nonprofit agencies have been able to introduce new programs and services, and in some cases, voluntary agencies have been created as a direct result of the availability of public funds to finance particular types of services, such as assistance to victims of crime (Smith, 1989).

The negative byproducts of these public-private relationships, however, are formidable. Questions about the autonomy of nonprofits have increasingly been raised (Gibelman, 1995), as these contracted agencies must modify their service delivery systems to align with public program priorities and as the public sector becomes more demanding in its accountability requirements. The consequences of contracting have been seen as so pervasive that nonprofits have been accused of becoming agents of the state (Goldstein, 1993). The key factor in this transformation has been the growing reliance of nonprofits on contract funds, which makes them dependent on government resources.

Beneficial Public Policies

In addition to their relationship with government through contracts, nonprofits benefit from public policies that help finance their work. For example, nonprofits have historically benefited from government largess through federally subsidized postage rates. However, a 1993 law changed the way that Congress subsidizes the Postal Service for delivering nonprofit mail; federal subsidies are gradually being phased out (Hall, 1998).

The IRS sets interest rates (typically below market rates) for computing charitable deductions for trusts, gift annuities, charitable trusts, and some other deferred gifts (Billitteri & Stehle, 1998). Of course, taxpayers benefit from their ability to claim tax deductions for charitable giving in cash and kind. There is increased pressure on Congress to pass new tax incentives to encourage charitable giving, particularly at a time when nonprofit organizations are seen as key players in solving the country's problems ("Panel on Civil Renewal," 1998). The idea of increasing charitable giving through greater tax incentives was also a cornerstone of proposals during the early days of the Bush administration (Williams, 2001).

Competition for Funds

Nonprofits and for-profits now compete for the same sources of funds, most notably government or managed care contracts. This competition has made it imperative for all human service organizations to establish a cost basis for units of services and to be able to calculate how many clients are needed for a specific program to break even (Ezell, 2000; Meyer & Sherraden, 1985). When reimbursement rates are part of the competitive bidding process, for-profits, by virtue of volume of services, may be able to underbid nonprofits and win the contracts.

A high level of expertise is needed to monitor all potential funding sources. To stay competitive, many nonprofits have borrowed fund-raising strategies from the business world. In this process, organizations have had to become more sophisticated about identifying sources of funding and fine-tune budgeting practices to "cost out" how much money it takes to fund particular programs and services. This may include hiring fund-raisers and fund developers.

Diversification of Funding Sources

The greatest source of stability for a nonprofit lies in diversifying its funding base. When an organization has only limited sources of funds, it may become resource dependent, a position in which the funder or funders can exercise enormous influence over the programs and operations of the agency. Such influence may translate to "life or death power" over the organization (Elkin, 1987, p. 625).

Nonprofit organizations tend to have multiple and diverse sources of funding, particularly in comparison to other types of organizations. It is very common for both large and small nonprofit organizations to receive funds from managed care agreements, government contracts, United Way, individual contributions, and other sources (Ezell, 2000). Diversification is seen as positive, as it allows organizations to avoid overdependence on any one source, such as charitable contributions, contracts, or grants, control of which lies outside the province of the organization.

Although there is substantial overlap in the funding base of nonprofits and for-profits, the relative weight of each funding source differs substantially. For example, fees-for-service constitute a larger proportion of revenues for for-profits than for nonprofits. Examples include nursing homes and day care centers. These often are unsubsidized, and the costs are borne solely by the users of the service.

Another important factor for the financial health of an organization is stable and predictable sources of revenues to support its core programs and operations. No organization can operate with any degree of predictability if it is unsure of its revenue sources. Agencies that assume that the contract they have had from state government for many years is guaranteed for the future may find themselves in trouble. Legislative cutbacks to public agencies may mean fewer contract funds or cancellation of contracts altogether.

The search for funds to develop and maintain the programs of human service organizations is ongoing and a constant concern. The methods used for fund-raising as well as the range of possible funding sources are both varied and complex (Turner, 1995). The sources, of course, depend on the nature of the programs the organization provides. Organizations that offer a diverse range of programs tend to have a larger range of revenue sources. The single-program agency, on the other hand, may have only two or three funding sources. For example, a homeless shelter may receive government contracts from both the U.S.

Department of Housing and Urban Development and the U.S. Department of Health and Human Services and/or the state equivalents of these agencies. In addition, the shelter may be part of the United Way and receive donations from that source. Businesses and individuals within the community served by the shelter may also be the source of some donations. Fees-for-service are not a likely source of funding for a homeless shelter, by virtue of the nature of the problems experienced by clients.

The organization may also have its own fund-raising activities, such as special events, planned (estate) giving, and solicitation of corporate and individual contributions. An organization may rely on fund-raising specialists, or the board of directors or a subcommittee of the board may be charged with certain fund-raising responsibilities. However, generating revenues for the organization is everyone's job. All staff must be knowledgeable about grant and contract writing and opportunities to expand programs through the support of individuals, corporations, and/or foundations.

Corporate Contributions

Corporate contributions fall within the category of private giving. In 2006, corporate contributions to charity rose 18.5 percent from the previous year (National Philanthropic Trust, 2007) to a total of $4.2 billion. This is a substantial increase over 2000, when corporate giving was $2.5 billion (Blum, 2000b; Moore, 1998). Of the 1999 total in corporate giving, $2.5 billion was in cash and $1.1 billion in product donations (such as clothing, food, pharmaceuticals).

The growth in contributions is consistent with the growth in corporate profits, the result of a heretofore robust economy. Nevertheless, companies have not become more generous. Giving as a percentage of corporate net income has remained consistent at about 1 percent (Blum, 2000b). Among the big donors are Merck & Company, Johnson & Johnson, Pfizer, Walmart Stores, Philip Morris Companies, Bank of America, and the ExxonMobil Corporation.

Corporations give cash or goods for charitable causes for two key reasons: tax incentives and public image. Although some corporations support a variety of organizations and causes, corporate donations are often earmarked for specific purposes. For example, the Goldman Sachs Group, an investment company, created the Goldman Sachs Foundation, which has its own criteria for giving. These criteria tend to relate to the interests of the sponsoring corporation. Goldman-Sachs gave a $3 million grant to the Institute for International Education, in New York, to establish the Goldman Sachs Global Leaders Program (Blum, 2000a).

Another characteristic of corporate giving is geography—corporations tend to donate to organizations and causes within the communities in which they operate. Prudential Insurance Company of America, headquartered in Newark, New Jersey, donates a sizable portion of its charitable funds to nonprofit groups in that city.

In addition to direct dollar contributions for general purposes or specific programs, corporations may also enter into joint ventures with nonprofits, described as cause-related marketing.

Cause-Related Marketing

Cause-related marketing is an increasingly used strategy to raise money for charitable organizations and is based on a relationship between a corporate sponsor and a charitable organization. These ventures usually take one of three forms:

1. Arrangements in which companies give a portion of proceeds from the sale of a product or service to a designated charity
2. Sponsorships, in which businesses underwrite the cost of charity events or programs in exchange for publicity
3. Licensing, in which manufacturers pay to use a charity's name and logo on its products (Gray & Hall, 1998)

A survey of 211 companies conducted by a communications company in Boston and the Harvard Business School's Social Marketing Task Force found that 92 percent of them support a charitable cause (Blum, 2000b). The motivation was partially to make a difference in regard to a social issue but also to enhance employee loyalty and the reputation of the company (Blum, 2000b). Considerations in forming the charity-business partnerships include the ability of the charity to carry out a cause-related program at the local level and the specific social needs of the community in which the business is located.

A particularly good example of such a partnership venture is the Boys & Girls Clubs of America, which won a $60 million marketing contract with the Coca-Cola Company. This contract allowed Coca-Cola to install vending machines in many of the charity's more than two thousand clubs (Gray & Hall, 1998). The charity receives a small profit from each product sold, and Coca-Cola uses the Boys & Girls Clubs' name in its promotional campaign. Another example of a charity that has profited from corporate sponsorship is Habitat for Humanity, whose promotions include the use of corporate banners at new building sites.

Available data suggest that these arrangements work positively for both partners. Surveys conducted in 1993 and 1998 showed that four out of five consumers have a more positive image of companies that support a charitable cause than of those that do not. Consumers also are likely to switch to a brand or store associated with a good cause ("Study Says Business and Charity Mix," 1999).

These arrangements are not without critics. Some health charities have been criticized for endorsing specific products. Sponsors may request donor or membership lists to market credit cards or products, risking the wrath of organizational supporters. Nevertheless, cause-related marketing has been shown to be a fruitful source of income for some organizations.

Foundations

The Carnegie Foundation. The Ford Foundation. The Bill and Melinda Gates Foundation. The William Randolph Hearst Foundation. The Lily Endowment. The Rockefeller Foundation. The Soros Foundation. What comes to mind? Big philanthropic dollars! Although this perception is accurate—foundations are a significant source of funds for the nonprofit sector—such funding is seldom for general purposes. Foundations provide grants for specific purposes that are consistent with their mission and priorities. Unlike charitable giving on the part of corporations, which represent big businesses' social consciousness, the very purpose of foundations is to fund programs to bring attention to the causes, social problems, or concerns within their purview.

There are over 50,000 private, community, corporate, and operating foundations in the United States. In 2006, foundations increased their total giving by 9.1 percent, to a total of over $36 billion. This is a continuation of a decade-long trend that can be attributed to the growth in foundation assets, a direct result of a booming economy. Foundations are required to give an average of at least 5 percent of their assets to charity over a three-year period; thus, the more their assets grow, the more they are required to give (Lipman, 2000).

Requests for funds for nonprofit programs almost always require an application on the part of the organization seeking support. Homework is an essential first step before any application is made. The Foundation Center, for example, produces several directories of funding sources that provide information about the program priorities and funding histories of foundations. Human service organizations should first establish the match between their needs and the foundations that support such needs.

As with corporate funding, foundations often restrict their giving. Location is one important criterion; many foundations provide support to nonprofits only within specific regions, states, or cities. Some foundations designate specific funding priorities each year. To receive serious consideration, applications from nonprofits are expected to address these priority concerns.

The specifications for grant submission, a list of programs supported in the past, and current foundation program priorities can be obtained by contacting foundations directly or through their websites. Early and thorough research enhances the chances of successful submissions.

Individual Donations

Charitable contributions from individuals were over $250 billion in 2005 (National Philanthropic Trust, 2007). It is estimated that taxpayers who itemize deductions on their tax returns give slightly above 3 percent of their earnings to charity, for which they receive a total of $107.4 billion in deductions (Lipman, 2000). It is interesting to note that people in the lower-income brackets tend to give a higher percentage of their income to charity than more affluent people.

In the 1990s, individual charitable contributions exceeded $1 trillion. Clearly, a much larger proportion of donations came from individuals than from corporations. Even with this largess, the Clinton administration indicated that "there's a lot more we can do to tap into the country's generosity" (Sinclair, 2000, p. 5).

The post-9/11 economic downturn and the recent recession have impacted individual donations to nonprofits and the human services, but not as much as one might anticipate. In the second year of the recession, individual giving to nonprofits dropped only a total of 2 percent (Giving USA Foundation, 2009). This demonstrates that human service organizations should not abandon attempting to seek individual donations in spite of difficult times. In fact, given that some organizations may erroneously assume that giving will be tight and may not focus their efforts on fundraising, organizations should see this as an opportunity to reevaluate and refocus their fundraising efforts.

Big Donors

Your office door may bear a plaque noting that the room and its contents are a gift from a specific donor, as an acknowledgment of a large contribution. Many nonprofit organizations seek to raise a portion of their funds by securing large donations from individuals. Determining who may qualify to be a big donor and gaining access to him or her may be the responsibility of members of the board of directors, a fund-raiser, or even the executive director. An example of a director-initiated effort to gain a large contribution for an agency is presented in box 3.2.

BOX 3.2
Thanks, Frank!

At a recent meeting of the board of directors of a community service center, a board member, Frank, a retired businessman, brought up the need to raise funds for equipment for the center's job training and job search program. Frank, a volunteer, mentioned that computer skills were now essential to anyone entering or reentering the workforce and that the center should be a place where program participants could learn to use computers. Because there was a full board agenda, the president acknowledged the importance of the subject but respectfully asked that the issue be tabled until the next meeting.

The next day the executive director wrote a letter to Frank in which he expressed great interest in this training program and supplied Frank with a draft of a budget that he thought would be necessary to bring this program to fruition. This draft budget included money for six computers and two printers and an allowance to recarpet, paint, and decorate the office space used for the job training and job search program. In total, the initial start-up costs, minus monies for an instructor (which would be paid from program participant fees), came to about $16,000. The

(*continued on next page*)

executive director asked Frank for his advice about this draft budget and wanted Frank to call him with his comments.

About a week later, during a meeting of the advisory committee for the job training and job search program, Frank referred to the letter from the executive director and announced to a stunned advisory committee that he would fund the entire program. In fact, during a subsequent conversation, Frank told the executive director that he would send a check to the community service center for this purpose in the amount of $18,000, or $2,000 more than the draft budget indicated. Frank said that the extra $2,000 should be used to "make the place look nice."

The executive director immediately wrote to Frank to express the appreciation of the center for this wonderful and generous gift. The executive director also e-mailed members of the board's executive committee to inform them of this gift and to suggest that the officers also write to Frank to express appreciation for his support of the center and for his deep commitment to the job training program.

Frank gave a sizable gift. Some members of boards have personal resources that they are able and willing to donate to the organization. Other board members or key constituents of the agency have access to potential donors. Board members, in general, are expected to be important links to potential individual or corporate donors.

The executive director of the community service center did not ask outright for a gift but laid the foundation for Frank to provide a program-specific donation. The executive director sized up the situation, saw the potential, and knew of Frank's keen interest in the program. The moment was opportune and resulted in an important contribution to the center. The executive director also followed an important axiom of fund-raising: acknowledge the contribution immediately, publicly, and graciously.

The securing of major gifts involves the development of relationships over years rather than weeks or months (Lindahl, 1995). It involves careful investigation of the potential interest of the donor and his or her willingness to give (Turner, 1995). In other words, people with large financial resources are important friends for nonprofit organizations. Requests for donations should be based on research of past giving patterns, ability to give, and relationship—past and present—to the organization. Other relevant information about potential donors may include their religious affiliation, cultural traditions, and personal and professional interests (Turner, 1995). Fund-raising is about building relationships and finding a fit between philanthropic impulses and institutional and social needs. Social workers who hope to become executive directors will be heartened to know that, with some modification, the relational skills they possess will serve them well as fund-raisers. As human service workers and students read this book, they may find that many of the tasks of administrators require core human service skills, repackaged in different ways and in different contexts. While being a good social worker does not directly translate into being a good administrator, many of the skills necessary for these positions are similar.

Fund-Raising Practices

Mail solicitation has become a major means of raising funds for charitable causes. You may want to know why you receive so many solicitations. In addition to revenue from solicitations, organizations sell their mailing lists to other organizations. For example, if you donate to the National Wildlife Foundation, you are likely to receive solicitations from other animal rights or animal protection groups. This is because your name is now on a list of contributors, and there is a belief in the fund-raising world that those who give are the most likely to give again.

Fund-raising is a specialty occupation. Large organizations may have at least one person on staff whose job is to raise money. He or she may do this by organizing special events such as dinners or theater parties. This often means that the agency "upfronts" some of the costs, such as theater tickets, before contributors have bought the tickets. (The costs to donors, in this case, would include the theater ticket, transportation, perhaps dinner, plus a contribution.) Thus, agencies take a risk that the event will be a success. The organization makes money by deducting the cost of the event from the amount charged to participants. What remains after expenses constitutes the income to the organization. If the agency is left with fifty unpurchased tickets from the block of tickets bought, it loses money.

Fund-raising practices are monitored by a number of public and private entities, including the Consumer Protection Department of the state and/or local government, the Better Business Bureau, and voluntary accrediting agencies, such as the Council on Accreditation of Services for Families and Children. Their interest in organizational fund-raising practices is the protection of the public interest. They are concerned about how money is raised and the purposes for which donated funds are used. For this reason, fund-raising practices are reviewed and regulated.

The Council on Accreditation is one accrediting body that requires organizations that seek to raise funds through individual solicitation from the general public do so in an ethical and fiscally responsible manner. Ethical considerations include providing potential donors with an accurate description of the organization, its purposes and programs, and the financial needs for which the solicitation is being made. How the Council on Accreditation further delineates the responsibilities of the organization is described in box 3.3.

Other Sources of Revenue

Fees-for-Service

Fees are defined as money payments in exchange for a product or a service (Lohmann, 1980). Suppose, for example, that a family service agency runs a counseling service subsidized to a large degree by the local United Way. Typi-

---

BOX 3.3
Ethical Fund-Raising Practices

◆ The governing body and management establish and exercise controls over fund-raising activities carried out on behalf of the organization by its personnel, volunteers, contractors and/or consultants.

◆ In solicitation materials, the organization provides accurate descriptions of the organization, its identity and purpose, its programs and the financial needs for which the solicitation is being made, with no material omissions, misstatements of fact, or misrepresentation of the use of the funds.

◆ The organization spends the funds for the purposes for which they were solicited, with the exception of reasonable costs for administration of the fund-raising program.

◆ The organization analyzes the costs and benefits of each of its fund-raising activities, including the factors which affect the reasonableness of fund-raising costs to dollars raised.

◆ The organization establishes controls on how donated funds are to be handled and for acknowledging such contributions.

◆ When donors wish to remain anonymous, their wishes are protected.

◆ The organization discloses descriptive and financial information about its fund-raising activities, on request of a donor.

Source: Council on Accreditation of Services to Families and Children (1997).

---

cally, the agency has a fee structure so that clients will be asked to pay some portion, or perhaps all, of the fee.

Most nonprofit agencies have sliding fee scales, which take into account the client's ability to pay. However, setting the fee involves obtaining details about the client's financial status that may be irrelevant to the presenting problem or service provided and that some clients might see as invasive of their privacy. Judgments must be made in setting the fee scale and also in how these scales are administered (Lohmann, 1980).

The fee may be collected directly from the client or from a third party, such as an insurance company, or both. Managed care companies, for example, typically require a co-payment. In these arrangements, the insurer pays a certain amount for a service and the client is expected to pay either a predetermined amount (say, $10) or the difference between the actual cost of the service as set by the agency and the amount allowed by the insurer.

Fees-for-service raise some fundamental issues for human service organizations, excluding proprietary organizations, for which the profit motive is straightforward. Because human service organizations, by definition, seek to fulfill a public need, the fees charged must reflect the ability of the targeted populations to pay. Charging a person near the poverty level a $50 counseling fee when the client has no insurance coverage would be inappropriate. Recruiting clients who can pay for services has been termed *creaming,* a form of discrimination in which people are given preference for service on the basis of their ability to pay. (*Creaming* has also been used to describe exclusionary service practices in regard to gender, race, and ethnicity, or even the severity or type of the client's problem [Gibelman, 1983].) Fees, and the manner in which they are collected, should not pose a direct or serious threat to the physical, psychological, or social well-being of clients (Lohmann, 1980).

On the other hand, human service organizations are businesses and must have revenue in order to provide their programs of service. When clients can afford to pay, fees are seen as legitimate. Fees also allow the consumers of service—the clients—to choose when and where they will receive service. For most agencies, fees are an important source of revenue, but they are rarely the main source. Agencies and their workers must continuously grapple with the balance between meeting their financial obligations (survival) and providing services (mission). It is valuable for human service organizations to communicate with their constituents about such dilemmas. Including community members in these dialogues can empower them to be decision makers concerning the role and function of the organization—an important part of culturally competent practice. For instance, in response to a financial crisis, an agency serving Southeast Asian immigrants contemplated charging fees for English-as-a-second-language classes. The agency held a series of meetings with community leaders, who developed a sliding-scale fee structure. Most of these community leaders thought that many Vietnamese, Lao, and Cambodian residents would be more likely to take classes for a nominal fee, as this would distinguish the program from welfare. In Southeast Asian communities, the extended family primarily provides for the needs of the poor, and industry and hard work are core cultural values. Based upon the community leaders' recommendations, the new system of fee-for-service classes was published in the local paper. Over time, this greatly increased participation.

Business Ventures

Many larger nonprofit organizations engage in business activities that may or may not be related to their primary mission to generate revenues. Program-related initiatives are those that are closely related to or identified with the organization and are consistent with its mission. The best-known example is probably the sale of cookies by the Girl Scouts of the United States (Massarsky, 1994). Other revenue-seeking activities may be related to the organization's programs, such as food sales or vending machines, activities from which the agency receives a portion of the proceeds.

A related method of raising funds concerns unrelated business activity— business activity that is outside the main scope of the charitable purpose of the organization (Starkweather, 1993). For example, suppose a hospital owns an office building and rents space to tenants who are not connected with the hospital or even to the medical profession. This constitutes business activity unrelated to the primary purpose of providing health care. The income from this unrelated activity may be subject to tax, while the hospital (if a nonprofit) remains tax exempt.

Unrelated business income surfaced as a significant issue in the 1980s, and concerns have been voiced primarily by the proprietary community, particularly smaller businesses. The charge is that nonprofits are aggressively pursuing entrepreneurial activities (such as those discussed earlier—corporate partnerships, sale of items unrelated to their service purposes, and the like) that directly compete with and pose a threat to the business community. Criticism is aimed at those activities that may be considered peripheral to the tax-exempt purposes of the nonprofits. The business community believes tax exemption for purposes unrelated to the organization's purposes creates unfair competition, and it has repeatedly lobbied to change the exemption regulations (Wellford & Gallagher, 1988).

This issue of unfair competition remains, by and large, unresolved. However, nonprofits are increasingly being asked by the federal and state governments to justify tax, postage, and other privileges, particularly when nonprofits and proprietary organizations are competing in the same markets (Berger, 1999). As the boundaries between the sectors continue to blur and different organizational types compete for the same sources of revenue, the tax-exempt status of nonprofits will become an increasingly politicized issue.

Volunteer Labor

Some nonprofit organizations rely on volunteers as a way to offset costs that would otherwise be incurred in hiring full- or part-time staff. The use of volunteers is particularly notable among cause-related organizations, such as those related to health. For example, the Lupus Foundation of America, which has affiliates throughout the United States, relies on people suffering from lupus and their significant others to plan and lead support groups, manage some operations, and raise funds. Habitat for Humanity relies on volunteers to construct homes.

Valuation of volunteer labor is a thorny issue (Lohmann, 1995). Even without attaching a dollar value, the use of volunteers constitutes a cost savings to the organization. It is important to note, however, that there are also real costs to the organizations in using volunteers. Volunteers must be trained and supervised. Many organizations reward volunteers through some type of recognition event, such as dinners honoring them. Nevertheless, it can be assumed that organizations that recruit, train, and use volunteers do so because they assist in their work and, thus, the achievement of the organization's goals.

This discussion certainly does not touch on all possible sources of funds or fund-raising strategies. The intent here is to suggest the wide range of options available for raising dollars to support the programs of human service agencies.

Clearly, agencies have different track records of experience and success in their fund-raising initiatives; target different sources of funding depending on their legal status, mission, and programs of service; and formulate different fund-raising strategies based on tradition, expertise, and organizational purpose.

To varying degrees, social work practitioners are often called on to help plan, implement, and evaluate these fund-raising strategies. Such participation may range from identifying potential funding sources for a new program to developing the program components of a grant application or recruiting volunteers to assist in the logistics of a marathon to raise awareness of—and funds for—an issue or cause.

Managing Finances

Financial management concerns identifying and procuring the financial resources needed by the organization to deliver its services and ensuring that these resources are used effectively and that they are accounted for appropriately (Lohmann, 1995). All organizations—proprietary, nonprofit, and for-profit—must manage their finances in accord with sound financial practices, applicable laws, professional ethics, and community standards.

In human service organizations, financial management involves the control and planned use of money and other resources in a manner that furthers the organization's goals. Although these activities center on fiscal matters, how finances are handled has direct implications for the work of the organization (Lohmann, 1980). If the financial aspects are not handled well, the overall achievement of the organization's goals becomes impossible. In recognition of the interrelationship between program and finances, both public and private human service organizations attempt to bring program planning and budgeting together as part of an overall process. In this respect, the direct service practitioner is involved in the financial matters of the organization. Furthermore, the practitioner is also responsible for providing some of the data necessary to generate financial reports, such as the number of clients seen and the fees paid. These requests of the social worker may seem like just more paperwork, but agencies must be able to account for how money is spent and determine how much money is needed to serve their clients effectively. The input of social workers on these bread-and-butter issues is essential.

Financial Operations

Most organizations have specialists on staff to deal with money matters, because financial management involves a distinct set of knowledge and skills. The key finance person is the chief financial officer, or controller. This person works closely with the chief executive officer to ensure the appropriate integration of finances and programs.

There may be several bookkeepers on staff as well, depending on the size and resources of the agency. When possible, financial duties are separated among several staff members; the person who handles accounts receivable (income), for example, is not the same person who writes checks. These internal controls help to prevent misuse or abuse of agency funds.

Financial management is guided by organizational procedures that may include financial planning, a process in which the financial implications of program planning are considered. For example, when an agency is considering initiating a program to serve the mental health needs of older adults in the community, it must cost out, or estimate, the anticipated revenues and expenses associated with the program. Will they need one full-time social worker or two? How many hours of secretarial support will be needed per week? What about costs for program brochures? Where will the money to pay for the program come from? If fees-for-service are not a viable source of revenue, what private foundations might cover some of the costs? Are there public agencies that fund this kind of program, such as the State Department of Mental Health? Does the agency have the money to allocate to this program until external support can be secured?

Similar kinds of questions need to be asked and answered in regard to ongoing programs. If an agency's counseling program is supported primarily by fees-for-service, do the number of billable client contact hours over the past year show a continued or increased demand for services from that of the preceding year? A program of refugee resettlement has been underwritten by a contract with the United States Citizenship and Immigration Services (formerly Immigration and Naturalization Services). What are the prospects that this contract will be renewed? The agency has primarily served Russian immigrants, but immigration numbers have dropped off. Should the agency budget remain consistent? What happens if there is a delay in contract renewal? Financial planning includes examination of expected income under various contingencies and matching the expectations of cost and income (Lohmann, 1980).

Budgeting

Human service organizations engage in budgeting as part of financial planning both for the long term and for the short term (generally defined as one year). There are numerous approaches to the budgeting process. These include zero-based budgeting, program budgeting, and performance budgeting. The latter seeks to use program outcomes or results as the basis for budgeting. Contract budgeting refers to preparing a budget for submission to a government agency or a corporate or foundation sponsor for a specific program. A sample of a contract budget summary appears in box 3.4. Note that supporting information would also be submitted to explain and justify each item listed on the summary.

BOX 3.4 Sample Contract Budget Summary	
Category	*Total Budget*
Personnel	$374,432
Fringe benefits	49,937
Consultants	8,331
Equipment rental	0
Travel	20,800
Occupancy	8,076
Communications	6,440
Printing/supplies	4,325
Raw food	261,750
Catered food	0
Vehicle cost	30,000
Insurance cost	21,000
Other expenses	56,572
Total: Grant funds, income, & insurance	$841,663
Total direct operating budget	$841,663
– Anticipated income	(40,162)
Total direct costs	$801,501
+ Indirect costs at 8%	64,121
Total reimbursement	$865,622
Match	0
Anticipated income	$40,162
Central insurance	0
Income central insurance	0
Equipment/renovations	44,097
One-time payments	0
Contingency	0
Total project cost	$949,881

Organizations prepare a written budget usually several months in advance of their new fiscal year. The budget serves as the plan for managing the organization's financial resources. Budgets are a means of facilitating the provision of services; they are not an end in themselves (Ezell, 2000). The budget enables the agency's programs to be carried out by allocating the required resources. The budget is the primary financial model against which expenses are monitored.

The baseline for the next year's budget is that of the previous year together with year-to-date financial reports that show the accuracy of budget projections. Program directors may be asked to develop a budget that details both anticipated revenues and expenditures, using the baseline figures. For example, the senior services unit of an agency runs a number of bereavement groups, among other programs. In budget planning, program staff calculate the number of people the agency expects will participate in these groups during the coming year based on last year's figures and any other known information that may help in projecting numbers. Expenditures are then calculated, including the cost of advertising the program, staff salaries, room rental, refreshments, and other known expenses. The amount of fees likely to be generated is similarly calculated, along with any other known or projected sources of program support.

The CFO may be asked to compile and review the information provided by the program directors. The CFO will work with the CEO to review and make adjustments to the information provided and then incorporate administrative costs, capital expenditures, governance expenses, and the like. Not all programs are self-supporting, and an agency, through its financial planning process, may offset anticipated deficits in one program area by budgeting a surplus in another.

The need to make adjustments in revenue or expenditure estimates is normal. There is a tendency to overproject revenues based on a wish for it to be so rather than on past experience. There is also risk of potentially underestimating projected costs of planned activities. Adjustments are made until such time as projected revenues and expenses "zero out"—that is, until anticipated revenues and anticipated expenditures are equal or close to it. Alternatively, an agency, through its board of directors or other authority, may decide to accept a deficit budget, in which anticipated expenses are higher than anticipated revenues. In this case, the agency should have some idea as to where the difference will come from. Many agencies have financial reserves—cash or assets that are set aside, similar to individual saving accounts and investments. These reserves can be tapped or a line of credit may be obtained from a bank to make up for the shortfall.

Budget Responsibility

In nonprofit organizations, the budgeting process may involve many different staff members, as well as a budget and finance committee of the board of directors and the board itself. The board of directors is charged with the responsibility to review and approve the budget prior to the new fiscal year. Similarly, the board periodically reviews financial statements against the budget and must approve any planned deviations from and revisions to the budget.

The budgets of public agencies are subject to the approval of the appropriate legislative body, such as the city council, the state legislature, or Congress. The budget is not a benign document. Most of us can recall instances when the federal government has shut down on October 1 (the first day of the new fiscal year) because Congress had failed to reach agreement about the budget. At other times, the federal government and some state governments have operated on a "continuing resolution," which authorizes them to continue operations under the terms of the previous year's budget until a new budget is approved or a specific deadline is reached.

Monitoring Finances

Every organization uses some type of accounting system to provide information about revenues and expenditures. Information is needed for several reasons. First, there is accountability to outside parties, such as the government, corporate funders, and managed care companies with whom the organization contracts to carry out specific programs. Second, the organization must at all times know its true financial condition. Generating such information allows the organization to take corrective action when necessary.

Most organizations have written operational procedures that detail how finances are handled. Monthly financial statements are produced by most organizations for internal monitoring and external accountability purposes. These statements show actual financial performance (revenue and expenditures) compared to the budget.

Organizations also produce an annual financial report or audit. The audit is typically conducted by an independent public accounting firm that applies appropriate industry accounting standards. Nonprofit and for-profit organizations also are required to file income tax returns with the IRS.

The complexity of the financial operation depends on the size of the agency's budget and the number and types of revenue sources. Sources of revenues may include self-pay, commercial insurance, HMOs, PPOs, EAPs, Medicare, Medicaid, and philanthropic contributions. One of the major complications for agencies today is the large number of funding sources, each with its own set of accounting and reporting requirements. Accounts may need to be handled differently depending on their source. Box 3.5 illustrates the anticipated revenues, by source, for a large human service organization.

A Positive Bottom Line

For public and nonprofit human service organizations (unlike their for-profit counterparts), the end-of-year bottom line should be consistent with the budget. Surpluses are not the goal. The idea is to use available revenues to support service programs. However, the nonprofit agency can have a positive bottom line at the end of the year in which revenues surpass expenditures. This is not necessarily bad; the extra funds are then banked into reserves for future unforeseen expenditures. In fact, a reserve fund is an essential part of financial management and constitutes sound business practice (Raffa, 2002).

How much should be in reserves and how large a budget surplus is acceptable? According to Lohmann (1995), the critical issue for nonprofits is not whether they retain a surplus over operating expenses but how such surpluses are used. For the for-profit organization, the goal is to have a surplus of revenue over expenses at the end of the fiscal year. This is where the profit lies.

BOX 3.5
Where the Money Comes From

Sample Financial Statement
Statement of Activity*
Year Ending June 30, 2007

Revenue and Support	*Total*
State government grants—OASAS	$ 2,831,414
State government grants—OASAS—PRC	38,561
State government grants—OASAS—DOH	446,285
Federal grant—HUD	287,466
Federal grant—CDC	155,076
City government grant—DOH	297,010
City government grant—HRA	835,751
City government grant—DHS	1,093,952
Food stamps	92,225
Medicaid revenues—OASAS	3,653,294
Medicaid revenues—HIV	125,078
Client fees	76,081
Grants and donations	175,839
Consulting fees	96,600
Development fees	27,594
Tenant services	107,447
Rental income	84,530
Interest income	3,855
Other	26,820
Total revenues and support	**$10,454,878**
Expenses	
Program services:	
Methadone clinic	$ 3,695,188
Residential programs	1,356,302
Drug-free day service program	1,174,206
Primary care/health services	614,277
Other programs	536,861
Housing initiatives program	172,820
Casa Banome	432,559
Casa Esperanza	783,022
Total program expenses	$ 8,765,235
Administrative expenses	$ 1,133,363
Change in net assets	556,280
Total expenses	**$10,454,878**

*Based on audited financial statement
CDC—Centers for Disease Control
DHS—Department of Human Services
DOH—Department of Housing
HIV—Human Immune Deficiency
HRA—Human Resources Administration
HUD—Housing and Urban Development
OASAS—Office of Alcohol and Substance Abuse Services
PRC—Practice Research Colloboration

Unwanted Surprises

Given the diversity of funding sources for human service organizations and the inability of most organizations to control or prepare for all contingencies in either revenues or expenditures, unanticipated financial problems can and do occur. The scenario in box 3.6 shows how an unexpected shortfall in revenue can affect the organization.

In this instance, staff members assumed, erroneously, that because there had been raises in the past, there would always be raises. They were unwilling to consider grant writing or outreach to the community, which could bring new clients to the agency. However, the executive director also made some wrong assumptions. She thought that sharing general information about the budget with staff on a few occasions would prepare them for the possibility that there

---

BOX 3.6
What Happened to My Raise?

Most of the professional staff at Lutheran Social Services have been employed by the agency for four or more years. Each year they received a salary increase on January 1 for anywhere between 3 and 5 percent. The executive director has authority to grant slightly higher or lower raises based on the individual performance evaluations of staff.

Although staff had been informed of a projected budget shortfall for the current year, it came as a shock when the board voted against salary increases for the new fiscal year. The executive director was aware that the board's decision would not be well received by staff and consequently scheduled a special staff meeting to discuss the situation. The executive director was particularly concerned that the news be delivered quickly, before there were leaks of information.

Staff had come to expect the raise as a given, and the news of the board's decision was greeted with anger. The meeting turned into a blame session targeting the executive director. The executive director had earlier informed the staff of budget problems; these were the result of an unanticipated dip in the number of fee-for-service clients as well as lower-than-expected revenues from a planned fund-raising dinner. The executive director had tried in several earlier staff meetings to engage the staff in discussion about ways in which revenues might be increased or expenditures decreased. The response was uniformly "Fund-raising is not our job." They wanted to know what the board and executive director were doing about raising money. Staff were unwilling to consider ways in which to trim expenditures.

At this meeting, the executive director concluded that there was little she could say that would lessen the impact of the news that there would be no salary increases. She ended the meeting, sensing frustration among all concerned. In the following weeks, morale took a nosedive. Staff felt betrayed and unappreciated. They considered appealing to the board, until one employee pointed out that the board had approved the budget with full knowledge that funds for staff raises had not been allocated. Several employees discussed among themselves whether it was time to think about new jobs.

would be no raises. However, this connection between the budget shortfall and pay raises was never clearly articulated, and the information was not presented in a way that showed the relevancy of fiscal problems to day-to-day operations. This example demonstrates why collaborative leadership and staff empowerment are so important. When social workers feel included in the decision-making process, they are more likely to be supportive of management in times of crisis.

Some organizations try to avoid such surprises by practicing open book management. Each month, when financial statements are prepared and distributed to the board, staff also receive a copy. This allows staff to become more aware of the relationship between finances and programs and the factors that affect the financial bottom line. Such involvement, in the view of some managers, helps motivate staff to work together to make the organization more fiscally viable (Grimsley, 1995).

Mergers

A merger is one means that organizations can use to address scarce resources. It is an option an increasing number of human service organizations have exercised or are now considering.

We have become familiar with the term *merger* in relation to the corporate world because of the coverage mergers receive in the media and the dollars involved. For example, in early 2000, Time Warner and America Online announced their merger, a phenomenon that not only made the news worldwide but also had an instant effect on the stock market. In 1999, Bell Atlantic merged with GTE, and the pharmaceutical giants Warner-Lambert and Pfizer also merged (Blum, 2000b). The list of acquisitions and mergers is extensive. These mergers are known as industry consolidations and are not unique to the corporate sector.

Within the health care industry—both for-profit and nonprofit organizations—a major restructuring has been occurring. Market forces have been driving hospitals, for example, to initiate mergers and consolidations. Such restructuring efforts often take place among similar types of hospitals—nonprofits, for example, merging with other nonprofit hospitals. However, nonprofit hospitals have also been selling off to for-profit enterprises. HMOs have similarly been converting to for-profit status (Starkweather, 1993).

Such consolidations are also becoming commonplace among nonprofit human service organizations, ranging from service agencies to foundations to centralized fund-raising entities. There are several motivating factors: avoiding service duplication through economy of scale, reducing administrative costs, gaining a competitive edge, and extending the range of service offerings. A study of 192 charities that have merged or formally allied themselves with other groups found that chief among the motivating factors were:

◆ A sudden change in the status quo, such as a new opportunity to obtain funds or a change in leadership

- ◆ Forward-thinking leaders who promoted the idea
- ◆ External forces, such as a potential for government support, which prompted a reexamination of an organization's operations (Sommerfeld, 2000)

Some of these motivating factors are illustrated in the vignette in box 3.7.

BOX 3.7
Exploring Merger Options

Aurora Family Services is part of a network of loosely affiliated nonprofit family service agencies found throughout the United States. It is located in a relatively affluent county that is within close commuting distance of Chicago. However, the board has dubbed the agency "a best-kept secret" because its services are considered to be underutilized, there is no waiting list, and the professional staff often have unfilled hours.

One of the board members, Larry, is a former president of the agency and serves on the boards of other nonprofits. He is well connected in the community and is a take-charge type of person. At Larry's suggestion, an informal lunch meeting was arranged among Larry, the board president, and the executive director and their equivalent counterparts of Flemington Family Services, located in a neighboring county and part of the same network of agencies. Flemington Family Services has fewer staff members than Aurora and has operated at a deficit for several years. At the lunch, it was decided that exploration of a merger between the two organizations would be appropriate. Both sides were careful to avoid any language suggesting a commitment to merge; the term used was *explore*.

A committee was formed by the boards of directors of both agencies to study how the two agencies might collaborate. The chair of the committee then formed subcommittees to promote discussions between the two agencies in specific areas of concern, such as governance, financial management, and the separate program areas. On a selective basis, staff were also assigned to the subcommittees.

Consistent problems were encountered in scheduling subcommittee meetings. Even issues such as where to meet were not easily resolved. Larry reported back to the board at each subsequent meeting, as did his counterpart in Flemington. After several months, some board members began to raise questions as to whether it was worth the energy to proceed with these discussions. What benefits, they asked, would accrue to the respective agencies from a merger? Larry responded by saying that the fact-finding meetings were designed precisely to answer that question.

It became clear that merger discussions—and an ultimate decision—would take considerable time. Once the committee reports to the boards, each will have to engage in its own review and decision-making process. Legal consultation will be needed. Implementation plans will have to be drawn up. Approval will be needed from the Office of the Attorney General in which the agencies are registered. Voluntary accrediting bodies will also need to be consulted.

Mergers also cost money. There are legal costs, potential relocation costs, public relations costs, potential severance to staff, retraining, a need for new letterhead, and the like. The decision to merge will be made only after a careful assessment and planning process.

In this case, the potential merger may produce cost savings, in part by reducing duplicative services and administrative costs. However, at this point, it is too early to know. Neither agency is in a fiscally strong position. The merging of two agencies in financial difficulties does not necessarily produce a stronger single agency.

Examples of mergers among service-related organizations include the combining of Second Harvest, the nation's largest network of food banks, with Foodchain, its biggest competitor. The merged group is called America's Second Harvest and is touted as one of the largest mergers ever in the nonprofit world (Marchetti, 2000). Another example is Family Service America, which in 1998 merged with the National Association of Homes and Services for Children under the new name Alliance for Children and Families. The stated reason for the merger was an effort to cut costs and expand their reach to all fifty states ("Family-Aid Groups Announce Merger," 1998).

Mergers have been seen as a positive development in the nonprofit sector and as a potent means of addressing the competition between nonprofit groups and between nonprofits and for-profits. One large agency may be able to exercise more clout than two smaller agencies (Dundjerski, 1999). In addition, mergers offer a way to address the growing demands for accountability, in part by promoting efficiency in administrative operations (Marchetti, 2000). On the other hand, efficiency may not be the most important goal for nonprofits, particularly if it threatens the levels of commitment and connection to the original cause that inspired the formation of the organization.

Key Points

- ◆ The organization's financial position is integrally related to its ability to carry out its program of service.
- ◆ Nonprofits have been the beneficiary of public policies that provide direct and indirect financial support, including tax exemption and postal subsidies.
- ◆ Diversification of funding sources is an important strategy to reduce fiscal dependency.
- ◆ Corporate contributions to charities continue to rise, but most corporations establish their own priorities for giving.
- ◆ Joint ventures between corporations and nonprofits are common and often take the form of cause-related marketing, in which the corporation gains valuable publicity and the nonprofit gains revenue.
- ◆ For-profits have repeatedly raised concerns about what they see as unfair competition from business ventures by nonprofits.
- ◆ Individual contributions constitute a higher proportion of revenues for nonprofits than do corporate contributions.
- ◆ The use of volunteers is one way nonprofits can offset costs that would otherwise be incurred in services and/or operations, but there are often hidden costs in recruiting, training, and supervising volunteers.

◆ Financial management involves planning, securing, managing, and accounting for the appropriate expenditure of the organization's resources.
◆ All human service organizations must manage their finances according to sound financial practices, applicable laws, and professional standards.
◆ Budgeting and program planning are integrally related.
◆ Mergers between nonprofit organizations and between nonprofits and for-profits have become more common than they once were.

Suggested Learning Activities and Discussion Questions

1. Obtain a copy of your agency's budget for the current fiscal year. Identify each source of funding and the dollar amount expected from each source. Then identify the five largest expenditure items. What do these figures tell you about the agency?
2. Organize a group of three or four people who work in your program area within the same agency. Brainstorm businesses, foundations, and other community groups that might be interested or have a stake in this program. Then discuss how these potential stakeholders might be approached to contribute to your organization.
3. Put on your public relations hat. Using the specific program in which you work as your point of references, develop a preliminary marketing plan to promote and fund this program. Consider ways to work with corporate sponsors.
4. Conduct an Internet search of newspapers in your state or locality for articles about mergers of human service organizations. Assess how such mergers are portrayed; for example, what are the motivations behind such mergers, who is affected and in what way, and what impact is projected?

Recommended Readings

Arsenault, J. (1999). *Forging nonprofit alliances*. San Francisco: Jossey-Bass.
Austin, J. (2000). *The collaboration challenge: How nonprofits and businesses succeed through strategic alliances*. San Francisco: Jossey-Bass.
Cleverly, W. O., Song, P. H., & Cleverly, J. O. (2011). *Essentials of healthcare finance* (7th ed.). Sudbury, MA: Jones & Bartlett Learning.
Dropkin, M., & LaTouche, B. (1998). *The budget-building book for nonprofits: A step-by-step guide for managers and boards*. San Francisco: Jossey-Bass.
Freedman, H. A., & Feldman, K. (1998). *The business of special events: Fundraising strategies for changing times*. Sarasota, FL: Pineapple Press.
Lawrence, S., Camposeco, C., & Kendzior, J. (2000). *The foundation yearbook: Facts and figures on private and community foundations*. New York: Foundation Center.
Maddox, D. C. (1999). *Budgeting for not-for-profit organizations*. New York: John Wiley.
McCormick, D. H. (2000). *Nonprofit mergers: The power of successful partnerships*. Frederick, MD: Aspen Publishers.

McLaughlin, T. A. (1998). *Nonprofit mergers and alliances*. New York: John Wiley.

McLaughlin, T.A. (2009). *Streetsmart financial basics for nonprofit managers*. New York, NY: John Wiley & Sons.

Peters, J. B., & Schaffer, E. (2005). *Financial leadership for nonprofit executives*. St. Paul, MN: Fieldstone Alliance Publishing Center.

Reiss, A. H. (2000). *CPR for nonprofits: Creative strategies for successful fundraising, marketing, communications, and management*. San Francisco: Jossey-Bass.

Stevens, S. K., & Anderson, L. M. (1998). *All the way to the bank: Management for tomorrow's nonprofit*. St. Paul, MN: Stevens Group.

Sumariwalla, R. D., & Levis, W. C. (2001). *Unified financial reporting system for not-for-profit organizations*. San Francisco: Jossey-Bass.

References

Berger, H. (1999, October). Merger mania. *Nonprofit Times*, pp. 22-23.

Billitteri, T. J., & Stehle, V. (1998, July 16). Charities breathe easier after court decision on gift annuities; model law delayed. *Chronicle of Philanthropy*, p. 40.

Blum, D. E. (2000a, June 15). 9 of 10 companies have charity marketing deals. *Chronicle of Philanthropy*. Available: http://philanthropy.com/premium/articles/v12/i17/17003902.htm

Blum, D. E. (2000b, July 13). Corporate giving rises again. *Chronicle of Philanthropy*. Available: http://www.philanthropy.com/free/articles/v12/i18/18000101.htm

Council on Accreditation of Services to Families and Children. (1997). *1997 standards for behavioral health care services and community support and education services* (U.S. ed.). New York: Author.

Dundjerski, M. (1999, July 15). 2 philanthropies merge to trim overhead costs. *Chronicle of Philanthropy*. Available: http://www.philanthropy.com/premium/articles/v11/i18/18001802.htm

Elkin, R. (1987). Financial management. In A. Minahan (Ed.-in-chief), *Encyclopedia of social work* (18th ed., pp. 618-627). Silver Spring, MD: National Association of Social Workers.

Ezell, M. (2000). Financial management. In R. J. Patti (Ed.), *The handbook of social welfare management* (pp. 377-393). Thousand Oaks, CA: Sage Publications.

"Family-aid groups announce merger." (1998, February 26). *Chronicle of Philanthropy*. Available: http://philanthropy.com/premium/articles/v10/i09/0904706.htm

Gibelman, M. (1983). Using public funds to buy private services. In M. Dinerman (Ed.), *Social work in a turbulent world* (pp. 101-113). Silver Spring, MD: National Association of Social Workers.

Gibelman, M. (1995). Purchasing social services. In R. L. Edwards (Ed.-in-chief), *Encyclopedia of social work* (19th ed., pp. 1998-2007). Washington, DC: NASW Press.

Gibelman, M. (1998). Theory, practice, and experience in the purchase of services. In M. Gibelman, & H. W. Demone, Jr. (Eds.), *The privatization of human services: Policy and practice issues* (pp. 1-52). New York: Springer.

Giving USA Foundation. (2009). U.S. charitable giving estimated to be $307.65 in 2008. Retrieved on February 4, 2012, from http://www.givingusa.org/press_releases/gusa/GivingReaches300billion.pdf.

Goldstein, H. (1993). Government contracts are emasculating boards and turning charities into agents of the state. *Chronicle of Philanthropy*, p. 41.

Gray, S., & Hall, H. (1998, July 30). Cashing in on charity's good name. *Chronicle of Philanthropy*. Available: http://philanthropy.com/premium/articles/v10/i19/19002501.htm

Grimsley, K. D. (1995, September 17). Opening up the nuts and bolts of the bottom line. *Washington Post*, p. H6.

Hall, H. (1998, July 16). Non-profit groups gird for double-digit increases in postage rates. *Chronicle of Philanthropy*, p. 39.

Lindahl, W. E. (1995). The major gift donor relationship: An analysis of donors and contributions. *Nonprofit Leadership & Management, 5*(4), 411–432.

Lipman, H. (2000, August 10). Rise in giving tracks growth in Americans' income, IRS data show. *Chronicle of Philanthropy*, pp. 12–13, 15.

Lohmann, R. A. (1980). *Breaking even: Financial management in human service organizations*. Philadelphia: Temple University Press.

Lohmann, R. A. (1995). Financial management. In R. L. Edwards (Ed.-in-chief), *Encyclopedia of social work* (19th ed., pp. 1028–1036). Washington, DC: NASW Press.

Marchetti, D. (2000, May 4). Two food charities join forces in one of biggest non-profit mergers. *Chronicle of Philanthropy*. Available: http://philanthropy.com/premium/articles/v12/i14/14003301.htm

Massarsky, C. W. (1994). Enterprising strategies for generating revenue. In R. D. Herman & Associates (Eds.), *The Jossey-Bass handbook of nonprofit leadership and management* (pp. 382–402). San Francisco: Jossey-Bass.

Meyer, D. R., & Sherraden, M. W. (1985). Toward improved financial planning: Further applications of break-even analysis in not-for-profit organizations. *Administration in Social Work, 9*(3), 57–68.

Moore, J. (1998, August 13). A corporate challenge for charities. *Chronicle of Philanthropy*, p. 1, 34–36.

National Association of Social Workers. (1999). *Code of ethics*. Washington, DC: Author.

National Philanthropic Trust. (2007). *Philanthropy statistics*. Available: http://www.nptrust.org/philanthropy/philanthropy_stats.asp

"Panel on civic renewal adds another voice to calls for tax incentives to promote giving." (1998, July 16). *Chronicle of Philanthropy*, p. 51.

Raffa, T. J. (2002). *Criteria for nonprofits' operating reserves*. Available: http//www.iknow.org/pages/articles/criteria.htm

Sinclair, M. (2000, July). Clinton staff says Americans should give more. *Nonprofit Times*, p. 5.

Smith, S. R. (1989). Federal funding, nonprofit agencies, and victim services. In H. W. Demone, Jr., & M. Gibelman (Eds.), *Services for sale: Purchasing health and human services* (pp. 215–227). New Brunswick, NJ: Rutgers University Press.

Sommerfeld, M. (2000, July 13). New study of charity alliances. *Chronicle of Philanthropy*. Available: http://philanthropy.com/premium/articles/v12/i18/18005106.htm

Starkweather, D. B. (1993). Profit making by hospitals. In D. C. Hammack & D. R. Young (Eds.), *Nonprofit organizations in a market economy* (pp. 105–137). San Francisco: Jossey-Bass.

"Study says business and charity mix." (1999, March 11). *Chronicle of Philanthropy*. Available: http://philanthropy.com/premium/article/v11/i10/10003203.htm

Turner, J. B. (1995). Fundraising and philanthropy. In R. L. Edwards (Ed.-in-chief), *Encyclopedia of social work* (19th ed., pp. 1038–1044). Washington, DC: NASW Press.

Wellford, W. H., & Gallagher, J. G. (1988). *Unfair competition: The challenge to charitable exemption.* Washington, DC: National Assembly of National Voluntary Health and Social Welfare Organizations.

Williams, G. (2001, February 8). White House proposes tax breaks to spur giving to the nation's charities. *Chronicle of Philanthropy,* p. 30.

Chapter 4

Who Has the Power?
Roles in Human Service
Organizations

In this chapter, the major roles and responsibilities of some of the key players in human service organizations are identified, including the board of directors (in the case of a nonprofit organization) and the chief executive officer. The question of who leads the human service organization deserves special consideration, as it is the vision, priorities, work style and preferences, and management skills of the organization's leadership that set the tone for how the organization functions.

There are a host of other influential players who have a role in determining what the organization does and how well it functions. These other players include stockholders (in the case of publicly held for-profit organizations), volunteers, and the government, foundations, and corporate and individual contributors who provide the funds. For social workers in direct service positions, understanding the complex web of major players—both internal and external to the organization—helps explain accountability requirements and the time spent on documentation of both processes and outcomes. Many people are interested in how the organization conducts its business and with what results.

Each organization has a governing body responsible for adopting policies, defining services, guiding development, and ensuring accountability to the community the organization serves. In a nonprofit organization, this governance function resides with a board of directors (also known as a board of trustees). In the case of a for-profit agency, such as one that is owner operated, one person (a designated or managing partner or the owner/president) acts as the governing body and assumes responsibility for the operations of the organization and its services. The owner thus fulfills the functions of managerial leadership but may also choose to create an advisory board to provide input and feedback on programs, community relations, or other matters.

Public organizations may also create advisory boards composed of representatives of key constituency groups. Here, too, the advisory group provides a mechanism for input into decision making, but such input is not necessarily binding on the organization's management. The public agency's advisory board may, however, serve important symbolic and political purposes. The powers and responsibilities of advisory boards are not as broad as those of boards of nonprofit organizations. For this reason, the following discussion is limited to non-profit boards, as they constitute the legal authority for nonprofit organizations.

Role of the Board of Directors

Because the largest proportion of social workers are employed in nonprofit agencies (Gibelman & Schervish, 1997), the leadership role of the board of directors of these agencies deserves special attention. From the earliest days of organized philanthropy, interested and committed individuals have served as trustees, overseers, and board members of nonprofit organizations. These board members are volunteers, but their role is different from that of the volunteer who transports children or answers the crisis hotline.

In nonprofit organizations, the board of directors is responsible for devising and approving the policies of the organization. Boards act on behalf of the interests and values of the community and the constituents of the organization. Board members are entrusted to guide the nonprofit organization with care, skill, and integrity (Abzug & Galaskiewicz, 2001; Jackson & Holland, 1998). They share collective responsibility for the fiscal and programmatic aspects of the organization's performance.

In addition to planning and policy-making functions, the board is responsible for the general direction and control of the agency. Other roles include hiring and evaluating the CEO, facilitating fund-raising and access to necessary resources, and representing the organization within the larger community. Finally, the board is also responsible for evaluating the effectiveness of the organization and ensuring its accountability to funding sources, government, and the community (Axelrod, 1994; Callen, Klein, & Tinkelman, 2010; Gelman, 1995).

Staff, including the CEO, may be hired and fired; the board is elected. Although board members can be removed (for example, if they fail to attend meetings or engage in behaviors considered to pose a conflict of interest), their tenure is relatively secure for the length of their term of office. The board represents constancy and stability.

Standards

Although boards are expected to monitor and evaluate their own performance, external monitoring ensures greater accountability to constituents and the public. The National Charities Information Bureau (2000) is one of several standard-setting and oversight agencies concerned with charitable organizations. The Bureau established a list of fundamentals for board governance shown in box 4.1.

The directors of nonprofit corporations are required to exercise reasonable and ordinary care in the performance of their duties, exhibiting honesty and good faith. They must discharge their duties with care, skill, and diligence (Gibelman, Gelman, & Pollack, 1997). Although the board delegates day-to-day

---

BOX 4.1
NCIB Standards in Philanthropy: Governance

Board Governance
    The board is responsible for policy setting, fiscal guidance, and ongoing governance and should regularly review the organization's policies, programs, and operations.
    The board should have:
- An independent, volunteer membership
- A minimum of five voting members
- An individual attendance policy
- Specific terms of office for its officers and members
- In-person, evenly spaced face-to-face meetings, at least twice a year, with a majority of voting members in attendance at each meeting
- No fees to members for board service, but payments may be made for costs incurred due to board participation
- No more than one paid staff member, usually the chief officer, who shall not chair the board or serve as treasurer
- Policy guidelines to avoid material conflicts of interest involving board or staff
- A policy promoting pluralism and diversity within the organization's board, staff, and constituencies

Source: Adapted from National Charities Information Bureau (2000).

---

operational responsibility of the organization to the CEO, it cannot abdicate its responsibility for vigilant oversight. Box 4.2 highlights the functions of the board in relation to the CEO. In this chapter, we will also consider the role of

---

BOX 4.2
Functions of the Board of Directors vis-à-vis
the Chief Executive Officer

The board
- Appoints the chief executive officer
- Delegates authority and responsibility for the organization's management and implementation of policy
- Holds the CEO accountable for the organization's performance
- Develops criteria and systems for CEO evaluation, preferably with the participation of the CEO
- Evaluates the CEO's performance in writing at least biannually against written performance criteria and objectives that were previously provided to the executive and that were established for the time span between evaluations
- Provides that the executive participates in the evaluation process and reviews, signs, and responds to the evaluation before it is entered into the executive's record

Source: Adapted from Council on Accreditation of Services to Families and Children (1997).

line-level social workers in organizational transformation and change. Too often, change and leadership are considered in a top-down manner. New styles of management recognize that it is important to empower all levels of workers to take on leadership roles. New social workers often feel powerless in the context of agency work, yet have considerably more power than they believe. However, prior to engaging in systemic systems change, direct service workers must have a thorough understanding of the organizational climate and culture, and the manner in which power and change are viewed within the organization.

Board Performance

Effective performance on the part of the board is not guaranteed by its structure or by organizational policies and procedures, no matter how sound these may be. A review of empirical studies of nonprofit organizational effectiveness over a twenty-year period (1977-97) revealed that "effectiveness" has been conceptualized in many different ways, with more attention to organizational process than outcomes (Forbes, 1998).

Measuring effectiveness involves, first, clarification about desirable or effective behaviors. Six dimensions of board competency have been identified as essential to effective governance. Jackson and Holland (1998) summarize the research in this area, as follows:

> *Contextual.* The board understands and takes into account the cultural norms and values of the organization it governs.
> *Educational.* The board takes the necessary steps to ensure that members are well informed about the organization and the professions working there as well as the board's own roles, responsibilities, and performance.
> *Interpersonal.* The board nurtures the development of its members as a group, attends to the board's collective welfare, and fosters a sense of cohesiveness.
> *Analytical.* The board recognizes complexities and subtleties in the issues it faces, and draws on multiple perspectives to dissect complex problems and to synthesize appropriate responses.
> *Political.* The board accepts as one of its primary responsibilities the need to develop and maintain healthy relationships among all key constituencies.
> *Strategic.* The board envisions and shapes institutional direction and helps to ensure a strategic approach to the organization's future. (Pp. 160-161)

Although many nonprofits provide for the active recruitment of volunteer leaders, others tend to recycle their existing leadership. Turnover among leadership is vital for reinvigorating the organization with new ideas, new dynamics, and a fresh perspective. It also ensures greater accountability.

Elements of an effective board development program include orienting new and continuing board members on an annual basis, providing continuing education in policy making, and promoting continuous opportunities for the board to assess its own performance and that of the organization (Axelrod, 1994).

Clarifying Board and Staff Responsibilities

Who leads the nonprofit organization? Traditionally, the leadership function has been ascribed to the volunteer board of directors. In reality, leading an organization entails a complex set of activities carried out by the board, the executive leadership, middle management, and direct service workers. Each has an important role in translating the mission of the organization into action and helping to meet the needs of clients. Boards and senior management must listen carefully to the perspectives of the direct service staff, who may be more in touch with the needs of the client population. For instance, in an agency serving the Latino community, it was the workers who first recognized the need for change in the agency's substance abuse programs. The direct service staff found that their clients, especially teenaged Latina mothers, were increasingly wanting to include family members in counseling sessions. New billing structures and a new definition of services were needed. It was the direct service workers who pushed for a family-focused substance abuse program. The management was able to respond to the suggestions of the workers and presented the ideas to the board, who fully supported the change.

Human service organizations that are transitioning from largely volunteer-run to professionally managed tend to experience murky boundaries between the role of the board and that of the executive director, as the vignette in box 4.3 illustrates.

BOX 4.3
Hey, Let Me Do My Job

Donna was thrilled about her new job as executive director of a state nonprofit health advocacy agency. She had previously worked as the associate executive director of a large nonprofit, and her career plan, now actualized, was to take over as the CEO of an organization with a clear purpose, a heart, and a cause.

This was the first time the organization had hired its own executive director. In recent years, the board had hired a management firm to take care of some functions—producing the newsletter, collecting membership dues, and running the annual conference. Until Donna was hired, however, this was a volunteer-run organization. The decision to set up an office and hire an executive director was made by the board of directors because of the growing complexity of the organization's programs and the positive state of its resources. It was time to turn certain functions over to the professionals.

The board included several prominent physicians. The majority, however, were people suffering from Tourette's syndrome or close family members. There was relatively little turnover among the board or committees; because of the investment of volunteers in this organization, their involvement was long term and intense. The people affected by the disease were exceptionally motivated to work on public and community education, patient education, and membership services.

(continued on next page)

Donna faced several challenges. First, there was no precedent for dividing the work between volunteers and paid staff. Some board members seemed to feel that all functions should immediately be turned over to the office, even though the office consisted of a staff of two. Other board members, however, were afraid that their roles would be taken away from them. In addition, there was some covert resentment toward Donna because she did not suffer from Tourette's syndrome and therefore was thought to lack both investment and knowledge about the cause represented by the organization.

Another challenge concerned differing orientations. In Donna's past work experiences, she had not encountered the intensity and level of commitment that the volunteers of this organization exhibited. To them, the organization represented a lifeline. Some expected and demanded that Donna show the same commitment. Donna's commitment, however, was to doing the job she was hired to do, as she understood it. This included professionalizing the organization and its programs of service.

Boundaries were also an issue. The volunteers were in constant telephone contact. Donna began to receive evening and weekend calls at home from the volunteers on a regular basis. Setting limits did not seem to be effective; if she allowed the phone machine to pick up, the message left was that she should call back right away. Invariably, the caller wanted Donna to do something. Everyone was giving her orders. She began to feel that the emotional and time demands of the job were eating her up.

Donna's situation represents somewhat of an extreme in terms of lack of role clarification between board members and staff. This is understandable, given the transitional stage of the organization. However, even in many long-established and professionally oriented organizations, there can be substantial misunderstanding about respective board-staff responsibilities. The term *micro-management* is often used to describe the actions of board members who get overly involved in day-to-day operations, either instead of or in addition to their policy-making responsibilities.

In practice, it is common for there to be some confusion about the roles of the board and the CEO. This is because governance is more a shared function than classical organizational models suggest. For example, it is appropriate for the CEO to identify policy needs and make recommendations to the board. On the other hand, the board has some jurisdiction over the responsibilities of the CEO, such as the development of policy to guide the organization's management in personnel matters. A collegial working relationship between the board and the executive is essential, but the executive, no matter how seasoned, prominent, or well liked, remains an employee of the organization (Gibelman & Gelman, 1999).

The Job of the Chief Executive Officer

The chief executive officer (sometimes referred to as the executive director or executive vice president) maintains day-to-day managerial responsibility for the work of the agency. The CEO is an employee of the organization and serves at the pleasure of the board. He or she is a professional who is knowledgeable about people, management techniques, service provision, evaluation, fund-raising, and conflict resolution and excels as a politician and communicator (Herman & Heimovics, 1994; Menefee, 2000).

The CEO's job description varies depending on the organization's structure but typically includes the components listed in box 4.4 in relation to the board of directors.

The job tenure of the CEO tends to be shorter than that of staff. A 1997 study of CEOs in corporate America revealed that the average CEO stayed on the job for 6.3 years (Ginsberg, 1997). However, this statistic is overly optimistic. When the researchers controlled for a few top executives who had been in their positions for more than thirty years, the average tenure of a corporate CEO dropped to 3.9 years. The survey, conducted by Drake Beam Morin, a New York-based outplacement and management consulting firm, also revealed that nearly 9 percent of the companies surveyed had experienced a CEO change in the past six months and 34 percent had had a change in the past 2.5 years (Ginsberg, 1997).

Data on the nonprofit sector show a similar trend. A survey conducted by the David and Lucile Packard Foundation in 1997 found that 45 percent of its grantees had experienced a change in executive leadership in the previous three years (Marchetti, 1999). There are a variety of reasons why this is the case: turnover among board members may result in new expectations about the CEO's role; the organization may be struggling financially and the board may decide that it needs a new leader to turn the agency around; or the CEO may decide that it is time to move on to a different opportunity.

BOX 4.4
Components of the CEO's Job

- ◆ Implement board policy
- ◆ Plan and coordinate with the governing body the development of policies governing the organization's program of services
- ◆ Guide staff in formulating strategies designed to achieve organizational objectives
- ◆ Handle overall personnel management and ensure that the organization's personnel management is in accord with written organizational policy
- ◆ Attend all meetings of the board and their standing and ad hoc committees and task forces, with the possible exception of those held for the purpose of reviewing the executive's performance, status, or compensation
- ◆ Ensure that the board is kept informed about the finances, operations, and programs of the organization

Sources: Bradshaw, Murray, & Wolpin (1992); Council on Accreditation (1997); Heimovics & Herman (1990).

Despite all the concern in recent years about the downsizing of middle managers, it is actually the top-level manager (CEO) who is more vulnerable (Ginsberg, 1997). The importance of the longevity of the CEO has to do with organizational stability. Change at the top often means a period of disequilibrium and uncertainty for the organization and its staff. The length and severity of this period is affected by the reasons for the CEO's departure and the amount of time involved in searching for and hiring a new CEO.

During periods of such change, employees tend to exhibit higher-than-usual levels of stress, because they are concerned about how they will fit in under new executive leadership. Will their jobs be secure? What if the new person has a totally different management style? What if the staff person likes the way things are and knows that some level of change will occur? It is a given that the climate and ways of doing business will change when the new CEO takes over; the question is, to what extent?

Public organizations are particularly vulnerable to shifts in top-level management. With each election (mayoral, gubernatorial, or presidential), such changes are commonplace. The newly elected politicians want to bring in their own people and do so through political appointments. For example, the commissioners of major departments, such as mental health, human services, and health departments, occupy appointed positions. Even if the elected politician is of the same party as the previous occupant of the position, he or she may use the opportunity of an election to bring in new people.

No matter what the type of organization, change at the top occurs with some regularity and, almost always, with some disruption to business as usual. However, in many instances, an organizational shake-up is considered positive by key stakeholders. A new CEO is seen as an opportunity to bring fresh ideas and positive change to the agency.

Attributes of a Good CEO

Effective leadership is an essential factor in creating organizational change and innovation. However, despite the widespread use of and reference to the term *leadership* in the literature and in practice, agreement about the attributes of a leader or the qualities of leadership is lacking. What makes for a good CEO? "It depends" may not be a clear answer, but it is accurate. It depends on the organizational culture, the status of the organization (financial and programmatic stability), the preferences and predilections of the board of directors, and the environmental influences impinging on the organization at any given period of time.

Ask several employees about their views on the attributes of a good boss, and each will indicate different characteristics or at least prioritize them differently. Some prefer a take-charge type of person. Others prefer someone who is visible and communicates with staff. Still others prefer a boss who leaves them alone.

Differences in perception about the most important qualities of a good CEO also depend on one's position within the organization or community. The board, for example, will see competitiveness, vision, leadership, ability to get along with diverse constituencies, and financial acuity as important characteristics of a CEO. Anecdotal evidence derived from conversations with social work practitioners suggests the following attributes of the effective CEO from a staff perspective:

- ◆ Accessibility
- ◆ Availability
- ◆ Sense of humor
- ◆ Empathy and concern
- ◆ Candid forthright approach
- ◆ Good listener
- ◆ Responsive to concerns
- ◆ Hard working
- ◆ Role model

These humanistic characteristics are augmented, of course, by desired competencies. The required competencies of a CEO include problem solving, planning, controlling, managing self, managing relationships, leading, and communicating (Gibelman & Gelman, 2001; Herman & Heimovics, 1994).

Not all CEOs of human service organizations are educated as social workers. As human service organizations have sought to develop business acumen to survive and thrive in a competitive environment, experienced managers schooled in business, law, public administration, and related fields have been recruited to CEO positions. Board members may perceive that business savvy and fundraising skills are as important CEO attributes as (or more important than) knowledge of human need and social services.

There are mixed views about the use of non–social workers in top management roles. One view is that the use of non–social workers in key management posts promotes a mismatch of ethical orientations. Those educated in business and finance, for example, hold to their own set of ethical norms that are quite different from those to which social workers ascribe. Social justice, for example, would not be expected to be a strong ethical norm among those with MBAs. An emphasis on the bottom line financial may be more characteristic of the businessperson, to the potential detriment of services to clients. The principles of law and finance may overrule principles of fairness, honesty, and good faith, with unknown consequences (Oakley & Lynch, 2000).

The job of CEOs, whatever their background, is to manage and lead. The CEO has ultimate responsibility for running the day-to-day operations of the organization; hiring, deploying, and firing; raising and accounting for funds; creating and implementing programs; and accounting to multiple constituencies with regard to outcomes. The job is multifaceted and demanding.

Someone Is Watching: External Key Players

It bears repeating that the human service organization is an open system, one that constantly interacts with and influences (and is influenced by) its larger environment. Thus, role prescriptions and relationships within human service organizations are affected by external forces. In a sense, there are "bosses" outside the agency who have a say in what is done inside the agency.

Standard-Setting Organizations

Out of recognition of the need to define standards of quality for the services provided by human service organizations and to increase accountability for the outcomes of services, various organizations have evolved to formulate standards in specialized service areas and to enforce them through an accreditation process. The Council on Accreditation for Services to Families and Children is one such body. It is the largest independent accrediting body for agencies providing behavioral health care, social services, counseling, and other community services to families, children, and other individuals. Other accrediting organizations include the Joint Commission on Accreditation of Health Care Organizations and the Accreditation Council for People with Developmental Disabilities.

The Council on Accreditation's standards are referred to throughout this book, as they have significant applicability to the social service organizations that employ a large proportion of social workers. The Council's standards are rooted in the values of the social work profession and are based on the following assumptions: at least some personnel have been professionally trained in social work or a related human service profession, often at the supervisory and leadership levels; there is interdisciplinary collaboration and professional supervision and consultation; human service organizations are accountable to the community; there is commitment to the central role of consumers in making decisions about services provided on their behalf; and a holistic person-in-environment approach is used, which recognizes the interaction of social, cultural, environmental, and psychodynamic factors (Council on Accreditation, 1997). The standards represent professional consensus about organizational practices distilled and synthesized from the practice field (Council on Accreditation, 1997).

Accreditation serves a variety of purposes. The process itself forces the organization to periodically examine its programs and operations in regard to its overall mission. Once accredited, the organization provides evidence to the community that it has met accepted standards of operation—a kind of seal of approval; private and public funders have a basis for determining that the organization is worthy of financial support; and goals for organizational improvement are established (Council on Accreditation, 1997).

Watchdog Agencies

Historically, there have been two primary national groups that devise standards for and review compliance of charitable nonprofit organizations: the National Charities Information Bureau (NCIB) and the Philanthropic Advisory Bureau (PAS) of the Council of Better Business Bureaus (CBBB). NCIB and PAS, which merged in 2001, each developed standards against which to evaluate nonprofits. NCIB and PAS reviews carry significant influence, foremost among donors. These organizations are not accrediting bodies like the Council on Accreditation but rather serve as watchdogs to ensure the accountability of charitable groups to the public.

National Charities Information Bureau   The NCIB was founded in 1918 by a group of national leaders to provide information to donors, government agencies, the media, and the general public about charitable organizations. The originating concern was that Americans were donating millions of dollars to charities without knowing very much about them. The mission of NCIB, itself a charitable organization dependent on contributions, was to provide information to donors to enable them to give wisely to charitable organizations.

The results of the NCIB review could have an unanticipated but consequential impact on the organization, as illustrated in the vignette in box 4.5.

Evelyn learned an important lesson: Watchdog agencies are to be taken seriously! A bad report can cause potential damage to the organization's fund-

---

BOX 4.5
When the Report Card Isn't So Good

Evelyn's first encounter with the National Charities Information Bureau was one she will always remember. Evelyn was the newly appointed CEO of a national agency that ran an annual conference on social welfare and conducted research on social issues for use by public and nonprofit agencies. One day she opened an envelope from NCIB that contained a prepublication copy of an evaluation report prepared by NCIB staff analysts. In sum, the report noted that, based on information available to NCIB, the organization was out of compliance in regard to three of its standards: (1) it lacked a policy promoting pluralism and diversity within the organization's board, staff, and constituencies; (2) it had a persistent budget deficit; and (3) it did not produce an annual report. The report further noted that the organization had failed to respond to NCIB's request to submit information. Thus, the report was based on information available from public sources.

Evelyn consulted with legal counsel and was advised to contact NCIB directly and request an appointment. Evelyn did so and met with one of NCIB's program staff. She was given a copy of the original and follow-up letters of request for information sent by NCIB to the organization. She was told what documents had been reviewed as the basis for the evaluation. She took notes and asked what steps would be necessary for NCIB to conduct another evaluation based on full information disclosure. She learned that this process might take several months and, until such time, the report stood.

raising abilities as well as its public reputation. Moreover, it can take significant time to rectify the situation. Sometimes differences can be resolved easily. At other times, a particular point of disagreement may require voluminous correspondence and several meetings. Sometimes there is no agreement, and NCIB releases the report to the public. In all cases, however, NCIB gives the charity an opportunity to respond to the report before its release (National Charities Information Bureau, 2000).

Philanthropic Advisory Service   The Philanthropic Advisory Service was a service of the Council of Better Business Bureaus. The CBBB is the umbrella organization for the Better Business Bureau system, which is supported by 250,000 local business members throughout the United States.

The purpose of the PAS was to promote ethical standards within the charitable community, provide information to the public about charitable organizations, and educate individual and corporate donors to make wise giving decisions (Better Business Bureau, 2000). Like the NCIB, the PAS had, until the merger, its own set of ethical practices outlined in the Council of Better Business Bureau's *Standards for Charitable Solicitations* (Better Business Bureau, 2000). In addition, like the NCIB, the PAS focus was on national or international organizations. Information was requested from charitable organizations about their programs, governance, fund-raising practices, and finances when the charities were the subject of inquiries. In this respect, PAS differred from NCIB because NCIB selected the organizations it wished to evaluate. PAS initiated inquiries when a question or complaint was received about a charity. The information collected and analyzed by PAS was disseminated through local Better Business Bureaus.

A Merger   In 2001, NCIB and PAS merged. The new Better Business Bureau Wise Giving Alliance, as the merged organization is called, now uses the Council of Better Business Bureau's *Standards for Charitable Solicitations,* which are the standards previously used by PAS (Better Business Bureau Wise Giving Alliance, 2001). New standards are under development. The intent of the new group is to evaluate a large number of charities and reach more donors (Blum, 2000).

Government Agencies

The Internal Revenue Service is an important player in the world of nonprofit organizations. The IRS approves and authorizes tax-exemption status for nonprofits and monitors the activities of these organizations to ensure that they relate to the purposes for which they were founded. Congress, of course, delegates authority to the IRS, and such authority appears to be on the increase. For example, the Joint Tax Committee of Congress has recommended an expanded federal government role in the amount of information it releases to the public about nonprofit organizations, including the results of IRS audits, rulings on tax issues, and applications filed by charities for tax-exempt status ("A Call for

Disclosure," 2000). Furthermore, the Joint Tax Committee is considering request-ing more financial information from nonprofits as part of their annual tax filing.

The Federal Trade Commission also has jurisdiction over some human ser-vice organizations, notably those that do business in multiple states. The FTC monitors interstate commerce and thus has jurisdiction over all businesses that cross state lines. One of its responsibilities is to ensure that business practices are appropriate.

Several other federal and state agencies exert powerful influence over hu-man service organizations. As noted in chapter 2, the U.S. Department of Health and Human Services and the state agency counterparts award and monitor grants and contracts. Included in this process is determining which agencies are eligible. These departments also demand accountability from human service agencies in terms of dollars spent.

The U.S. Postal Service regulates fund-raising campaigns conducted through the mail. It also monitors the use of the mail in regard to reduced postal rates for tax-exempt organizations and appropriate use of these special mail rates. The Department of Labor, through the Equal Employment Opportunity Com-mission, monitors compliance with workplace laws. The Department of Justice, through the Office of the Attorney General, issues licenses and hears and re-views citizen complaints about organizations. The Department of Regulatory Af-fairs in each state authorizes permits to do business in a state, grants state and local tax exemption, and hears public complaints. The Office of Personnel Man-agement issues regulations regarding agency participation in combined federal fund-raising campaigns. The list is extensive.

Because every nonprofit or for-profit human service organization is incor-porated in a state, there are state regulatory agencies that oversee and monitor organizational activities. Different states assign this function to different agen-cies. For example, in Arizona, the applicable state body is the Office of the Sec-retary of State; in Florida, it is the Attorney General's Office; in New Jersey, it is the Office of Consumer Protection; and in Pennsylvania, it is the Department of State.

Government agencies at the federal, state, and local levels, standard-setting agencies, and watchdog organizations, singularly and collectively, have an enor-mous impact on how human service organizations are structured and how they operate. A large number of internal and external "bosses" affect human service organizations.

Key Points

- ◆ In nonprofit organizations, the board of directors carries legal and pol-icy-making authority.
- ◆ The chief executive officer maintains day-to-day management responsi-bility for the work of the agency.
- ◆ The CEO serves at the pleasure of the board; the tenure of the CEO is often shorter than that of other staff.

◆ There are several voluntary accrediting organizations that define standards of quality in human service organizations; the assumption is that human service organizations should be self-regulating.

◆ There are numerous government agencies that have regulatory and oversight authority over human service organizations.

◆ The various accrediting, standard-setting, and oversight agencies exercise considerable influence over how nonprofit organizations operate.

Suggested Learning Activities and Discussion Questions

1. Review the bylaws or articles of incorporation of your agency. What do they say about the role and responsibilities of the board of directors? The executive director?

2. Conduct an Internet search of your city or state newspapers. Use key words such as *nonprofits, charities, human services*, and *chief executive officer* or *executive director*. Find two articles about the departure of a CEO from a human service organization. Describe the circumstances surrounding the departure.

3. What are the external environments to which your organization relates? What kinds of demands are imposed on the organization by relevant others (individuals, agencies, government bodies, and so on), and how do these demands influence day-to-day work within the agency setting?

4. Pretend you have been appointed to a search committee for a new CEO of a human service organization. The top two candidates would bring different but strong experience and expertise to the job. One has an MSW. The other has an MBA. List arguments either in favor of or against the hiring of the MBA.

5. Identify a charity about which you would like information. Then log on to the Better Business Bureau Wise Giving Alliance (www.give.org) and see what reports are available about this organization. Put yourself in the mind-set of a donor. How and in what way would this report influence your decision to give to the charity?

Recommended Readings

Fletcher, K. (2000). *The policy sampler: A resource for non-profit boards.* Washington, DC: National Center for Nonprofit Boards.

Nanus, B., & Dobbs, S. M. (1999). *Leaders who make a difference: Essential strategies for meeting the nonprofit challenge.* San Francisco: Jossey-Bass.

Sand, M. A. (2005). *How to manage an effective nonprofit organization.* Pompton Plains, NJ: Career Press.

Scott, K. T. (2000). *Creating caring and capable boards.* San Francisco: Jossey-Bass.

References

Abzug, R., & Galaskiewicz, J. (2001). Nonprofit boards: Crucibles of expertise or symbols of local identities? *Nonprofit and Voluntary Sector Quarterly, 30*(1), 51–73.

Axelrod, N. R. (1994). Board leadership and board development. In R. D. Herman & Associates (Eds.), *The Jossey-Bass handbook of nonprofit leadership and management* (pp. 119–136). San Francisco: Jossey-Bass.

Better Business Bureau. (2000). *Philanthropic advisory service (PAS)*. Available: http://www.bbb.org/about/pas.asp

Better Business Bureau Wise Giving Alliance. (2001). *About the BBB Wise Giving Alliance*. Available: http://www.give.org

Blum, D. E. (2000, September 2). Merger of 2 watchdog groups raises concern among observers. *Chronicle of Philanthropy*, p. 10.

Bradshaw, P., Murray, V., & Wolpin, J. (1992). Do nonprofit boards make a difference? An exploration of the relationships among board structure, process and effectiveness. *Nonprofit and Voluntary Sector Quarterly, 21*(3), 227–249.

"A call for disclosure." (2000, March 9). *Chronicle of Philanthropy*, p. 28.

Callen, J. L., Klein, A., & Tinkelman, D. (2010). The contextual impact of nonprofit board composition and structure on organizational performance: Agency and resource dependence perspectives. *Voluntas: International Journal of Voluntary and Nonprofit Organizations, 21*(1), 101–125.

Council on Accreditation of Services to Families and Children. (1997). *1997 standards for behavioral health care services and community support and education services* (U.S. ed.). New York: Author.

Forbes, D. P. (1998). Measuring the unmeasurable: Empirical studies of nonprofit organization effectiveness from 1977 to 1997. *Nonprofit and Voluntary Sector Quarterly, 27*(2), 183–202.

Gelman, S. R. (1995). Boards of directors. In R. L. Edwards (Ed.-in-chief), *Encyclopedia of social work* (19th ed., pp. 305–312). Washington, DC: NASW Press.

Gibelman, M., & Gelman, S. R. (1999). Safeguarding the nonprofit agency: The role of the board of directors in risk management. *Journal of Residential Treatment for Children and Youth, 16*(4), 19–37.

Gibelman, M., & Gelman, S. R. (2001). Very public scandals: An analysis of how and why nongovernmental organizations get in trouble. *Voluntas, 12*(1), 49–66.

Gibelman, M., Gelman, S. R., & Pollack, D. (1997). The credibility of nonprofit boards: A view from the 1990s. *Administration in Social Work, 21*(2), 29–40.

Gibelman, M., & Schervish, P. (1997). *Who we are: A second look*. Washington, DC: NASW Press.

Ginsberg, S. (1997, August 24). When departures produce uncertainty. *Washington Post*, p. H4.

Heimovics, R. D., & Herman, R. D. (1990). Responsibility for critical events in nonprofit organizations. *Nonprofit and Voluntary Sector Quarterly, 19*(1), 59–73.

Herman, R. D., & Heimovics, R. D. (1994). Executive leadership. In R. D. Herman & Associates (Eds.), *The Jossey-Bass handbook of nonprofit leadership and management* (pp. 137–153). San Francisco: Jossey-Bass.

Jackson, D. K., & Holland, T. P. (1998). Measuring the effectiveness of nonprofit boards. *Nonprofit and Voluntary Sector Quarterly, 27*(2), 159–182.

Marchetti, D. (1999, June 3). Managing turnover at the top. *Chronicle of Philanthropy*. Available: http://philanthropy.com/premium/articles/v11/i16/16000101.htm

Menefee, D. (2000). What managers do and why they do it. In R. J. Patti (Ed.), *The handbook of social welfare management* (pp. 247–266). Thousand Oaks, CA: Sage Publications.

National Charities Information Bureau. (2000). *About NCIB*. Available: http://www.ncib.org/about.cfm

Oakley, E. F., III, & Lynch, P. (2000). Promise-keeping: A low priority in a hierarchy of workplace values. *Journal of Business Ethics, 27*(4), 377–392.

Chapter 5

Supervision within the Organizational Setting

In chapter 4, discussion focused on the role of key players in the organization. In larger organizations, direct service staff may have little occasion to meet or interact with the board of directors and CEO on an ongoing basis. The most pertinent hierarchical relationship is between the social worker and the supervisor.

In this chapter, supervision is discussed primarily as an agency function to promote staff competence and to ensure that the work of the organization is carried out effectively. Attention is devoted to both the administrative and professional functions of supervision. Administrative purposes of supervision focus on the worker within the particular agency context and the way work is carried out. For example, supervision seeks to help staff become knowledgeable about and follow agency procedures in regard to client screening processes, reporting requirements, record keeping, and the like. The professional functions of supervision are to enhance worker knowledge and skills as necessary for effective job performance, to monitor the application of newly acquired skills, to increase self-awareness, to enhance culturally competent practice, and to evaluate worker performance.

Both the administrative and professional aspects of supervision involve an educational component. Thus, the supervisor also serves as trainer and gatekeeper for the continuing professional education of social work staff. The different forms of professional education are discussed in this chapter as they apply to on-the-job professional development. It is the supervisor who, in most cases, is responsible for performance evaluation. Thus, this chapter includes discussion of the evaluation of job performance.

Social work has been defined as a supervising profession (Kadushin & Harkness, 2002; Scott, 1966). The practice of social work supervision dates back to the very beginnings of the social work profession: "Social work practice was built on a foundation of supervision" (Harkness & Poertner, 1989, p. 115). The scholarly work on the subject of supervision by Kadushin and Harkness (2002), Shulman (1993, 1995), and others assumes an organizational base of practice. The relationship between social work supervision and enhanced practice has been repeatedly acknowledged and emphasized (see, for example, Menefee, 2000; Shulman, 1993).

Definitions of Supervision

Barker (1999) defines supervision as "an administrative and educational process used extensively in social agencies to help social workers further develop and refine their skills and to provide quality assurance for the clients" (p. 473). Traditional social work supervision, which meets this definition, is different from clinical supervision. Clinical supervision has taken on increased importance due to licensure, the need for ethical and self-aware practitioners, and the importance of staff development. Supervisors and agencies providing clinical services have an ethical obligation to help practitioners reflect upon their cases. This form of supervision focuses on the dynamics of the client situation and the work of the social worker in that regard (Barker, 1992). Traditional supervision is broader in scope, focusing on the worker within the agency context, including the impact of agency-imposed standards, rules, and regulations (Gibelman & Schervish, 1997a). Clinical supervision has a psychoeducational component, as the worker must develop insight into his or her professional use of self and its impact on the client (Campbell, 2002; Shier & Graham, 2011). Such supervision is particularly important in cross-cultural situations, when a worker is providing services to someone who is significantly different from him or herself (Delgado, 2006). Without supervision, misunderstandings can easily occur. For instance, a middle-aged Chinese man mandated for counseling for domestic violence may not talk about his family or his feelings to a social worker of a different cultural background. A social worker unfamiliar with this culture may see the man as resistant. However, with supervision, the worker may come to understand that in many Asian cultures, talking about family problems is seen as bringing shame upon the family (Nghe, Mahalik, & Lowe, 2003).

The Supervisor

A supervisor is a person assigned responsibility to carry out the supervision functions with authority to do so prescribed by the agency. The supervisor is expected to be a leader, a teacher, and a skilled master of the work to be done (Garthwait, 2011). The supervisor serves as the link between the practitioner and the agency, the external environment, and the profession itself. The organization delegates authority to the supervisor to direct, coordinate, enhance, and evaluate the job performance of supervisees (Kadushin & Harkness, 2002).

The supervisor is expected to be qualified for this role by virtue of experience and education. Relevant skills include the ability to motivate employees, coordinate work and workload, set goals and limits, provide corrective feedback, monitor and improve work processes, and educate and consult with employees (Kurland & Salmon, 1992; Menefee, 2000; Rauktis & Koeske, 1994; Walsh, 1990). Typically, a social worker assumes the role of supervisor after working in the field for several years (Gibelman & Schervish, 1997b). Ideally, specialized training is provided before the supervisor assumes this position. Supervisors may, and often do, maintain a small active caseload as well.

The *Code of Ethics* and Supervision

The vision of the profession and its obligations, as reflected in the National Association of Social Workers (1999) *Code of Ethics*, elaborates on and clarifies several aspects of the purposes and nature of social work supervision. The *Code* also reflects the most current thinking within the profession about the place of supervision in the profession and in social work practice.

Under the heading "Social Workers' Ethical Responsibilities in Practice Settings," the *Code* sets forth specific expectations regarding the role and nature of supervision and the qualifications of those providing supervision. For example, the *Code* specifies that:

- ◆ Social workers who provide supervision or consultation should have the necessary knowledge and skill to supervise or consult appropriately and should do so only within their areas of knowledge and competence.
- ◆ Social workers who provide supervision or consultation are responsible for setting clear, appropriate, and culturally sensitive boundaries.
- ◆ Social workers should not engage in any dual or multiple relationships with supervisees in which there is a risk of exploitation of or potential harm to the supervisee.
- ◆ Social workers who provide supervision should evaluate supervisees' performance in a manner that is fair and respectful. (P. 27)

These ethical standards suggest several elements of interest in the supervisory relationship, including the existence of a skill and knowledge base unique to the supervisory role, the potential power relationship inherent in the supervisor-supervisee relationship, and the evaluation role of the supervisor.

Other sections of the *Code* clarify the central role of supervision in social work. For example, Section 3.07, "Administration," obligates administrators to take "reasonable steps to ensure that adequate agency or organizational resources are available to provide appropriate staff supervision" (National Association of Social Workers, 1999, p. 30). The relationship between supervision and professional growth and development is also evident in Section 3.08, "Continuing Education and Staff Development," which provides that "social work administrators and supervisors should take reasonable steps to provide or arrange for continuing education and staff development for all staff for whom they are responsible" (p. 31). The central role of supervision is thus clearly articulated in the *Code of Ethics*.

The Role of Social Work Supervision within the Organization

Expectations about the broad parameters of supervision can be discerned from standards developed by human service accrediting bodies in regard to agency-based supervision. Box 5.1 provides an example of such standards.

These standards illustrate several key points. First, the job of the supervisor is delegated by those higher up in the organization. The job of the supervisor involves holding the supervisee accountable and, through the process of

---

BOX 5.1
Standards Regarding Supervision

◆ The organization delegates supervisory responsibility and holds personnel accountable for the performance of assigned duties and responsibilities.

◆ Frequency and type of individual or group supervision is arranged according to the level of skills of the supervisor, the complexity and size of the workload, and the newness of the assignment.

◆ Personnel assigned supervisory responsibility are provided sufficient time to hold supervisory conferences and to carry out their evaluation and training responsibilities.

◆ When the organization provides field placements or internships for students, it provides supervision of and accountability for the work carried out by those persons.

Source: Council on Accreditation of Services to Families and Children (1997), p. 24.

---

performance review, documenting how well the supervisee has met accountability expectations.

The organization has a responsibility to establish and maintain the conditions under which appropriate supervision can take place. This means that the organization supports the supervisory process and that supervision is considered an integral part of the supervisor's workload. However, in some cases, the organization may elect to purchase supervision for employees or students in field placement from outside the agency, particularly when qualified supervisory personnel are lacking or are otherwise deployed.

What constitutes supervision depends on a variety of circumstances. It may take place on a one-to-one basis or in a group format. How often, for how much time, and with what focus depends on the experience and skills of the person being supervised, the complexity of the job demands, and the skills, style, and available time of the supervisor. The focus of supervisory sessions may be negotiated between supervisor and supervisee and may vary in intensity and substance based on agency context, supervisor style, supervisee need, and presenting problems of clients.

The Functions of Supervision

An important goal of supervision is to maximize the effective and efficient delivery of services by the agency's staff through the day-to-day operations of the unit (Menefee, 2000). An additional goal is to contribute to the professional development of the social worker. It is not enough for supervisors to focus only on agency tasks; building healthy organizations and professions demands that attention be paid to the advancement of human service personnel. To accomplish these goals, the supervisor may function in the roles of enabler, teacher, broker, and advocate, among others, as the needs of the supervisee and the situation/environment demand. Central to these three components is the concept of accountability.

The Educational Function

To the extent that social work supervision centers on helping workers to sharpen their practice skills and acquire knowledge of how to better meet the needs of clients, supervision can be considered educational in nature. This supervisory function helps the supervisee become a more effective professional, which, in turn, ensures the provision of high-quality services to clients.

The educational component has been important since the beginning of the profession and remains so (Golensky, 2011). It is perhaps most emphasized in the early stages of a social worker's professional life in an agency (Nathanson, 1992). Here, a supervisor's responsibilities include orienting and training new staff. The knowledge the supervisor may impart during this process includes the nature of the helping process; the dynamics of the client population and the systems that impinge on the client's life; the agency's mission, goals, structure, and operations; and the agency's interaction with funding sources and the implications of funder demands on practice. The supervisor, in addition to imparting knowledge, also facilitates the supervisee's learning through role modeling, observing, discussing, critiquing case records, and exploring optional interventions (Shulman, 1993).

The supervisory function of fostering the professional development of staff continues after the worker's initial orientation to the agency and spans, in differing degrees, the entire period of time in which the worker is employed by the organization. In-service training and staff development, explored in more detail later in this chapter, are the mechanisms by which staff are trained for job-specific functions and tasks.

Support

Social workers who deal with the psychosocial problems of the consumers of human service organizations on a day-to-day basis can experience a high level of stress (Kurland & Salmon, 1992). The supervisor helps workers deal with stress, sustains workers' morale, cultivates teamwork, builds and sustains workers' commitment to the organization, and addresses work-related problems of conflict and frustration (Garthwait, 2011; Kadushin & Harkness, 2002). The supervisor must provide the needed support while directing and guiding the worker in the delivery of services (Menefee, 2000).

A positive relationship between supervisor and worker is important and consists of three elements: (1) rapport (general ability to get along); (2) caring (as evidenced in the communication by the supervisor of concern for the social worker); and (3) trust (the ability of the social worker to be open about mistakes and failures as well as successes) (Shulman, 1993, 1995). The supportive component of supervision, according to Kurland and Salmon (1992), includes helping workers set realistic work goals while encouraging them to recognize and appreciate the small successes achieved by their clients and develop positive norms and set limits in their work with clients.

The supportive supervisory role takes into account and addresses some of the underlying problems staff encounter that produce stress and burnout. These include workload size, client-worker relationships, and the nature of the problems clients experience. Supportive supervision helps workers manage day-to-day problems, a process of continuing resolution of the conflicting demands and pressures of social work practice (Shulman, 1993). Kurland and Salmon (1992) suggest that, through appropriate supervision, burnout can be prevented and worker enthusiasm maintained.

You may notice that aspects of the supportive function appear to be similar to the therapeutic relationship. It is true that supervisors in their supportive role, and in their role as professional developers (to be discussed later in this chapter), engage in skills and tasks that appear to be similar to those used with clients. Perhaps one of the most difficult aspects of the supervisory relationship is to learn how to establish good, healthy boundaries without being unnecessarily closed. Supervisors must seek their own supervision and should discuss with their own supervisors any concerns. In general, a good rule of thumb is that supervision should always focus on the tasks and cases in which workers are engaged and should delve into personal aspects of a supervisee's life only when they interfere with their work. That said, should these concerns be chronic and difficult to resolve, the supervisor should suggest that their supervisees seek additional therapeutic support.

Administrative Function

The supervisor assigns and coordinates the work of staff, monitors and evaluates staff performance, and facilitates communication within the organization. The supervisor may, to varying degrees, advocate for staff, serve as a buffer between staff and administration, and encourage needed change within the agency (Garthwait, 2011).

Supervision is an important element in establishing the climate of an organization. The immediate working environment includes the interactions social workers have with their colleagues and their supervisors. Supervisors can help set the tone for how and to what extent colleagues interact. Supervisors also can challenge workers to grow, thus stimulating a positive work environment.

Sometimes supervisors are involved in recruiting and selecting new staff (Kadushin & Harkness, 2002). The extent of this type of involvement is significantly influenced by the organization's size. For example, in large organizations where there is a human resources department, the supervisor may be brought in to participate in the screening process. In small agencies, the supervisor may be the person primarily responsible for recruitment and selection.

One of the most importance areas in which supervisors must educate their supervisees and offer guidance is that of culturally sensitive practice. Human service workers often find themselves working with people from different backgrounds. Differences in terms of race, culture, ethnicity, religion, and sexual identity appropriately may affect the experiences and social workers. Social workers must be able to handle these differences appropriately and sensitively. In recent years, social work education has increasingly recognized the importance of educating students for practice with people from different cultures. For instance, Furman, Bender, Shears, and Lewis (2006) found that nearly 80 percent of social work faculty feel that it is important to educate students for practice with diverse populations. However, the same group of professors was less certain that the profession is adequately preparing students for culturally sensitive practice. Fifty percent of social work faculty in the study, for example, believe that social work students are not prepared for culturally sensitive social work practice with Latinos.

It is important for human service workers to understand how their own background and experiences affect their practice with people who are different from themselves. For instance, Julie, a social worker in a large city in the South, found that she had difficulty accepting GLBT clients. At first, she focused on what she believed was their need to change. Over time, she began to realize that she was inappropriately imposing her personal religious beliefs on her clients, and that this was negatively affecting her relationships with her clients. She began to work with her supervisor on being more tolerant and accepting of different sexual orientations. As noted by Lewis, Packard, and Lewis (2007),

> It would be difficult for a supervisor to help practitioners work effectively with clients and systems without a high degree of multicultural competence. Multicultural competence always involves self-interrogation as well as knowledge and awareness about the cultural factors affecting others, and this is no less true for the supervisory relationship. (P. 144)

Another area where these conflicts often arise is in work with recent immigrants. The current social discourse is strongly critical of residents of the United States who are not legal residents or citizens and even those who are here legally but do not speak English. Furman, Langer, Sanchez, and Negi (2007) explored the value dilemmas that social workers encounter when current or proposed legislation seeks to deny services to these populations. They found that the majority of social work students in their study recognized the ethical mandate to serve the most oppressed and disenfranchised people, regardless of their linguistic abilities or migration status. In working with immigrant populations, social workers should help other workers, their agencies, and society at large understand the incredible strengths that immigrants possess. It takes a great deal of courage and resourcefulness to cross hostile borders and survive in a country in which you do not speak the language and whose citizens and government may be hostile to your very presence.

Supervision and Accountability

In social work's quest for legitimation as a profession, a central issue has been the extent to which social workers practice autonomously. The organizational base of practice has been a recurrent theme in regard to the limits on autonomous social work practice. Established structures of accountability and oversight, primarily through supervision, are essential to the provision of quality services.

Supervision is the means to enforce agency rules and regulations. For the worker, interaction with clients is most important in the allocation of time. The supervisor, however, must oversee and enforce compliance with record keeping, fiscal, procedural, and reporting requirements. The supervisor must also provide continuity in carrying out the work of the organization and therefore must be vigilant in ensuring compliance with agency procedures.

The goal of supervision, in this instance, is to hold supervisees accountable for their performance. The supervisor evaluates supervisees and influences decisions regarding their retention in the position, salary increases, and promotions. Thus, supervision also helps the organization maintain internal and external accountability by ensuring that the clients are receiving the correct types and adequate quality of care.

Difficulties Encountered in Supervision

Relationship Issues

The fact that the supervisor exercises a substantial amount of control over the worker is a source of potential friction in the relationship. This may or may not be a problem, depending on the personal dimensions of the relationship and the way in which the worker responds to authority and the supervisor handles authority.

Some personalities and styles simply don't mesh. Supervision is a relationship. If, for example, the supervisor is a highly controlling type of person and the supervisee takes pride in seeking help only when it is needed, there may be a clash of personalities. Differences in gender, age, or background may also affect the relationship. In such instances, the first step is to talk about the conflict—a step that can be initiated by either the supervisor or supervisee (Garthwait, 2011). If the problem cannot be worked out, there may be agreement that a change of supervisor is in order. If this is not a realistic option, the relationship will have to accommodate the differences or the supervisee may have to consider other job options. This may seem harsh, but the reality is that the supervisor is the boss.

Expectations about the supervisory relationship may also differ. For example, supervisees may feel that their supervisors are not available and do not devote enough time to them. The quantity of supervisory time has been found to be a significant predictor of satisfaction with supervision (Nathanson, 1992).

What constitutes reasonable expectations of time should be established by the supervisor and supervisee at the outset of the relationship. Will they meet once a week? Under what circumstances might the supervisory session be postponed or canceled? What about emergency situations when the supervisee needs consultation? The parameters of the relationship can form an agreement between the two parties.

These personal factors are also affected by the fact that there is often an absence of choice about the match between supervisor and supervisee. Supervisees rarely have a choice of supervisor. And almost as often, the supervisor lacks freedom to choose supervisees. Supervisees should not passively hope to get what they need, but rather should be active participants in their own growth and development. Supervisors are not mind readers; it is essential that you make suggestions for your supervision and take ownership of your own growth and development.

Constraints on the Supervisor

To be effective in carrying out the supervisor's responsibilities the supervisory role must be legitimized and supported by the organization. It is the agency that sanctions supervision, in part through the delegation of authority to the supervisor. The increased demands on social workers in agencies to carry larger caseloads, brought on in part by hiring freezes and attrition, have placed time constraints on many supervisors, particularly those who also have a direct service function. Concurrently, resources to support the allocation of personnel to provide supervision are shrinking because of tight budgets and the need to conserve and use agency funds more efficiently (Gibelman & Schervish, 1997a). The problems that can arise from these factors are illustrated in box 5.2.

BOX 5.2
Caught in a Bind

Michelle is a supervisor in the foster care unit of a voluntary child welfare agency. She has been on the job for five years, and although she finds the type of case situations she encounters to be emotionally taxing and professionally challenging, she feels that the agency has done its best to create a positive work environment. There are tight restrictions on supervisor-supervisee ratios; at no time has Michelle been assigned more than five supervisees. This has enabled Michelle to carry a reduced caseload of her own while allowing sufficient time to meet formally once a week with each supervisee and be available to them as needed.

The foster care program was entirely funded through a contract with the State Department of Human Services. The contract was first awarded in 1990 and had been renewed each year. In fact, there had been a steady increase in the program's scope, as well as in program funds. Staff had come to regard contract renewal as automatic and a given.

(continued on next page)

Last year, another voluntary agency in a neighboring community decided to extend its range of program offerings to include, for the first time, foster care services. Agency administrators were well connected with key state officials who encouraged them to bid on a contract. The agency was able to price the cost of services below that of Michelle's agency because it has a large endowment. The board of directors decided to use some of this endowment to subsidize the new foster care program. The hope was that if the agency was successful in its bid for the contract, in future renewals the state allocation would be increased and the subsidization could then cease.

The Department of Human Services has been under tight scrutiny regarding the expenditure of funds for all its programs, including foster care. The nation of a new agency in this particular locale that could offer the same service at lower cost was very appealing, and the contract was awarded. Michelle's agency was given sixty days' notice of contract termination; however, the agency was awarded a very small continuation contract to serve current clients until the cases could be closed.

Michelle met with the agency's director. They discussd various other funding sources for the foster care program but concluded that there were no realistic options, as the public agency was the only body authorized to provide or contract for foster care services. They calculated that with the small continuation contract, they could continue to employ three of the five social workers for no longer than one year. Two of the social workers would either have to be redeployed or let go. Before any decisions could be made about redeployment, it was first decided that the staffing of the other agency programs would need to be assessed. Similarly, Michelle was instructed to evaluate the skills of the five workers under her supervision in regard to their transferability to other program areas. Finally, she was asked to think about the worst case scenario: which two social workers would immediately lose their jobs?

Michelle has interpreted her supervisory job to include advocating for her staff. She now feels that she is letting her staff down. Despite their uniformly excellent performance, it is unlikely that all five workers will remain employed. Even the three who remain may have only a year left on the job.

Because supervisors are mentors and trainers to supervisees, they are sometimes caught between direct service social workers and the higher-level administrators to whom they report (Garthwait, 2011). This is the case with Michelle. As a middle manager, she is responsible for carrying out the organization's policies and procedures, which, in this instance, may mean reassigning or terminating staff. As a social work supervisor, her role also includes advocating for and supporting staff. In this instance, she is faced with a conflict of loyalties and duties. The resolution of the conflict, however, must take into account financial realities, over which she has no control.

The emphasis on job management and implementation of agency policies and procedures is likely to be more extreme in times of scarce fiscal resources. The supervisor becomes the mediating force between the agency administration and the direct service workers.

In less extreme circumstances, the supervisor may need to intervene about caseload issues with administrators. The supervisor may also be called on to mediate between workers and clients who are dissatisfied with the services they are receiving. Thus, the supervisor may frequently be in the position of interpreting, representing, and negotiating the interests of workers in dealings with clients and administrators.

Supervisory Style

There is no one prescribed supervisory style. Even within one agency, supervisors may approach their supervisory roles very differently. These different approaches are a matter of emphasis: the primary purpose of supervision may be seen, for example, as accountability, education and training, professional development, support, or some combination of these. In the example cited earlier, Michelle had to emphasize the accountability function of her supervisory role, even though she may have preferred to accentuate other roles.

Even though the emphasis and style of supervision are subject to variation, there is a core set of dynamics and skills characteristic of the supervisory process; these constant elements of supervision are observable in different settings and with different professionals (Brashears, 1995). In general, the similarities pertain to the nature of the relationship between supervisor and supervisee, the sanctioning of the relationship by the organization, and the structure of the relationship, for example, individual and group, formal and informal.

Enhancing Professional Development

Supervision includes an educational component. The supervisor is responsible for helping individual employees learn about the agency, the clients, the way services are provided, records maintenance, and a host of other job-specific knowledge and skills. The supervisor also serves as the gatekeeper for a portion of employees' continuing education. The supervisor may directly provide in-service training or refer employees to agency-sponsored staff development programs. The supervisor can also recommend and/or approve employees' participation in continuing education offered outside the agency.

In this book, it is assumed that the social worker is currently working toward or has already completed a formal degree in social work. There are two points of entry into the profession based on education: the baccalaureate in social work and the master of social work. The BSW is awarded to qualified students who major in social work in a Council on Social Work Education—accredited college or university (Barker, 1999). The baccalaureate social work curriculum prepares students for entry-level professional practice (Frumkin & Lloyd, 1995).

Graduates of formal degree-granting programs are expected to have the ability to maintain "reciprocal relationships with social work practitioners, groups, organizations, and communities" (Council on Social Work Education, 2001, p. 6). These outcomes are intended to ensure the relevance of professional training to the present and changing needs of the practice community. The Educational

Policy Statement and CSWE accreditation standards acknowledge the organizational base of practice and the necessity for practitioners to function within the structure of organizations. "Professional social workers are leaders in a variety of organizational settings and service delivery systems within a global context" (Council on Social Work Education, 2001, p. 5).

Formal education is not the end of one's education, and it is expected that BSW and MSW graduates will continue to grow and develop as professionals.

Continuing Professional Education

Social work education ranges from university-based degree-granting programs to continuing professional education through staff development and/or in-service training. Each component of the educational process falls under the sponsorship of institutions of higher education, independent providers, or agencies themselves.

Continuing education has been accepted within all professions as the way to keep professionals updated on knowledge and skills to ensure competent practice. Continuing education has been defined as "training taken by social workers and other professionals who have already completed their formal education required to enter the field" (Barker, 1999, p. 103).

Continuing education is a mechanism to address rising professional and societal concerns about accountability and performance standards. The NASW (1999) *Code of Ethics* acknowledges the ethical responsibility of social workers to participate in continuing education: "Social workers practice within their areas of competence and develop and enhance their professional expertise" (p. 6).

Continuing education is also a requirement for obtaining and sustaining practice credentials. There are several types of credentials in social work, each designed to assure the profession, clients, and the public that a practitioner has competence for safe practice (Biggerstaff, 1995). Every state, as well as the District of Columbia, Puerto Rico, and the U.S. Virgin Islands, has some form of legal regulation of social work practice. These laws control who can practice, what services they can provide, methods they can use, and the titles they can present to the public (Biggerstaff, 1995; Whiting, 1995). Many public and private agencies now require licensing or registration, or eligibility for these, as a prerequisite for employment. Many licensing and certification laws require, as a condition of renewal, participation in a specified number of continuing education units per year. Human service organizations thus have a vested interest in assisting their employees to maintain their credentials and ensuring that employees update and enhance their knowledge and skills.

Human service organizations typically include in their personnel policies and procedures a statement about the continuing professional development of staff. A sample of one such statement appears in box 5.3.

BOX 5.3
Professional Development: A Sample Agency Policy

Agency employees are encouraged to participate in professional development activities. However, attendance at such programs is contingent on the needs of the agency. Regular, full-time employees with two or more years of agency employment are eligible for reimbursement for professional development costs, but exceptions may be made with the approval of the executive director.

The agency may reimburse employees, in whole or part, for the cost of tuition, enrollment fees, and books for non-degree-related programs taken at a recognized institution, professional conference, or institute up to $250 per year. The intent is to provide assistance in covering the costs of professional development programs that, in the opinion of management, increase employees' competence in their present jobs or prepare them for advancement in the agency.

Participation in professional development programs can be granted, with pay, at the discretion of the executive director. Employees are also encouraged to participate in relevant professional development programs on their own time, for which reimbursement at the rate indicated also applies.

An employee must submit a written request for professional development reimbursement prior to enrollment to his or her immediate supervisor, who will request approval from the management. Receipts for tuition, enrollment or conference fees, books, and mileage, as applicable, should be submitted to the supervisor for reimbursement. The executive director retains ultimate discretion to approve requests and specific items to be reimbursed.

In-service training is provided by the agency, on a regular basis, either by agency personnel or by expert outside professionals at no cost to employees.

In-Service Training

Orientation programs for new employees, one form of in-service training, focus on the organization's objectives, resources, policies, and services. The new employee learns about operational procedures—how work is conducted in the particular agency setting. Content may include information about eligibility criteria, purposes, and service elements of the organization's programs; the organization's structure, service mandates, policies, and limitations; and lines of accountability and authority within the organization (Council on Accreditation, 1997).

In-service training is not limited to the orientation of new employees. As new procedures are developed, for example, agency employees are often required to participate in in-service training to become familiar with these changes and their impact on work assignments. The important point of differentiation between in-service and other types of training is the focus on the specific procedures and services of the organization.

Organizations may have a specialist on staff who is responsible for planning and conducting such training. However, it is the supervisor who is responsible for monitoring the extent to which the content learned in training is transferred to on-the-job performance. In smaller agencies, the supervisor may be both teacher and monitor. No matter what the size of the organization, the supervisor identifies training needs, preferably collaboratively with their supervisees, and refers the supervisee to the appropriate training. It is the supervisor's responsibility to ensure that workers know how to do their job and how to do it well (Garthwait, 2011).

In-service training has its origins in the earliest days of the profession. Social work can be considered one of the pioneering professions in instituting on-the-job training. In recent years, corporate America has adopted this approach for white-collar employees, based on the rationale that the pace of technological change requires organizations to give workers the skills and knowledge to handle changes (Ginsberg, 1997). Companies have found that outside education is expensive and often ineffective, as the content may not be immediately applicable to the work setting. In-service training offers the opportunity to tailor the curriculum to the specific needs of the organization.

Staff Development

Staff development, like in-service training, is usually an internal agency program. The goal of staff development is to improve employees' knowledge, skills, and abilities in relation to the agency's programs and services. The scope and breadth of such programs will depend on the agency's size and resources. Smaller agencies may collaborate with other human service organizations to conduct training in areas of mutual interest and in response to similar staff needs. Again, the focus is on the relatedness of the training content to the specifics of the job. However, administrative procedures are usually emphasized less than is the case with in-service training. Instead, staff development may focus on promoting awareness of and sensitivity to the particular characteristics, cultures, and needs of the clients, as well as the practice technologies and methodologies relevant to effective service provision and positive service outcomes.

The decision about what content to offer through staff development is made by the organization based on performance indicators, consumer feedback, and the organization's plan for continuous improvement of performance. Agencies that are part of a network of providers and/or are affiliated with managed care organizations (MCOs) are also likely to offer training relevant to devising and monitoring treatment plans and protocols in accord with MCO expectations.

Professional Development

Continuing professional education is typically offered by providers external to the organization. Although continuing education is an umbrella term, it is used here to refer to the vast array of university, commercial, and professional association offerings that pertain to updating professional knowledge and skills independent of their applicability to a specific job.

Some agencies promote employees' professional development by funding such participation (e.g., paying the registration fees and travel expenses associated with attending a professional conference). It is usually up to employees to select the conference or program they wish to attend; the agency may require only that the content be broadly related to its programs and services.

Support for professional development is based on the assumption that staff participation in these activities is beneficial to employees' morale, productivity, and longevity on the job. Such assumptions have been validated by empirical studies that have shown a positive relationship between continuing education participation and staff morale. For example, Kushnir, Cohen, and Kitai (2000) explored the association between opportunities for continuing medical education and primary physicians' job stress, burnout, and job dissatisfaction. They found that continuing medical education and perceived opportunities at work for keeping up to date on medical and professional developments were correlated negatively with job stress and burnout, and positively with job satisfaction.

Evaluating Job Performance

The supervisor is responsible for overseeing the work of the social worker. Worker performance appraisal, commonly referred to as evaluation, is the systematic assessment of how well the agency's employees are performing their jobs during a specified and predetermined period of time (Pecora & Wagner, 2000). Such evaluations are frequently used for determining salary increases and for considering promotional opportunities.

As the supervisee's superior, the supervisor can demand changes in style, action, or results as a condition of employment—receiving organizational rewards and benefits and maintaining an ongoing relationship with the agency. This may mean facilitating the supervisee's understanding of standards of social work practice, as well as organizational priorities and how they can best be achieved.

Clarifying Needs and Expectations

The assessment of a worker's performance implies that there is (1) a detailed job description, (2) a clear understanding of performance expectations, and (3) criteria for evaluation that are known from the outset of the evaluation period. The job description is the beginning point for an evaluation. The greater the degree of job clarity, the greater the likelihood that staff will understand their responsibilities and what is expected of them (Pecora & Wagner, 2000).

Specifying performance criteria is necessary for evaluation. How much, how often, and how well are some of the issues that need to be clarified up front. For example, if the job description specifies that the worker is to "conduct home studies," this leaves unanswered expectations about the scope of the home study or how many home studies must be conducted to be considered satisfactory in terms of productivity.

Imagine being in a situation in which there were expectations of you, only no one communicated to you what they were. Then suppose you are given a job description with no priorities attached to the many tasks detailed in it and no notion of what constitutes acceptable performance. Expectations must be clearly stated, understood, and agreed on.

The performance expectations of employees change over time, depending on the stage of the organization's development and the internal and external environmental factors affecting the status of the organization. Thus, job descriptions and job performance criteria should be reviewed periodically, preferably with active discussion between the supervisor and the employee.

Performance Evaluations

Worker performance appraisal is designed to determine to what extent workers are achieving the requirements of their job (Pecora & Wagner, 2000). Evaluations should be based on clearly stated, realistic, and achievable criteria (Kadushin & Harkness, 2002). The job performance goals must also be realistic and measurable (Pecora & Wagner, 2000). The system for performance assessment should be objective and fair. Box 5.4 illustrates the purposes of evaluation from the perspective of one agency.

BOX 5.4
Sample Agency Policy on Performance Appraisal

Performance appraisals provide a means to monitor and guide employees' job performance and are used to help determine eligibility for salary increases. The employee appraisal process seeks to accomplish the following objectives:

- ◆ To enhance individual employee performance and ensure effective agency operations
- ◆ To summarize both formal and informal performance discussions held with employees throughout the review period
- ◆ To document performance areas in which employees do well and those areas that require improvement
- ◆ To establish performance goals and plans to correct performance shortcomings
- ◆ To link employee performance with salary increase considerations

The employee's supervisor is responsible for setting and communicating clear performance standards at the beginning of and throughout the review period. The supervisor is also responsible for observing and discussing with the employee the positive and negative aspects of his or her performance in relation to standards throughout the review period. The performance appraisal is based on the job description. Employees are held responsible for carrying out the activities related to this description. The specific criteria for evaluation should be discussed by the supervisor and

(continued on next page)

---

the employee at each anniversary date so that the employee is clear about expectations for the following year. The evaluation also notes areas in which improvement is needed, as applicable.

Prior to the anniversary date of hiring or on a date corresponding with salary reviews, each employee has an opportunity to discuss his or her performance and receives a written evaluation from the designated supervisor, which is also subject to review by the executive director. The employee may add comments to the written evaluation and receives a copy of the evaluation. The employee is asked to acknowledge receipt and review of the written appraisal with his or her signature. The performance appraisal becomes an official part of the employee's record.

Staff evaluation is one of the dimensions of organizational performance of concern to professional associations, as reflected in the NASW (1999) *Code of Ethics*, state licensing boards (which require a set number of hours of supervised practice for licensing), and voluntary accrediting bodies, such as the Council on Accreditation (which prescribes staff evaluation as one measure of quality control). Box 5.5 provides one example of guidelines for performance review.

Key concepts found within the standards include the notion that evaluations occur at least on an annual basis, that they begin at the point in time of the last evaluation (or at the time of hire), and that they are meant as a tool to improve performance, not to punish. Evaluation is not a replacement for regular supervision. It provides a formal process by which to review performance and progress during the past year and to plan for the future.

BOX 5.5
Performance Review Standards

At least once a year, performance reviews are conducted jointly between each employee and the person to whom the employee is accountable.

Performance reviews include:
>An assessment of job performance in relation to the quality and quantity of work defined in the job description and to the objectives established in the most recent evaluation.
>Clearly stated objectives for future performance.
>Recommendations for further training and skill-building, if applicable.

Personnel are given the opportunity to sign the performance review, to obtain a copy, and to include written comments before entry of the report into the personnel records.
The organization follows established operating procedures regarding conditions for disciplinary action and nonvoluntary termination of personnel, as appropriate, including:
>Violations of organization policy.
>Documented substandard performance.

Source: Council on Accreditation of Services to Families and Children (1997), pp. 24–25.

Performance evaluations are an important mechanism for identifying performance problems and devising a corrective action plan. Corrective measures might include a recommendation for further training or skill building. The evaluation process also may serve to highlight obstacles to performance that relate to unclear or inconsistent agency policies, the conditions of work, such as caseload size, or a shortage of resources. Pecora and Wagner (2000) highlight the usefulness of identifying conditions inherent in the work environment that may impede performance: "Sound performance evaluations help supervisors and managers to distinguish agency-related problems that should be corrected through some form of organizational change from worker-related performance difficulties that may be corrected by in-service training or formal staff development programs" (p. 413).

Each evaluation should include clearly stated performance expectations. "Do better" is not enough. Better in regard to what? What are the behavioral manifestations of the desired change? If a worker is consistently late for work, the performance expectation—to be on time—is easily understood and communicated. However, if the employee needs to improve relationships with other workers, what exactly does this mean? What are the dimensions of positive relationships with colleagues? How will the worker and supervisor know when these relationships are successful? These are difficult questions that require substantial discussion and exploration by the worker and supervisor. The end result may be an agreement between the supervisor and supervisee detailing benchmarks and/or indicators of progress toward achievement of the performance goals.

Performance objectives should provide the worker with some sense of priorities for the work ahead. It is insufficient to set forth as a performance objective "to conduct more home studies." By what percentage? Over what period of time? What about events over which the employee has no control, such as a reduced demand for child placement or a reduction in the number of families served? Human service organizations constantly struggle with how to clearly specify the basis on which a worker's performance is judged and how it can be measured (Pecora & Wagner, 2000).

At a minimum, performance measures should include an assessment of job performance in relation to both quality and quantity of work as defined in the worker's job description and in the objectives established in the most recent evaluation. There should be no surprises; staff should not be held accountable for performance in areas not explicitly delineated. Box 5.6 provides an example of an evaluation form used by human service organizations. The intent is to measure quality and quantity of work performed, work habits and attitudes, problem-solving ability, collegial relationships, initiative, and attendance.

A key component of evaluation is that it is (or should be) an interactional process. In some organizations, staff are invited to assess their own accomplishments; this information can be used as a basis of discussion with the supervisor. The self-assessment should tap employee satisfaction with job duties, support, training, opportunities for personal growth, and so on. This provides an opportunity for the worker to detail his or her accomplishments, areas in need

BOX 5.6
Sample Performance Evaluation Form

Employee's Name_____   Job Title _____

Department _____   S.S. # _____

_____   _____
Date of Last Evaluation   Date of This Evaluation

General Factors	Rating			Comments
	Very Good	Satisfactory	Unsatisfactory	
Punctuality and overall attendance record				
Quantity: Completes assigned work and meets contractual standards; can be relied on for completion of all tasks and follow-up independent of direction from supervisor				
Initiative: Voluntarily starts projects to enhance program and maximize the services provided, going beyond program mandates				
Attitude: The ability to cooperate with coworkers, supervisors, funding sources, and community linkages in a courteous and effective manner				
Agency Activities: Participates/volunteers for interagency activities and special events				
Community Involvement: Regularly participates in community meetings and events				

EMPLOYEE'S OVERALL RATING IS:

Additional Comments: _____
_____
_____
_____

_____   _____
Prepared By: Signature and Date   Employee's Signature* and Date

*If employee disagrees with this appraisal, he/she may write a response that will be appended to this evaluation.

of improvement, and future activities as these relate to the accomplishment of overall organizational goals and objectives.

The use of outcome measures has become increasingly popular within the human services, borrowing principles long used in for-profit enterprises. Funding sources have begun to tie reimbursements and future contracts to the ability of an organization to document that its programs and services have achieved their stated goals, for example, changed the behavior of clients in the desired direction. Efforts are being made in some agencies to include outcomes or results achieved, as measured by some predetermined criteria, as part of the evaluation process. For example, the evaluation may seek to determine how many children were returned from foster care to their biological parents or how many patients were discharged from the psychiatric hospital into a community halfway house.

Agencies are also applying outcome criteria to measure organizational productivity in general and to the evaluation of personnel. Caution is needed, however, in using outcome measures to evaluate a worker's performance. This is because the science of measuring outcomes is imprecise. Furthermore, to what extent can workers be held responsible for positive outcomes that involve people rather than products? Because changes in the human condition or the health of a community are affected by a host of complex factors over which the worker or agency has no control, agencies have generally relied on input or process measures of performance rather than on client outcomes (Gibelman, 1998).

Studies have shown that employees value performance reviews and that they are significantly related to increasing motivation (Moore, 1998). Such evaluations constitute an investment by the organization in its staff. Similarly, evaluations help to provide a climate in which employees can grow, thus contributing to the agency and to its clients.

Key Points

- ◆ Professional and ethical standards acknowledge and support the role of supervision in promoting good practice.
- ◆ Supervisors receive their authority from the organization, and they are the link between the practitioner and the agency.
- ◆ Supervisors are qualified for their position by virtue of education, experience, and a specific set of skills that includes the ability to motivate employees and monitor and improve work processes.
- ◆ Within the agency context, three major supervisory functions can be identified: administrative, supportive, and educational.
- ◆ The overall purpose of supervision is to ensure the effective, efficient, and accountable delivery of services to the agency's clients.
- ◆ Continuing education has been found to reduce job stress and burnout and increase job satisfaction.
- ◆ Evaluating worker performance is predicated on a clear and detailed job description, a mutual understanding of performance expectations, and articulated criteria for evaluation.

◆ Evaluations are used to assess progress, provide feedback, identify areas in need of improvement, and recognize achievements.
◆ The evaluation process may help to identify obstacles within the agency itself that affect worker performance.

Suggested Learning Activities and Discussion Questions

1. Describe the process of supervision in which you are involved. What do you consider to be the most useful aspects of your supervision? What aspects of supervision would you like to see emphasized more? What steps have you taken to address your needs so that supervision is effective for you?

2. Secure a copy of your agency's policies and procedures concerning professional continuing education. What is covered? Does the agency express preferences about the form or type of professional continuing education it wants for its staff? Compare your agency's continuing education policies to those listed in box 5.3 and identify their differences. How do these differences shed light on the organization's philosophy and its priorities?

3. Speak to two or three experienced practitioners in your agency who work in different divisions or carry different roles. Ask them for details about the professional continuing education activities in which they participated during the past year. Ask them why they chose the particular programs, conferences, or courses, what motivated them to participate, and how they applied what they learned to the job.

4. Recollect the process used for the last field work or job performance evaluation you received. Describe the interactional elements of this process and the opportunities you had to provide input and feedback about issues of concern to you. Discuss the extent to which the evaluation was useful to you in clarifying work expectations and priorities.

Recommended Readings

Golensky, M. (2011). *Strategic leadership and management in nonprofit organizations: Theory and practice.* Chicago: Lyceum Books.

Kadushin, A. & Harkness, D. (2002). *Supervision in social work* (4th ed.). New York: Columbia University Press.

Kaiser, T. (1997). *Supervisory relationships: Exploring the human element.* Boston: Brooks/Cole.

Perlmutter, F. D., Bailey, D., & Netting, F. E. (2000). *Managing human resources in the human services.* New York: Oxford University Press.

Shulman, L. (1993). *Interactional supervision.* Washington, DC: NASW Press.

References

Barker, R. L. (1992). *Social work in private practice* (2nd ed.). Washington, DC: NASW Press.

Barker, R. L. (1999). *Social work dictionary* (4th ed.). Washington, DC: NASW Press.

Biggerstaff, M. (1995). Licensing, regulation, and certification. In R. L. Edwards (Ed.-in-chief), *Encyclopedia of social work* (19th ed., pp. 1616–1624). Washington, DC: NASW Press.

Brashears, F. (1995). Supervision as social work practice: A reconceptualization. *Social Work*, *40*(5), 692-699.

Campbell, J. M. (2002). *Becoming an effective supervisor*. Philadelphia: Accelerated Development.

Council on Accreditation of Services to Families and Children. (1997). *1997 standards for behavioral health care services and community support and education services* (U.S. ed.). New York: Author.

Council on Social Work Education. (2001). *Educational policy and accreditation standards*. Alexandria, VA: Author.

Delgado, M. (2006). *Social work with Latinos: A cultural assets paradigm*. New York: Oxford University Press.

Frumkin, M., & Lloyd, G. A. (1995). Social work education. In R. L. Edwards (Ed.-in-chief), *Encyclopedia of social work* (19th ed., pp. 2238-2247). Washington, DC: NASW Press.

Furman, R., Bender, K., Shears, J., & Lewis. C. W. (2006). Faculty perceptions regarding MSW curricular deficits for education students for practice with Latinos. *Advances in Social Work*, *7*(1), 36-48.

Furman, R., Langer, C. L., Sanchez, T. W., & Negi, N. J. (2007). A qualitative study of immigration policy and practice dilemmas for social work students. *Journal of Social Work Education*, *43*(1), 133-146.

Garthwait, C. (2011). *The social work practicum: A guide and workbook for students* (5th ed.). Boston, MA: Allyn and Bacon.

Gibelman, M. (1998). Theory, practice, and experience in the purchase of services. In M. Gibelman & H. W. Demone, Jr. (Eds.), *The privatization of human services: Policy and practice issues* (pp. 1-52). New York: Springer.

Gibelman, M., & Schervish, P. (1997a). Supervision in social work: Characteristics and trends in a changing environment. *The Clinical Supervisor*, *16*(2), 1-15.

Gibelman, M., & Schervish, P. (1997b). *Who we are: A second look*. Washington, DC: NASW Press.

Ginsberg, S. (1997, September 14). More companies now come with a campus. *Washington Post*, p. H4.

Golensky, M. (2011). *Strategic leadership and managements in nonprofit organizations: Theory and practice*. Chicago: Lyceum Books.

Harkness, D., & Poertner, J. (1989). Research and social work supervision: A conceptual review. *Social Work*, *34*(2), 115-119.

Kadushin, A., & Harkness, D. (2002). *Supervision in social work* (4th ed.). New York: Columbia University Press.

Kurland, R., & Salmon, R. (1992). When problems seem overwhelming: Emphases in teaching, supervision, and consultation. *Social Work*, *37*(3), 240-244.

Kushnir, T., Cohen, A. H., & Kitai, E. (2000). Continuing medical education and primary physicians' job stress, burnout and dissatisfaction. *Medical Education*, *34*(6), 430-436.

Lewis, J. A., Packard, T. R., & Lewis, M. D. (2007). *Management of human service programs* (4th ed.). Belmont, CA: Brooks/Cole.

Menefee, D. (2000). What managers do and why they do it. In R. J. Patti (Ed.), *The handbook of social welfare management* (pp. 247-266). Thousand Oaks, CA: Sage Publications.

Moore, K. (1998, January 4). Love those evaluations. *Washington Post*, p. H4.

Nathanson, A. (1992). *New social workers' satisfaction with supervision and with their job overall*. Unpublished DSW dissertation. New York: Yeshiva University, Wurzweiler School of Social Work.

National Association of Social Workers. (1999). *Code of ethics*. Washington, DC: Author.

Nghe, L. T., Mahalik, J. R., & Lowe, S. M. (2003). Influences on Vietnamese men: Examining traditional gender roles, the refugee experience, acculturation, and racism in the United States. *Journal of Multicultural Counseling, 31*(4), 245-261.

Pecora, P. J., & Wagner, M. (2000). Managing personnel. In R. J. Patti (Ed.), *The handbook of social welfare management* (pp. 395-423). Thousand Oaks, CA: Sage Publications.

Rauktis, M. E., & Koeske, G. F. (1994). Maintaining social work morale: When supportive supervision is not enough. *Administration in Social Work, 18*(1), 39-60.

Scott, R. W. (1966). Professionals in bureaucracies—areas of conflict. In H. M. Vollmer & D. L. Mills (Eds.), *Professionalization* (pp. 264-275). Englewood Cliffs, NJ: Prentice Hall.

Shier, M. L., & Graham, J. R. (2011). Mindfulness, subjective well-being and social work: Insight into their interconnection from social work practitioners. *Social Work Education, 30*(1), 29-44.

Shulman, L. (1993). *Interactional supervision*. Washington, DC: NASW Press.

Shulman, L. (1995). Supervision and consultation. In R. L. Edwards (Ed.-in-chief), *Encyclopedia of social work* (19th ed., pp. 2373-2379). Washington, DC: NASW Press.

Walsh, J. A. (1990). From clinician to supervisor: Essential ingredients for training. *Families in Society, 71*(2), 82-87.

Whiting, L. (1995). Vendorship. In R. L Edwards (Ed.-in-chief), *Encyclopedia of social work* (19th ed., pp. 2427-2431). Washington, DC: NASW Press.

Chapter 6

The Work Environment

The work environment is a reflection of complex organizational, professional, and interpersonal factors. This chapter focuses on a few of these influencing factors. Topics include the impact of managerial style, the culture and climate of the organization, the workforce composition, the physical environment of the organization, the informal environment, and the causes, manifestations, and impact of burnout on staff, the organization, and, directly or indirectly, the clients. Social workers are encouraged to consider other factors within their workplace that influence attitudes toward the job and affect how work is accomplished.

The Impact of Managerial Style

In earlier chapters the key players within human service organizations, including the board of directors, executive director, and supervisor, were identified. These organizational leaders often set the tone for the organization through their management style. Where are the CEO and other senior managers physically located in relation to staff? Is the CEO a hands-on manager? Does he or she pitch in? Is there an open door policy? Is there access to management?

Many human service organizations operate in an open style, in which authority may be delegated, communication flow is two way, and staff are valued for their contributions.

Two-way communication means that there are formal or informal mechanisms and a supportive environment in which employees have the opportunity to deal directly with their supervisors and other members of management regarding the work environment. Employees are encouraged to go beyond complaints about actual or perceived workplace issues or problems. Their ideas are actively sought regarding program initiatives, procedures, and workplace improvement. The mechanisms for eliciting employee input might range from a suggestion box to periodic meetings with management for the purpose of brainstorming.

Participatory management has been recognized as both appropriate and facilitative within the human service organizational environment. The Council on Accreditation of Services to Families and Children (1997), for example, includes among its standards: "The organization uses a participatory management style and a team approach for the effective coordination of consumer service, management, marketing, and support functions to achieve good communication, smooth flow of information and positive relations with external stakeholders such as purchasers/payers, managers of care, and others" (p. 29).

An open management style might take the form of collaboration. In collaborative management, workers at all levels are expected and encouraged to provide input and feedback, and there is a strong emphasis on interpersonal as well as technical skills (Walsh, 1995). Reward systems value group as well as individual contributions.

The attributes associated with a collaborative, open style of leadership have been supported empirically. A survey of 801 employees in for-profit and nonprofit organizations with twenty-five or more employees revealed that they generally view efforts to involve them in organizational decision making as desirable. They also believe that even more involvement would be beneficial to themselves and to the organization. Furthermore, employees indicated that they were motivated to work harder when management listened to their suggestions (Swoboda, 1995).

In recent years, there has been considerable discussion of the merits of a "flat" organization—one in which all staff have a voice in how business is conducted (Chawla & Joshi, 2010). Unlike a hierarchical structure, a flat structure allows and encourages input into decision making, with the assumption that those "on the line" know better, or at least as well, what the organization needs to do and how to do it. While few true flat organizational structures exist in the human services, many grassroots and community-based organizations seek to establish a culture and atmosphere in which the principles of this approach are practiced. Based upon models of empowerment, equality, collaboration, and inclusivity, this structure may be particularly valuable for organizations that use paraprofessionals from diverse populations. In many organizations, non-degreed workers provide many direct services and represent community voices. By including diverse constituents in their leadership, agencies may better reflect the needs of their constituents.

Management Style and Gender

A common theme in the literature concerns gender differences in management style. Some stereotypes hold that women are reluctant to exercise authority or handle conflict; they promote a kinder, more gentle environment. Men, on the other hand, are believed to be take-charge types—efficient and more businesslike—but aloof and distant. Other assumptions are that men and women share leadership traits, such as vision, intelligence, and commitment, but their leadership styles are quite different. How accurate are these views?

The nonprofit Foundation for Future Leadership studied the issue of gender and management style and found that women do better than men in twenty-eight of thirty-one key management categories, including keeping productivity high and generating ideas. Findings also showed that women were even stronger than men in more logic-based skills such as getting things done on time, producing high-quality work, generating ideas, problem solving, and planning. These findings refute traditional stereotypes. Women lagged behind men in only one key area—self-promotion ("High Marks for Women," 1996).

The empirical evidence, however, is mixed. Rosener (1995) studied differences in management style and concluded that there is a "gender paradox." This paradox holds that when attributes commonly associated with women are considered to be negative or of little value, gender is seen as relevant. When attributes associated with women are considered to be positive or valuable, gender is considered irrelevant. This paradoxical thinking, Rosener concluded, is one of the reasons why women remain an untapped management resource.

Women achieving high-level positions in management is a phenomenon of the latter part of the twentieth century. The women's movement of the 1960s and 1970s was an impetus to opening doors for women. Still, women are underrepresented in upper levels of management, including management of human service organizations (Gibelman, 2000). Even though women predominate in the human services by a wide margin, men are disproportionately represented in management. The notion of one type of management—the male type—has lingered. Effective management has been equated with "command and control methods" (Walsh, 1995, p. H6). It took substantial time for women's styles, which are often equated with interactivity, to be considered both legitimate and effective. Books such as Deborah Tannen's (1994) *Talking from 9 to 5* illustrated how styles associated with gender influence who gets heard and who gets ahead.

When women achieve top management positions, they sometimes experience mixed messages and a culture clash (Rosener, 1995). Men (usually white) hold most of the positions of authority in the workplace. Thus, expectations of managers reflect the experience and values associated with male leadership. Women and minorities have had to adapt to this culture. According to Rosener (1995), men want women in management to stop being defensive and to be more assertive, less emotional, and more self-confident. At the same time, the workplace follows a masculine model. There is time off for drug and alcohol abuse treatment but often not for child care; business socializing still revolves around golf and drinking but not activities that might be more appealing to women.

It is important to remember that gender differences and power can break down at the level of the individual. It is essential that human service workers respond to their supervisors as individual human beings and to be careful not to respond to them based solely on their gender. While it is true that many male supervisors, and certainly the system overall, support patriarchy and inequality, it is equally true that many male leaders work hard at being empowering and sensitive leaders. These leaders should be seen as allies and not enemies. To respond to them with anger and scorn only serves to heighten differences and difficulties and does no one, especially line workers, any good.

The CEO exercises substantial influence over the day-to-day operations of the organization. Obviously, the style of the CEO affects the overall management of the organization and the nature of the work environment.

The Agency's Workforce

The CEO is responsible for developing, implementing, and evaluating a personnel plan that will ensure the efficient and effective operation of the agency's programs. Many factors may be involved in making decisions about the type and qualifications of the agency's workforce. Money may be very limited, and this may negatively affect the agency's ability to hire experienced staff who command higher salaries. The organization may be rooted in the self-help tradition and thus emphasize the use of volunteers. New programs may require specialized personnel to help plan and implement them. Fund-raising may be a priority, and there may be hiring preferences for candidates who have experience in grant writing or special event fund-raising.

Staffing Patterns

Human service organizations vary substantially in the types of staff they hire and how they are deployed. Larger agencies, for example, tend to hire specialists—those with expertise in distinct areas, such as discharge planning or short-term behaviorally oriented treatment, to fill particular niches or service needs.

Although many public human service organizations employ a large number of professional social workers, public agencies are generally perceived to be less professional than nonprofits. This perception has some empirical foundation. A demographic analysis of the membership of the National Association of Social Workers showed that a high proportion of MSW and doctoral-level members worked in nonprofit organizations and that a relatively small proportion worked in public organizations (Gibelman & Schervish, 1997). There were also differences in educational background based on the major service areas of agencies. For example, residential facilities and social service agencies employed a relatively high proportion of social workers at the BSW level, while mental health and managed care organizations employed very few social workers at that level. Both inpatient and outpatient health facilities tended to employ MSW-level social workers and would thus be considered to have a higher level of professionalization (Gibelman & Schervish, 1997). These data suggest that hiring and utilization of staff differ according to the auspices of the organization (for-profit, nonprofit, or public), the type of services provided, and the primary problems and needs of the population served by the agency.

Agencies providing public child welfare services have been found to experience an unusually high turnover rate among social workers and a consequent reliance on less experienced workers (Anderson, 1998). Problems of staffing tend to be circular. When less experienced or less educationally qualified workers are hired, they are often unable to contend with the heavy caseloads and the complexity of child welfare cases. Thus, they tend to leave their positions quickly.

A number of child welfare agencies under public jurisdiction, such as those located in New York City and Washington, D.C., have sought, in recent years, to professionalize their workforce by hiring more MSWs and providing financial support for existing staff to pursue advanced studies in social work. An example is the North Carolina Child Welfare Collaborative. BSW and MSW students interested in working in the field of child welfare receive child welfare training, are placed in child welfare agencies, and receive substantial stipends. They make a commitment to work in a public child welfare agency for one year following graduation. Other public agencies have tried to remedy their organizational deficiencies by decentralizing operations and moving professional staff into neighborhood centers. By and large, such efforts have not had widespread success in overcoming the problems that are often blamed on big bureaucracy (Bernstein, 2001; Gibelman, 1998) but also pertain to caseload size and the complex nature of clients' problems.

Use of Part-Time and Temporary Personnel

Workforce flexibility and downsizing have prompted a growing use of temporary and part-time employees. In recent years, the number of part-time employees has increased due to budget cutbacks, job sharing, and employees wanting to work fewer hours, among other reasons. In general, however, the driving force is cost savings for the organization (Pynes, 2008; "'Temp' Ranks Growing," 1995).

A study conducted by Catalyst, a New York–based research group, revealed that more women than men are employed part-time. An overwhelming number of those surveyed who had reduced their hours from full to part time agreed that the flexible work program offered by their organization had made them want to stay with the organization. Opportunities for promotion, however, may be limited because of the reduced work hours. Fifty percent of those surveyed by Catalyst reported that their workload did not decrease after their hours and salary decreased; 10 percent reported an increase in their workload after their hours were reduced ("Part-Timers Have Impact," 1997).

These overall trends in the labor market mirror those within human service organizations. Available data on the human services workforce suggest that the proportion of social workers employed part-time is growing (Gibelman & Schervish, 1997). Similarly, the use of independent contractors (a social worker who works on a per diem or contract basis with organizations for specified periods of times to accomplish certain tasks or functions on behalf of the organization and its clientele) is on the rise. For example, a social worker may be hired by an adoption agency to conduct home studies; he or she is paid on the basis of the number of home studies completed. A study of social workers' attitudes about salaries and working conditions revealed that independent contracting is perceived to be a reflection of the preferences and needs of employers, not employees (Gibelman & Whiting, 1999).

The human services are labor intensive; the major cost item to the agency is personnel salaries and benefits. Today, organizations providing human services are constantly looking for ways to maintain an acceptable level of service while decreasing costs ("Jobs, Salaries Drive an Array of Actions," 1999). Hiring part-time or hiring on a contract basis allows the organization flexibility and some control over its long-term financial commitments. Laying off regular staff can cause low morale and other problems, including potential legal liability. There are no such issues with the use of a contingency workforce.

From the vantage point of the social worker, contingency work offers flexibility, the chance to gain experience, diversity in assignments, and the possibility of future full-time employment (Ginsberg, 1997). For some social workers, the dual demands of parenthood and work may make part-time work attractive. For still others, temporary or contractual arrangements may offer less involvement in office politics and less of the stress associated with competition for raises and promotions (Uchitelle, 1996).

Staffing patterns vary to some extent by organizational type. Unionization offers a certain level of protection of jobs and positive working conditions. Hospitals, schools, and state and local public agencies are more likely to be unionized than are voluntary social service agencies or mental health clinics. Another factor influencing the use of human services personnel is the civil service. Confined to the public sector, civil service status confers a high level of job security, although it may be offset by bureaucratically oriented working conditions.

The use of part-time and contingency workers, however, crosscuts organizational types. Its most profound impact is probably on the nonprofit and for-profit sectors that are not unionized. For-profits, in particular, may seek alternatives to the traditional full-time social worker as part of an overall business orientation. How the human service organization plans and carries out its personnel policies and the impact of these policies on the work environment are explored in depth in chapter 8.

Volunteers

The use of volunteers is generally limited to the nonprofit sector. (Exceptions may include parental involvement and mentoring in public schools and candy striping in hospitals, some of which may be under for-profit auspices.) The charity organization societies and settlement houses of the late 1800s and early 1900s, for example, were staffed primarily by volunteers (Lubove, 1965; Trattner, 1999). Formal volunteering is regular but unpaid work within organizations;

informal volunteering, on the other hand, is more ad hoc in nature, such as help-ing a church set up its computer equipment (Dunn, 1995). The primary moti-vations for volunteering are helping others, supporting an important cause, and compassion for people in need (Independent Sector, 1992). For the year 2000, volunteer time was calculated to be worth about $250 billion (Independent Sector, 2003). In general, the more professional the organization, the more re-liant it is on paid employees. Volunteers provide many different services, such as raising funds through special events, delivering Meals on Wheels, and serving as receptionists, home visitors, and teachers' aides. About 61.2 million people volunteered through or for an organization at least once between September 2005 and September 2006 (Bureau of Labor Statistics, 2007).

Volunteers benefit the organization in a number of ways: by delivering ser-vices at a reduced cost and by offering access to additional sources of exper-tise, closer contacts with the community, and better client assistance. There are also some disadvantages. Recruiting, training, evaluating, and rewarding volun-teers are often complex processes that involve the assignment of organizational resources. There also may be potential conflicts with paid staff and difficulties in recruiting a sufficient number of qualified volunteers (Liao-Troth, 2001; McCurley, 1994).

Many volunteers are older people who have a wealth of skills and experi-ence to contribute. However, matching volunteer talents with organizational needs may be problematic, as described in box 6.1.

BOX 6.1
Finding Appropriate Roles for Volunteers

Don Spieler retired after thirty-three years as a senior executive of Kodak. He saw retirement as a chance to give something back to his community through vol-unteering. His first stop was the Rochester chapter of the United Way, where he met with the director, who seemed pleased to have him on board. Spieler had considered what roles he might play—perhaps joining a committee to evaluate grantees or serv-ing on the board of directors. When he received a phone call to tell him about his as-signment, he was stunned: fund-raising! This was not one of his interests, and he had not even mentioned fund-raising during his interview. Spieler was angry.

Over the next two years, Spieler visited seven different nonprofit organizations and, overall, he was offered work that was boring or that did not utilize his business expertise. One organization wanted him to volunteer two days a week as office man-ager. Another offered him the volunteer job of writing up minutes of meetings. Spieler concluded that these were "an entrenched group of agencies that did not ac-cept the skills I could provide for them."

Source: Adapted from Tanz & Spencer (2000).

Don Spieler's experiences illustrate the complexities of balancing the need and desire to use volunteers and designating appropriate assignments for them that use their special skills and contribute effectively to the work of the organization. Self-help organizations rely primarily on a volunteer workforce and have significant success in recruiting, utilizing, and retaining volunteers. This success is attributed to the unique attributes of self-help movements and the emotional investment volunteers bring to their roles.

The Physical Environment

The physical surroundings in which employees work influence their attitudes toward the job, the organization, and clients. The physical environment encompasses the employee's specific work area (do social workers spend their day in cubicles or do they have small private offices?), the furnishings (early Salvation Army or basic furniture in good condition that matches?), the reception area (folding chairs or comfortable couches and chairs?), the kitchen (if there is one), the conference room (a good-sized table in good condition with appropriate chairs?), and even the paint on the walls (is it fresh and clean?).

And what about the equipment? Does the copy machine work, and is it accessible to staff? Do staff have their own computers or easy access to one? Are the telephones early rotary style or is the phone system up to date? Are there filing cabinets with sufficient room for easy maintenance of records? These physical features do matter. When the furnishings and equipment are of poor quality, then employees are likely to feel that they are not valued.

Cost is an obvious consideration, especially for small neighborhood agencies that may function on a shoestring. However, there are many creative ways to get community businesses or even large corporations to donate equipment. Individuals, too, can be encouraged to donate funds for furniture and equipment. Such options are clearly more available to nonprofits than to public organizations.

The look of public child welfare and public assistance offices seems to reflect their lack of status within state and local government, and perhaps the views of public citizens about this type of work or the clients served. Some public offices have been called "downright dreadful" in appearance (Lewis, 1994), uninviting to both clients and the professional workforce. Such physical environments are demoralizing to staff and clients. However, staff can be encouraged to think of creative ways to surmount the physical limitations. For example, workers can be encouraged to bring in their own decorations—paintings, pictures, desk organizers. Occasionally, time for staff meetings might be devoted to a collective activity such as painting a room. In general, for-profit organizations tend to have more attractive offices, a reflection of the corporate culture. Such organizations may serve a different clientele from that of nonprofit or public agencies—people of higher socioeconomic status or with different kinds of psychosocial problems. The rationale may be that clients expect the offices to look a certain way. A visit to a for-profit nursing home, for example, and then a nonprofit nursing home may reveal differences in the style and quality of furnishings and the overall decor. This does not mean that the nonprofit nursing home is less adequate but only that it takes a more modest approach to the use of organizational funds for the facility.

Any discussion of the physical environment must include the organization's compliance with legal mandates. The physical setting in which services are delivered must be accessible to actual or potential clients of the organization. The Americans with Disabilities Act of 1990 (P.L. 101-336) established specific requirements regarding physical access to the facility by individuals with disabilities who are eligible to receive services. Standard-setting organizations have also established stringent guidelines concerning adapting facilities to accommodate the visual, auditory, linguistic, and motor limitations of its service population (Council on Accreditation, 1997). Aesthetics of the work environment aside, the characteristics of many consumers of health and human services—the elderly, people with disabilities, families with young children—require the elimination of structural barriers to be a high priority. It is both a matter of law and moral obligation among people-serving organizations (Stein & Teplin, 2011).

Organizational Culture and Climate

Every organization has its own culture and climate. The culture and climate of organizations are widely believed to influence the attitudes, behaviors, and health of employees (Brown & Leigh, 1996; Osborne & Gaebler, 1992; Peters & Waterman, 1982; Schorr, 1997).

The climate of an organization is defined in terms of employees' perceptions of their work environment. Glisson (2000) terms it "a property of the individual (perception) that is shared by other individuals in the same work environment. . . . Organizational climate is the shared perceptions that employees have of the psychological impact that their work environment has on those who work there" (p. 198). Psychological climate refers to how the work environment affects the employee's own personal well-being (Brown & Leigh, 1996). A positive work environment is perceived as nonthreatening, enhancing personal self-image, and career promoting. Organizational climates are created by shared psychological climates; employees have the same or similar perception of the work environment (Glisson, 2000). A positive organizational climate may be influenced by a number of factors, including opportunities to use one's skills and abilities; promotional opportunities; salary; congruity between one's expectations about a job and the reality of the job; opportunities for learning; opportunities for creativity, variety, and challenge; increasing responsibility; and control over the means to accomplish tasks.

Organizational culture is different from organizational climate, although there is substantial overlap between the concepts. Definitions are generally drawn from parallels to societal culture and emphasize shared values, beliefs, and behavioral norms in an organization. Glisson (2000) defines organizational culture as "a property of the collective social system. It comprises the norms and values of the social system that drive the way things are done in the organization" (p. 198). Culture is seen as a component of the social system, while climate is a property of the individuals within the social system (Glisson, 2000; James & McIntyre, 1996).

Organizations that engage in long-term and/or strategic planning often seek to define and articulate the shared values of their key constituents (Pynes, 2008). Box 6.2 illustrates the outcome of the efforts of the elected and appointed leadership of a national organization concerned with the issues of children and youth to define a set of shared values. These values were intended to serve as operating principles to achieve the organization's goals and objectives.

BOX 6.2
Shared Values as Expressed by Leadership of a National Organization

- ◆ We will treat each other with mutual respect, trust, and support.
- ◆ We will be receptive to new ideas.
- ◆ We will have realistic perceptions and expectations about everyone's time, energy, and limitations.
- ◆ We will have clear, realistic goals.
- ◆ We will work openly and honestly to reach organizational goals.
- ◆ We will face problems rather than hide from them.
- ◆ We will communicate openly and honestly.
- ◆ We will share responsibility.
- ◆ We will make commitments to accept tasks and honestly make our capabilities and limitations known to each other.
- ◆ There is life outside the organization; we are people first.
- ◆ We will maintain positive attitudes and interactions.
- ◆ We have a commitment to high-quality professional-level work.
- ◆ We care about children, each other, and ourselves.
- ◆ Laughter is on our agenda.
- ◆ Every member of the team has a unique and important contribution to make.
- ◆ When we make commitments, we keep them.
- ◆ Success belongs to the group, not to the individual.

Source: Adapted from McAdoo (1992), p. 4.

This example of shared values represents the ideal, not the actuality. Notice, for example, the use of the affirmative future tense "We will" rather than "We are" or "We do." In fact, the shared values identified may represent key stakeholder perceptions about the difference between how things are and how they ought to be. The articulation of these differences between the actual and the ideal can be addressed through group processes similar to those in which the shared values were originally formulated. For example, an analysis of key issues for the same organization focused on the identification of enabling and inhibiting factors in building an effective board-staff partnership, as described in box 6.3.

In a positive work environment, delineation of enabling and inhibiting influences on board-staff relationships or any other identified organizational issue is a first, not a final, step. The next step is the development of an action plan to enhance strengths and remove barriers. Plans to remove barriers might

---

BOX 6.3
Key Issues Analysis: Enabling and Inhibiting Factors in Building an Effective Board-Staff Partnership

Enabling	Inhibiting
Willingness to learn and grow	Not sure how to effectively relate to
Strong commitment to the organization	staff
and to children	Most board members have little experi-
Talent and skills of the board	ence relating to staff
Genuinely like one another	Self-gratification relating to power is-
Training sessions to improve culture	sues
Receptivity to direct, open remarks	Insecurity about the nature of staff/vol-
Reasonable expectations	unteer relationships
Experienced, competent staff	Issues about favoritism
History of quality programs	Lack of orientation for new board mem-
Staff understanding of personalities and	bers [in regard to] staff and peer rela-
operating modes of volunteers	tionships
Opportunities to socialize with peers	Naiveté about partnership expectations
	on the part of volunteers and staff
	Lack of defined action plans about
	work to be done
	Board members are unsure about their
	fiduciary responsibility for evaluating
	staff performance

Source: McAdoo (1992), p. 7.

---

include, in this example, learning to prioritize issues; developing clear guidelines about what information needs to be communicated to whom; and initiating a training program for new volunteers. Strength enhancement might focus on scheduling time for joint staff-board planning sessions; encouraging a culture that promotes understanding of and respect for differing opinions; and investing time and money in planning activities focused on clarifying the organization's mission, programs, and services.

A countervailing force to the implementation of these or any prescriptive principles is the existing organizational culture and climate. A turnaround in the climate of an organization takes more than declarations; routinized ways of interacting are easier and more comfortable than conscious alterations in the way business is conducted. Culture is affected by the organization's traditions and history and the CEO's management style, including the extent to which management is able to foster a supportive and challenging environment. Both the climate and culture of the organization provide the parameters in which certain behaviors and orientations—risk taking, collaboration, outcome orientations, innovation, flexibility, adaptability, competitiveness, and ethical behavior—may or may not be manifest (Rousseau, 1990).

Use of Teams

Teamwork has, in recent years, received substantial attention as a means to empower and use staff to address organizational issues and achieve desired ends. Teams may be formal or informal, depending on who initiates them and for what purpose. Most often, a team approach is sanctioned and formal. The use of teams is also a reflection of the organization's culture and suggests an open system.

Teams can be used within the organization for a number of purposes, such as identifying, analyzing, and solving problems related to agency performance and promoting creativity and innovation (Hodge-Williams, Doub, & Busky, 1995; Menefee, 2000). Suppose, for example, management sees a need to revise the agency's personnel policies and procedures. Administrators ask for volunteers among agency staff to work on an ad hoc committee to provide input. Committee members are asked to review and comment on drafts of the document. They may also be asked to draft certain parts of the revised policies, such as dress codes, professional conduct provisions, and the like.

Another example is the selection of new computer software. A team might be assigned responsibility to poll staff about their computer software needs and their experiences with various software packages. Staff might be involved in meeting with vendors to ask questions about the software.

Collaboration is viewed as the key to successful organizations (Rees, 1997). The use of teams promotes a high level of staff involvement, often resulting in a higher level of investment in the organization. Morale may increase as workers perceive that their opinions count. Studies support the belief that higher levels of involvement in problem solving and decision making induce higher levels of feelings of personal accomplishment and lower levels of burnout (Savich & Cooley, 1994). Workers who feel that they have some control over their environment also experience a higher level of professional effectiveness (Guterman & Jayaratne, 1994).

Some caution must be exercised with the use of teams. Managers may ask for feedback through open discussion but then reject any comments or suggestions that are not what they want or expect to hear. Managers can sometimes respond to staff input defensively. The results may be negative if staff feel that their input is not valued or their opinions are ignored. Such problems can be avoided if managers interested in utilizing a team approach to problem solving understand the need to be receptive to ideas. Social workers, too, can aid in ensuring a constructive process by taking care to communicate in a nonthreatening and nonhostile manner. In fact, social workers are trained to be active listeners, to respect the opinions of others, and to mediate and compromise. These skills can be applied within the organizational environment. Suggestions and recommendations from staff should be realistic, practical, and well thought out.

The efforts of employees to engage in creative problem solving are likely to be reinforced if the results are observable and tangible. Management can reward the contributions of staff by recognizing them in memos and articles in internal newsletters, or at annual events. Such public acknowledgment can go a long way toward making staff feel good about their efforts and, in the process, motivating them to take part in group problem solving in the future.

Communication

Because the services provided by human service organizations depend on people—foremost, social workers and consumers/clients—the centrality of communication is usually acknowledged.The importance of communication beyond the worker-client relationship is less often recognized.

Formal Communication

In a people-oriented profession in which verbal exchanges are characteristic, social workers also need to engage in a substantial amount of written communication.This involves, for example, maintenance of case records, memos, and reports to organizations and members of other professions involved in a case (teachers, lawyers, physicians), preparation of grant proposals, and progress and outcome reports to funding sources. Such communications occur within the organization itself (case records, for example) and between organizations and individuals (grant applications, reports to the court).

Internal communications often reflect the organization's structure and climate. In larger organizations, where face-to-face communication between staff and management may be less frequent, memos may be used to transmit information. Modern technology has largely replaced paper with e-mail. Downward communications are those that come from management to employees. Upward communications are those from the employees to management. Horizontal communications are those between people at the same level of the organization (Garthwait, 2011).

Some required communications—either sent or received—are mundane in nature. Others are vital in regard to the well-being of the clients served or to the continued funding or very existence of a program. Much of the social worker's communication concerns the agency's relationship to its clients and other agencies. Responses to the court about a child under protective custody may be required yesterday. A physical skirmish in a residential facility must be immediately documented. New directives come from management.The state legislature issues new regulations that must be read, understood, and immediately applied in work with clients in a program. An outside review team is coming to the agency for a site inspection and wants to meet with staff.Written reports must first be submitted.

Unfortunately, there are few time-saving alternatives to the use of written communications. Some information can be shared at staff meetings, but this does not necessarily save time. In addition, written memos ensure some level of accountability. A response is expected, and reminders can be sent.The tone of such communications, particularly those from management, both reflect and affect the organization's climate. Requests to "do something" and "do it now" are less well received than requests that are sensitive to the time demands being made and an explanation as to why the information is needed. On the other hand, managers may be justifiably concerned when requests for reports are ignored or deadlines are missed. The use of good communication skills, with sensitivity to the tone of the communication as well as the message itself, has important ramifications within the formal and informal organizational environment. Excellent writing skills may be viewed as an ethical imperative. Since social workers often advocate for the most vulnerable and oppressed people within society, it is important that all written communications represent them powerfully. The ability to write effectively is a powerful tool in policy advancement and the advocacy process.

Informal Communication

Informal communications are exchanges that are separate from and outside of the agency's codified, regular, and planned communication channels (Skidmore, 1990). Such informal communication systems can be effective and powerful. Rumors, for example, may circulate through the informal network long before an official communication about, say, the resignation of a key manager. Because human service organizations are staff dependent (e.g., personnel are the "doers" in regard to implementing agency programs), the nature of their informal communications can strongly influence how and how well work is carried out.

Informal Environment

An important part of the organization's culture and climate can be found in its informal environment. Although the informal environment includes communications, its breadth is more extensive. The informal environment may be as or more influential in determining the way in which work is done, by whom, and how well. Glisson (1985) described such informal arrangements under the rubric of a "psycho-social subsystem," involving the psychological and social relationship factors that affect the behavior of personnel and, consequently, the performance of the entire organization (p. 97).

One manifestation of the informal environment is a set of "unwritten rules" (Garthwait, 2011). Informal rules apply in the absence of formal rules or sometimes instead of them; they reflect established normative behaviors that prescribe how employees are to act in situations that, typically, have an impact on others. Such rules, for example, may relate to whether or not it is okay to eat or drink during a staff meeting, submit certain reports after the due date, or come into work late on a consistent basis. Another term that describes the expectations that surround informal rules is *normative behavior*. The norms are established by the group. Although they are usually unwritten, most employees know about them.

Breaking an informal rule has an effect on coworkers and clients. After a holiday, it is common for one or more staff members to call in sick. However, phone calls from clients may be at a higher volume than usual, perhaps because of the emotions people experience during holiday family gatherings. Extending one's holiday by calling in sick when this is not really the case places an added burden on others who must cover the emergencies. Thus, an informal rule may be that it is *not* okay to call in sick after a holiday. Under other circumstances, taking a day off may be considered to be perfectly alright.

One learns about informal rules through observation of the interactions of one's colleagues. Being sensitive to the nuances of the workplace helps employees to adapt to the culture of the organization and to fit in. Sometimes, a coworker can assist the new employee in learning the ropes (informal rules). More often, it may be a matter of trial and error. If only one person is eating during a staff meeting and all eyes are on him or her, it is unlikely that this behavior will be repeated.

In the work setting, we need to work with different types of people. The "people" element of work can have a profound influence on the work environment and the ability of social workers to carry out their jobs. When the formal or informal working environment is negative, morale suffers, as does productivity.

Staff Morale

From the point of view of employees, the conditions of work are as, and sometimes more, important than the nature of the work itself (Barber, 1986; Oberlander, 1990). Social workers may be highly committed and motivated to providing quality services to their clients. Yet when agency resources are scarce and there are too many cases and too few practitioners, the toll may be substantial.

Several studies have documented a relationship between work stress and people-serving occupations. Greenglass, Burke, and Konarski (1999), for example, studied burnout and concluded that high empathy may predispose helping professionals to emotional exhaustion. Higher degrees of stress are also associated with work involving life-and-death situations (EMS workers, emergency room staff, firefighters) or when judgment calls must constantly be made that affect the safety and life of others, such as police and air traffic controllers (Maslach, 1982). Within social work, such areas of practice as child protective services and oncology services involve a high level of stress independent of the work environment (Goodman & Boss, 1999; Ratliff, 1988). Lack of control over working conditions has also been found to be a factor in job stress (Killu, 1994; Leiter & Harvie, 1996; Ratliff, 1988).

Stress has a negative influence on morale. In turn, low morale is often symptomatic or a component of burnout. Many people use the word *burnout* to describe a state of malaise typically associated with overwork—large caseloads, long hours, difficult clientele (Beemsterboer & Baum, 1984; Snibbe, Radcliffe,

Weisberger, Richards, & Kelly, 1989). For example social workers in a hospital setting who work with people who are terminally ill or those who work with battered women, rape victims, or incest situations may experience depression, fatigue, or general dissatisfaction. The nature of social work practice itself can take a toll. As Hagan (1999) notes, "The helping relationship exists for the primary benefit of the client, and the emotional giving in the relationship is exclusively from the practitioner to the client. Constant emotional giving and sharing the intense feelings of others may result in emotional depletion" (p. 503). When there is a gap between what practitioners feel they should be accomplishing on the job (as may be measured, for example, by positive client outcomes) and what actually occurs, the level of disillusionment rises.

Burnout comes not only from our work with clients, but also from the conditions surrounding our work. Social work receives its mandates primarily from legislative actions—social policies. What we do, how much emphasis the service receives in funding, and what shape the programs and services take are all products of policy decisions made at the local, state, and federal levels. These externally controlled decisions often contain the seeds of practitioner frustration. There may be insufficient funds to do what the laws tell us must be done. The program's approach may be punitive rather than facilitative of clients' move toward independence; an example of this is many of the provisions of the Personal Responsibility and Work Opportunity Reconciliation Act of 1996 (P.L. 104-193), commonly known as welfare reform (Lens, 2000).

A survey conducted by the American Society of Chartered Life Underwriters and Chartered Financial Consultants and the Ethics Officer Association found that 57 percent of the more than sixteen hundred U.S. workers polled reported various levels of job-related stress. Such stress was manifest in loss of sleep or insomnia. Forty-eight percent of respondents reported having headaches, while 37 percent reported that pressure on the job made them depressed. Thirty-five percent reported that work pressure had caused them to gain or lose weight ("Feeling the Pressure at Work," 1997).

These symptoms have also been recognized among social workers. Burnout may manifest itself in fatigue, physical symptoms, estrangement from friends and relatives, and anxiety or depression. Other manifestations may include feelings of helplessness and hopelessness and the development of personal problems, such as marital conflict and substance abuse (Hagan, 1999). Hagan (1999) notes that burnout produces at least three outcomes:

1. Emotional exhaustion, which may take the form of a lack of emotional energy
2. Depersonalization, when one responds to others in a detached, uncaring, and dehumanizing manner
3. A reduced sense of personal accomplishment and a sense of inadequacy about the process and outcome of one's work

Such symptoms are costly to the practitioner and also have an impact on the organization and clients. Burnout may translate to ineffective or uncaring client services.

The Impact of Burnout on the Organization

On the organizational level, burnout means inefficient workers, absenteeism, low morale, unwillingness to pitch in, and high turnover (Ginsberg, 1998; Hagan, 1999). A study that explored the three dimensions of the Maslach Burnout Inventory and their relationship to actual turnover in a hospital found that employees who left had significantly higher burnout on all three dimensions than those who stayed. Employees who left voluntarily had higher emotional exhaustion scores and a lower sense of personal accomplishment than those who were terminated (Goodman & Boss, 1999).

Each time an employee leaves, the agency incurs the costs of recruiting and screening applicants and then providing on-the-job training. There is always a learning curve for new employees—it takes time for them to become familiar with and master their jobs.

These scenarios also affect the clients served. Continuity is an important component of service and care (Hromco, Lyons, & Nikkel, 1995). Worker turnover may result in clients withdrawing from service. Even if the unhappy social worker stays, the quality of service can be affected, in that creativity and productivity are often greatly diminished when burnout occurs (Ginsberg, 1998). It is difficult to hide the manifestations of burnout, which include hostility, withdrawal, indifference, nonresponsiveness, absence, and missed appointments (Maslach, 1982).

Some organizations establish policies to prevent or stem burnout. These include flexible work arrangements. Some organizations even provide workplace perks—such as yoga classes—to lighten the stress (Ginsberg, 1998). Spontaneous events, such as a surprise party for a staff member's birthday, can also lighten the atmosphere. Agencies also deal with burnout by providing staff development opportunities that enhance workers' feelings of competence or programs that deal with stress and stress management.

At times, some of the factors that lead to burnout are beyond an organization's control. However, involving staff in decision making and empowering them to be full participants in the organizational life can decrease the likelihood of burnout among staff. Agencies that invest in the well-being of their staff and help them to understand what can and cannot be changed help prevent burnout. Agencies should take a long-term developmental approach to nurturing their workers as a means of improving clients services and eliminating the costs of excessive employee turnover. That being said, it is important for social workers to take control of their own propensity toward burnout. Each social worker must develop the self-care skills needed to survive in times of change and transition. Social workers should access employment assistance programs and other resources to make sure they are as emotionally healthy as possible.

Dealing with Burnout

Burnout can occur as the result of one factor or a combination of factors, such as a worker's individual characteristics, the job setting, and the nature of the work with individual clients. Most social workers experience some level of stress and tension from time to time; this is to be expected. This is especially true during difficult economic times, when anxieties are high. Since the last recession, social workers have increasingly worked with clients whose lives are filled with financial chaos and uncertainty in addition to various psychosocial problems and concerns. Being around trauma, day after day, has a significant effect on the lives of social workers. In fact, social workers can face many of the same symptoms of those who have actually undergone life-course trauma. This condition, known as compassion fatigue or secondary trauma, may be fairly prevalent and is to be taken seriously by workers and their agencies (Bride, 2007). Ideally, the agency will have systems in place to recognize and deal with workplace stress. However, more realistically, it is up to social workers to recognize their own symptoms of burnout.

Social workers assist clients in developing self-awareness. We diagnose stress in our clients but may not be able to recognize the symptoms within ourselves. Developing and maintaining self-awareness is a starting point for preventing or dealing with burnout. Such self-awareness allows us to recognize the trigger points associated with accumulating stress. Awareness of our own limitations is also important. There are likely to be many aspects of our work that are outside of our personal control; a realistic assessment of what we can and cannot accomplish in our work influences our mind-set in regard to work responsibilities.

Your supervisor may be able to assist you in dealing with your own reactions to client situations, in having realistic expectations about the outcomes of interventions, and in setting limits on client demands (Compton, Galaway, & Cournoyer, 2005). Ongoing development of social work skills through continuing education programs can heighten feelings of competence (Hagan, 1999). Such participation will also bring you in contact with colleagues in other agencies who may have strategies to share, include coping strategies.

Another way of dealing with burnout is through support groups. These may be formal—when workers get together at a specific time, perhaps once a week, to discuss issues related to practice—or informal, as need or desire dictates. Such groups provide the opportunity for social workers to talk about frustrations, successes, and what works and doesn't work, and to pick up suggestions from coworkers about how to deal with particular situations (Compton, Galaway, & Cournoyer, 2005; Koeske & Koeske, 1989).

Equally important from a prevention standpoint are healthy activities, such as exercise, eating well, taking short breaks throughout the day, attending stress management seminars, communicating regularly with people in a support network, and getting enough sleep. Maintaining relationships and interests outside of work is of paramount importance as well (Skovholt, 2011).

Key Points

- The executive director's management style often sets the tone for the organization.
- Workforce specialization is associated with the size of the agency and the breadth of programs offered.
- Human service organizations are hiring more part-time and contingency workers as a cost-saving measure.
- Volunteers are used primarily in nonprofit organizations.
- The physical environment of the organization influences workers' attitudes toward the organization, their jobs, and clients.
- Human service organizations have a responsibility to ensure that the physical environment is free of barriers.
- Organizational culture is a component of the social system, whereas organizational climate is a property of the individuals within that system.
- The climate and culture of the organization inhibit or encourage risk taking, collaboration, and innovation, among other change-oriented behaviors.
- Teamwork, geared toward mutual support and problem solving, is one way to empower and utilize staff resources.
- Higher levels of staff involvement in decision making are positively associated with feelings of personal accomplishment and lower levels of burnout.
- The informal environment of the organization can be a powerful influence on the way that work is carried out.
- Burnout is one of the side effects of poor morale. It is associated with large caseloads, long working hours, and difficult client situations.
- Each social worker needs to be attuned to his or her own level of stress and make time for stress-reducing activities.

Suggested Learning Activities and Discussion Questions

1. Observe the physical environment of your agency. If you were seeing it for the first time, as a client would, what impression would you have?
2. Within your field or work setting, identify some environmental issues that you think relate directly to employee morale, both positively (enhancing morale) and negatively (decreasing morale).

3. Conduct an interview with a friend who works in an unrelated field and in another type of organizational setting. Ask your friend to describe the climate of the organization in which he or she works, worker morale, and how issues within the work environment are handled. If morale is viewed as positive, what factors account for it? If morale is low, what are the attributing causes? Make note of the descriptive terms used. Then compare these responses with those of one of your colleagues when asked the same series of questions.

4. To what extent do you think that burnout is inevitable in social work jobs? Are there strategies you can think of to prevent burnout?

Recommended Readings

Gabriel, Y., Fineman, S., & Sims, D. (2000). *Organizing and organizations* (2nd ed.). Thousand Oaks, CA: Sage Publications.

Murphy, K. R. (Ed.). (1996). *Individual differences and behavior in organizations*. San Francisco: Jossey-Bass.

Nutt, P. (1996). *Making tough decisions*. San Francisco: Jossey-Bass.

Ott, J. S. (1989). *The organizational culture perspective*. Belmont, CA: Dorsey Press.

Schein, E. H. (1992). *Organizational culture and leadership*. San Francisco: Jossey-Bass.

Schneider, B. (1990). *Organizational climate and culture*. San Francisco: Jossey-Bass.

Schorr, L. B. (1997). *Common purpose*. New York: Doubleday.

Skovholt, M. T. (2011). *The resilient practitioner.* New York: Taylor and Francis Group.

Trice, H., & Beyer, J. (1993). *The cultures of work organizations*. Englewood Cliffs, NJ: Prentice Hall.

References

Anderson, R. (1998, August 17). Critics find flaws in new foster care. *Topeka Capital-Journal*. Available: http://cjonline.com/stories/081798/com_fostercare.shtml

Barber, G. (1986). Correlates of job satisfaction among human service workers. *Administration in Social Work, 10*, 25–38.

Beemsterboer, J., & Baum, B. J. (1984). "Burnout": Definitions and health care management. *Social Work in Health Care, 10*(1), 97–109.

Bernstein, N. (2001, August 29). City will close office running foster program. *New York Times*. Available: http://www.nytimes.com/2001/08/29/nyregion/29FOST.html

Bride, B. (2007). Prevalence of secondary traumatic stress among social workers. *Social Work, 25*(1), 63–70.

Brown, S. P., & Leigh, T. W. (1996). A new look at psychological climate and its relationship to job involvement, effort, and performance. *Journal of Applied Psychology, 81*(4), 358–368.

Bureau of Labor Statistics. (2007). *Volunteering in the United States, 2006*. Available: www.bls.gov.news.release/volun.nr0.htm

Chawla, D., & Joshi, H. (2010). Knowledge management initiatives in Indian public and private sector organizations. *Journal of Knowledge Management, 14*(6), 811–827.

Compton, B. R., Galaway, B., & Cournoyer, B. R. (2005). *Social work processes* (7th ed.). Belmont, CA: Brooks/Cole.

Council on Accreditation of Services to Families and Children. (1997). *1997 standards for behavioral health care services and community support and education services* (U.S. ed.). New York: Author.

Dunn, P. C. (1995). Volunteer management. In R. L. Edwards (Ed.-in-chief), *Encyclopedia of social work* (19th ed., pp. 2483-2490). Washington, DC: NASW Press.

"Feeling the pressure at work." (1997, September 14). *Washington Post*, p. H14.

Garthwait, C. (2011). *The social work practicum: A guide and workbook for students* (5th ed.). Boston, MA: Allyn and Bacon.

Gibelman, M. (1998). Contracting for child welfare and related services in the District of Columbia. In M. Gibelman & H. W. Demone, Jr. (Eds.), *The privatization of human services: Case studies in the purchase of services* (Vol. 2, pp. 103-122). New York: Springer.

Gibelman, M. (2000). The nonprofit sector and gender discrimination: A preliminary investigation into the glass ceiling. *Journal of Nonprofit Management & Leadership, 10*(3), 251-269.

Gibelman, M., & Schervish, P. (1997). *Who we are: A second look.* Washington, DC: NASW Press.

Gibelman, M., & Whiting, L. (1999). Negotiation and contracting in a managed care environment: Considerations for practitioners. *Health & Social Work, 24*(3), 180-190.

Ginsberg, S. (1997, April 6). Temp services find the time is ripe for specializing. *Washington Post*, p. H6.

Ginsberg, S. (1998, January 4). After long days' journey into burnout, a grinding halt; learning to manage marathon hours can prevent workers from reaching the breaking point, and reduce companies' cost. *Washington Post*, p. H4.

Glisson, C. (1985). A contingency model of social welfare administration. In S. Slavin (Ed.), *An introduction to human services management* (Vol. 1, 2nd ed., pp. 95-109). New York: Haworth Press.

Glisson, C. (2000). Organizational climate and culture. In R. J. Patti (Ed.), *The handbook of social welfare management* (pp. 195-218). Thousand Oaks, CA: Sage Publications.

Goodman, E. A., & Boss, R. W. (1999). Burnout dimensions and voluntary and involuntary turnover in a health care setting. *Journal of Health and Human Services Administration, 21*(4), 462-471.

Greenglass, E. R., Burke, R. J., & Konarski, R. (1999). A study of the consistency of burnout over time. *Journal of Health and Human Services Administration, 21*(4), 429-440.

Guterman, N. B., & Jayaratne, S. (1994). "Responsibility at-risk": Perceptions of stress, control, and professional effectiveness in child welfare direct practitioners. *Journal of Social Service Research, 20*(1/2), 99-119.

Hagan, J. K. (1999) Burnout: An occupational hazard for social workers. In B. R. Compton & B. Galaway (Eds.), *Social work processes* (6th ed., pp. 501-507). Pacific Grove, CA: Brooks/Cole.

"High marks for women." (1996, September 22). *Washington Post*, p. H9.

Hodge-Williams, J., Doub, N. H., & Busky, R. (1995). Total quality management (TQM) in the nonprofit setting: The Woodbourne experience. *Residential Treatment for Children and Youth, 12*(3), 19-30.

Hromco, J. G., Lyons, J. S., & Nikkel, R. E. (1995). Mental health case management: Characteristics, job function, and occupational stress. *Community Mental Health Journal, 31,* 111-125.

Independent Sector. (1992). *Giving and volunteering in the United States.* Washington, DC: Author.

Independent Sector. (2003). *The value of volunteer time.* Available: http://www.independent sector.org/programs/research/volunteer_time.html

James, L. R., & McIntyre, M. D. (1996). Perceptions of organizational culture. In K. R. Murphy (Ed.), *Individual differences and behavior in organizations* (pp. 416–450). San Francisco: Jossey-Bass.

"Jobs, salaries drive an array of actions." (1999, January). *NASW News*, pp. 1, 6.

Killu, K. (1994). The role of direct care staff. *Behavioral Interventions, 9*(3), 169–176.

Koeske, G. F., & Koeske, R. D. (1998). Workload and burnout: Can social support and perceived accomplishment help? *Social Work, 34*(3), 243–248.

Leiter, M. P., & Harvie, P. L. (1996). Burnout among mental health workers: A review and a research agenda. *International Journal of Social Psychiatry, 42*(2), 90–101.

Lens, V. (2000). *Welfare reform and the media.* Unpublished doctoral dissertation. New York: Yeshiva University, Wurzweiler School of Social Work.

Lewis, R. K. (1994, September 17). Government workplaces often lack aesthetic appeal of private businesses. *Washington Post*, F1, F12.

Liao-Troth, M. A. (2001). Attitude differences between paid workers and volunteers. *Nonprofit Management & Leadership, 11*(4), 423–442.

Lubove, R. (1965). *The professional altruist: The emergence of social work as a career, 1880–1930.* New York: Atheneum.

Maslach, C. (1982). *Burnout: The cost of caring.* Englewood Cliffs, NJ: Prentice Hall.

McAdoo, R. F. (1992). *Partnership session summary.* Silver Spring, MD: National Association of School Psychologists.

McCurley, S. (1994). Recruiting and retaining volunteers. In R. D. Herman & Associates (Eds.), *The Jossey-Bass handbook of nonprofit leadership and management* (pp. 511–534). San Francisco: Jossey-Bass.

Menefee, D. (2000). What managers do and why they do it. In R. J. Patti (Ed.), *The handbook of social welfare management* (pp. 247–266). Thousand Oaks, CA: Sage Publications.

Oberlander, L. B. (1990). Work satisfaction among community-based mental health service providers: The association between work environment and work satisfaction. *Community Mental Health Journal, 26*, 517–532.

Osborne, D., & Gaebler, T. A. (1992). *Reinventing government.* Reading, MA: Addison-Wesley.

"Part-timers have impact." (1997, November 30). *Washington Post*, p. H4.

Peters, T., & Waterman, R. (1982). *In search of excellence: Lessons from America's best-run corporations.* New York: Warner.

Pynes, J. E. (2008). *Human resource management for public and nonprofit organizations: A strategic approach.* San Francisco: Jossey-Bass.

Ratliff, N. (1988). Stress and burnout in the helping professions. *Social Casework, 69*(3), 147–154.

Rees, F. (1997). *Teamwork from start to finish.* San Francisco: Jossey-Bass.

Rosener, J. B. (1995). *America's competitive secret: Utilizing women as a management strategy.* New York: Oxford University Press.

Rousseau, D. M. (1990). Assessing organizational culture: The case for multiple methods. In B. Schneider (Ed.), *Organizational climate and culture* (pp. 153–192). San Francisco: Jossey-Bass.

Savich, V., & Cooley, E. J. (1994). Burnout in child protective service workers: A longitudinal study. *Journal of Organizational Behavior, 15*, 655–666.

Schorr, L. B. (1997). *Common purpose*. New York: Doubleday.

Skidmore, R. A. (1990). *Social work administration* (2nd ed.). Englewood Cliffs, NJ: Prentice Hall.

Skovholt, M. T. (2011). *The resilient practitioner.* New York: Taylor and Francis Group.

Snibbe, J. R., Radcliffe, T., Weisberger, C., Richards, M., & Kelly, J. (1989). Burnout among primary care physicians and mental health professionals in a managed care environment. *Psychological Reports, 65*(3), 775–780.

Stein, M. S., & Teplin, E. (2011). Rational discrimination and shared compliance: Lessons from Title VI of the Americans with Disabilities Act. *Valparaiso University Law Review, 45*(3), 1095–1141.

Swoboda, F. (1995, June 25). For most workers, sharing power is just an Olympian idea. *Washington Post,* p. H5.

Tannen, D. (1994). *Talking from 9 to 5*. New York: William Morrow.

Tanz, J., & Spencer, T. (2000, August 14). Candy striper, my ass! *Fortune.* Available: http://library.northernlight.com/LH20000728010000073.htlml

"'Temp' ranks growing." (1995, September 24). *Washington Post,* p. H6.

Trattner, W. I. (1999). *From poor law to welfare state: A history of social welfare in America* (6th ed.). New York: Free Press.

Uchitelle, L. (1996, December 8). More downsized workers are returning as rentals. *New York Times*, pp. 1, 34.

Walsh, S. (1995, May 28). Still looking for a path to the top. *Washington Post*, p. H6.

Chapter 7

Social Work Practice in Host Settings

In chapter 6, the work environment of human service organizations was explored. However, not all social work is practiced in human service organizations. In this chapter, we look at the dynamics related to working in a host setting, especially the impact of the setting on the social work practice within it. Included in this chapter is a discussion of human service organizations whose professional workforces are composed largely of professionals other than social workers, such as psychologists and psychiatrists. In these settings, social workers are guests, though less overtly than in non–human service organizations.

Work Challenges in Host Settings

Host settings are arenas that are defined and dominated by people who are not social workers (Dane & Simon, 1991; Kelly & Stone, 2009). The primary work of these organizations ranges from health care to incarceration of criminals. In these organizational settings, social work is a secondary or ancillary profession. It is physicians, teachers, recreational specialists, or correctional officers who carry out the major activities associated with the mission of the organization. Furthermore, professionals of other disciplines are typically responsible for the management and decision making in these settings. Thus, in host settings the work environment may be substantially different from in human service organizations.

Dane and Simon (1991) identified four challenges for social workers who practice as guests in host settings:

1. Discrepancies between professional mission and values and those of the dominant individuals in the employing institution
2. Marginality or token status within workplaces employing few social workers
3. The devaluing of social work as women's work in settings that are predominantly male in composition
4. Role ambiguity and role strain

Role Incongruity

In general, the knowledge, skills, and value base of social workers provide an appropriate and comfortable fit with the nature of work within human service organizations. Organizational and professional value orientations are similar. Typically, there is a high level of mutuality and reciprocity of expectations between professionals and the organization. Clarity about role expectations, in turn, positively influences professional behavior.

In host settings, on the other hand, there may be a discrepancy between professionals' perceptions of their roles and those of significant others in the organization, a situation that has been termed *role incongruity* (Compton, Galaway, & Cournoyer, 2005). For example, the school administrator may perceive that the function of the social worker is limited to conducting home studies, even though the job description may indicate a well-rounded set of responsibilities. Or the hospital administrator may think that the social worker's job is discharge planning and may emphasize accountability in terms of how many people are discharged per day. Social workers in hospitals, however, may devalue the discharge planning function and have a much more expansive interpretation of their roles, which may include the provision of individual therapy, support and therapeutic groups, and various methods of psychoeducation. While these are certainly important roles, in their quest for professionalization, social workers have undervalued the role of discharge planning, which is actually a case management function. This is lamentable, as nurses have increasingly filled this gap and are frequently hired as discharge planners. This is an important lesson for social workers: it is essential that we think through the long-term consequences of how we define our role and function within the context of our host organizations (Dziegielweski, 2004).

In some instances, the administrators in host settings may have little understanding of social workers' knowledge and skills. Their value base and ethical prescriptions may also differ. When role incongruity exists, it creates confusion for all concerned. The social worker is likely to be unclear about the functions and behaviors expected of him or her. The supervising personnel and/or administrators may be dissatisfied with worker performance because they have differing expectations about the professional role and standards of practice. Social workers in host settings face a unique set of problems and challenges. They must define themselves within the system and document their contributions to the host setting (Dane & Simon, 1991; Goren, 1981).

Health Care Settings as Hosts

Social workers are employed in a variety of settings whose chief purpose is health care, not human services. These include hospitals, hospices, medical clinics, health maintenance organizations, and nursing homes (Gibelman, 1995; Lee, 2010). Also included are national organizations and their state and local affiliates concerned with specific diseases, such as the Multiple Sclerosis Association, the American Cancer Society, the Asthma and Allergy Foundation, the American Lung Association, and the March of Dimes Birth Defects Association. These organizational settings are oriented to prevention, amelioration, and cure of physical illness. Human services are a means to an end or an adjunct, facilitative component of the work, rather than the mission or focus of the organization.

Hospital Social Work

Social work practice in the hospital organizational setting is oriented to facilitating good health, preventing illness, and aiding patients with physical illness and their families to address and resolve the illness-related social, financial, and psychological problems (Barker, 1999). Practice within this setting is defined as "the provision of social services in hospitals and similar health care centers, most often within a facility's department of social services or social work" (Barker, 1999, p. 221).

Social work practice in hospital settings expanded significantly following the enactment of Medicare and Medicaid in 1965, because hospitals were able to build reimbursable social work charges into their routine daily costs. As Medicare caseloads increased, so did the number of hospital social workers. The typical client was usually a patient over sixty-five years of age and his or her family. Although the elderly continue to constitute a large portion of clients, the role of hospital social workers has expanded significantly (Ross, 1995). For example, social workers provide services in outpatient programs and emergency rooms (Oktay, 1995).

In 1983, a prospective pricing system for Medicare was instituted through the creation of diagnostic related groups, a federally mandated payment mechanism designed to control the costs of medical and hospital care. Under this system, hospitals maximize their profit by decreasing the time the patient spends in the hospital. To help hospitals achieve this goal, social workers had to focus an increasing amount of their attention on timely discharge. Discharge planning responsibilities became a major component of hospital social work.

Because of this focus on discharge planning, social workers in hospital settings are often caught in difficult organizational binds. These troublesome situations often are ethical in nature. The emphasis on efficiency and cost containment may be in direct conflict with social workers' obligation to focus on patient problems and service needs. In fulfilling professional obligations to the patient, social workers may find themselves in conflict with hospital administrators and even physicians.

Challenges to the stability, if not the very future, of hospital social work are ongoing. As health care expenditures continue to grow and medical facilities are forced to cut costs, social work departments increasingly are seen as nonessential to the primary mission of the hospital. In recent years, hospital closures of social work departments have become more frequent. Also pervasive is the reorganizing of social work departments within hospitals. The move from a traditional social work department to a decentralized model, in which social work staff are reassigned to other departments, has raised concerns about proper supervision and the quality of treatment for patients. Reorganization has also meant, in some cases, replacing department directors with non–social work personnel, including physicians and nurses.

Hospital social workers must also manage the challenges of serving on interdisciplinary teams. For instance, social workers are trained to see the biopsychosocial aspects of health and disease, while medical professionals tend to focus on the biological realm. However, the medical profession has been increasingly incorporating the psychosocial domains of behavior into treatment plans. Social workers working in health care settings should familiarize themselves with the literature of the medical profession. Social workers in host institutions must gently assert their areas of expertise while respecting the norms and culture of the host organizations. The key is for practitioners to work at being assets and contributors to the work experience and the lives of their coworkers and clients. Issues related to interdisciplinary collaboration also influence the practice of social work in school settings.

The School as an Organizational Setting

School social work is "oriented toward helping students make satisfactory school adjustments and coordinating and influencing the efforts of the school, the family, and the community to help achieve this goal" (Barker, 1999, p. 426). Social workers represent a growing force within the field of education (National Association of Social Workers, 2000). There are over nine thousand social workers serving students in thirty-seven educational jurisdictions across the United States (Torres, 1996). Social workers serve as a link between the home, school, and community, a role that educational reformers believe is vital to improving educational outcomes (Gibelman & Lens, 2002). The role of the school social worker varies depending on such factors as the size of the school district, number of staff social workers, role distinctions between social workers and other helping professions, and the community in which the school is located. School social workers typically are called on to help students, families, teachers, and educational administrators deal with a range of problems that include truancy, depression, withdrawal, aggressive and/or violent behavior, rebelliousness, and the effects of physical or emotional problems.

The social worker is a guest to the major players in the school system—the educators. Within the special services department of the school, the social worker is part of an interdisciplinary team. Thus, even within the small human services division of a school or school district, social work is unlikely to be the main discipline.

Enabling Legislation

Since the passage of the Education for All Handicapped Children Act of 1975 (P.L. 94-142), social workers have played an important role in schools. This legislation and its successive amendments mandated the provision of appropriate free educational resources for children with disabilities; the educational system is required to provide services in the "least restrictive environment," which involves issues of equal access, supportive services, and procedural protections. Services include special testing, remedial lessons, counseling, and tutoring (Barker, 1999).

Passage of the Individuals with Disabilities Education Act of 1990 (IDEA; P.L. 101-476) and its subsequent amendments sought to further ensure the best education for students with special needs. Improvements aimed at increasing access for students and their families to needed services. Social work services were explicitly added to the definition of early intervention services.

In 1997, additional amendments to IDEA increased opportunities for a social work role within the schools (Huxtable, 1998). In November 1999, President Clinton signed the Omnibus Spending Measure, which provided federal funding for more school-based mental health personnel (National Association of Social Workers, 2000). President Bush, in his No Child Left Behind initiatives, focused considerable attention on the role of testing in education to the neglect of children's psychosocial needs. As such, social work and other supportive, family-centered services were not furthered. While the Obama administration's attention has been on helping cash-strapped states survive the recession, states have nonetheless been forced to cut school budgets significantly. As such, social work within school settings remains underdeveloped and at risk of further cuts for many years to come. Social workers will need to improve their advocacy of in-school services in order for social work within school settings to remain a vital field of practice.

The Reality

Legislation defines the boundaries of professional practice. However, legislatively authorized programs are subject to many state, local, and professional influences. Individually or in combination, these influences may affect how roles are delegated. Because several disciplines are represented in the special services divisions of schools (e.g., psychology, counseling), it is generally up to the specific school system to designate what role each is to play. Role assignments, as well as the value placed on the professional role, are influenced by the degree to which educational administrators understand what social workers do (Tower, 2000), as illustrated in the vignette in box 7.1.

Mary's situation is common in host settings. Administrators and supervisors who are unfamiliar with social workers' training and expertise may have preconceptions about their role and function within the school setting. In Mary's case, the supervisor had a very narrow view of the social work role.

It is not surprising that Mary experienced disillusionment. She felt that her skills were underutilized. Consequently, Mary became bored with the repetitious task of taking social histories. She could not do any follow-up other than to make recommendations to the school support team. Mary felt that she could

---

BOX 7.1
Let Me Use My Skills!

Mary received her MSW, and her first job out of graduate school was as a clinical social worker in a nonprofit mental health agency. As the mother of two small children, Mary sought a position that afforded more time off. She considered several possibilities and finally decided that a position as a school social worker would best meet her needs. In addition to having summers off, she would also be able to work directly with children, thus utilizing the skills she had developed in her master's program specialization: working with adolescents in a direct service capacity. She was delighted when she landed a job as a school social worker in a community close to her home.

Mary was the only social worker employed by this suburban school district. There were two psychologists, two learning disability specialists, and one speech and hearing therapist employed in the school support services department. The supervisor of the department was a learning disability specialist who, it quickly became apparent, had little idea about the knowledge and skills of social work professionals. Furthermore, her supervisor seemed to think that social workers had very little to contribute of a clinical nature.

Mary felt that her skills were not only poorly utilized but also undervalued. In a typical month, she completed twenty-eight social histories, all of which involved at-home or in-office interviews with the families of the children referred. When her supervisor remarked that this level of productivity was insufficient, Mary was ready to throw up her hands in despair. What she wanted to be doing was helping the students. The two school psychologists were actively engaged in direct work with the students and sometimes their families. In fact, their caseloads were so large that they frequently complained about being overburdened. When Mary mentioned to her supervisor that she would be happy to take on some of these cases, she was informed that this was not her job.

---

have adequately performed these tasks without the benefit of her MSW training. This "deskilling" of practitioners can lead to role conflict and burnout (Fabricant, 1985).

Mary tried to share her interpretation of her role with her supervisor but found an unreceptive audience. However, there were other options. First, the interpretation of the professional role is not a one-time occurrence. In addition, Mary had potential allies—the school psychologists—who were overburdened by their own caseloads and could use some help in counseling the many children who needed such services. Other coping capacities include building bridges through partnerships with administrators to better advance the social work agenda.

Criminal Justice

In the late 1970s, social workers maintained a visible presence within the criminal justice system, including juvenile detention and correctional facilities (Miller, 1995). Although social work has largely abdicated its role in this field, there are still a small proportion of social workers who practice within correctional facilities as guests. A notable exception has been the Criminal Justice Program of the University of Washington Tacoma, in which the criminal justice program is housed. This program infuses social work insights, values, and skills into a criminal justice curriculum.

The mission of the criminal justice system—to punish and protect—is in many ways the opposite of the mission of the social work profession—to help. The complexities of these ethical orientations can be seen in the different perspectives regarding the cause of criminal or deviant behavior. If, for example, the incarcerated individual has a history of abuse as a child and shows evidence of chronic mental illness, is the behavior a manifestation of criminality or mental illness? Is the appropriate solution punishment or treatment?

Social workers may work in a correctional setting with those accused or found guilty of crimes or with victims of crime, a battered women's shelter, a hospital, or a court's social services division, among other settings. Social workers may also be on call to local police departments to assess the needs of victims of violent crime and refer them to community services (Popple & Leighninger, 1993). For example, social workers may work with the police in cases of domestic violence; they may be employed directly by the police unit. Domestic violence response teams, which provide crisis intervention at the scene of domestic violence crimes, have been found to be effective and are positively viewed by law enforcement agents (Corcoran, Stephenson, Perryman, & Allen, 2001).

Roberts and Rock (2002) identify a number of professional functions of the social worker in the criminal justice system:

- ◆ Risk assessments of mentally ill and substance-abusing offenders, with particular focus on their risk of future violence and repeat criminality
- ◆ Assessment and treatment of mentally ill offenders in the criminal justice system and forensic mental health units
- ◆ Assessment of degree of danger posed among convicted sex offenders
- ◆ Assessment to determine whether an alleged offender is competent to stand trial and assessment of mental status in regard to responsibility standards in criminal cases
- ◆ Pre-sentence reports for juvenile court and criminal court judges
- ◆ Child custody evaluations and assessments to determine whether parental rights of people with mental illness, convicted felons, and/or abusive parents should be terminated
- ◆ Assessment and treatment of involuntary offenders (p. 661)

Social workers have obvious and clear value dilemmas when they practice in this setting (van Wormer, 2009). The role orientation of the host setting is that of surveillance and control. Social workers, on the other hand, perceive their role to be that of helper. For social workers practicing within the criminal justice system, issues of control, power, and communication frequently arise; these must be discussed and resolved if social workers are to be effective (Treger, 1995).

These questions are particularly vexing when the adjudicated parties are children or adolescents. Criminal behavior is no longer an adult-only phenomenon. In recent years, there has been an increasing number of heinous crimes committed by youth, who are sometimes prosecuted as adults. For society as a whole, and especially for the social worker in the criminal justice system, the moral questions center on how to balance the rehabilitative and accountability needs of the youth and family and at the same time achieve the public safety goals of criminal justice (Gilbert, Grimm, & Parnham, 2001).

As practitioners of the profession that has historically advocated for oppressed and disadvantaged populations, social workers must also be concerned about the disproportionate representation of African Americans in the criminal justice system (Bureau of Justice Statistics, 2005). In their role as advocates, social workers should question social inequalities and disparities. Individual social workers who work within the criminal justice system must balance this ethical concern with the needs of the host institution in which they work and the protection of society as a whole. This balancing act represents just the type of ethical dilemma that social workers face on a daily basis. Yet social workers understand that the vast majority of imprisoned minority women, for example, were sentenced for nonviolent crimes (Bureau of Justice Statistics, 2005). Social workers facing such dilemmas should seek out supervision and consultation from other social workers and should read as much of the literature in the field as they can. New social workers should be especially thoughtful when seeking systems change in their host institutions; it is easy to become marginalized and, ultimately, shunned. Systems change within organizations is often painstakingly slow. Social workers should always look for congruence between their values and those of their hosts and seek to work collaboratively with others. It is important to work from a strengths perspective in our encounters with other professionals as well as with clients.

The Legal System

Social workers also practice within the judicial system; in this case, the organizational setting may be the courts or law firms. One example is the Legal Aid Society, the oldest and largest public interest law firm in the world. Since 1876, the Legal Aid Society has sought to provide quality legal representations for people who cannot afford to pay a private attorney. The Defender Services Program, part of the Legal Aid Society services offered in New York City, employs social workers to work hand-in-hand with more than nine hundred attorneys to protect the legal rights of the more than 300,000 people served each year.

Box 7.2 highlights both the essential role of the social worker in legal proceedings and the relationship between the social worker and the attorney. The social worker assists in the accomplishment of the major organizational mission: to obtain a favorable legal disposition for the client. The social worker's ser-

---

BOX 7.2
The Defender Services Program

The Defender Services Program (DSP) is a unit of the Criminal Defense Division of the Legal Aid Society. Its function is to provide a wide range of services to the client at the request of the client's attorney. The program utilizes social service and paralegal staff to complement the work of the defense attorney in an effort to obtain a favorable disposition for the client. The staff is composed of masters-level social workers, paraprofessional case aides, and paralegal staff.

Requests for DSP services can occur at arraignment, plea negotiations, or at the pretrial, postconviction, and presentencing phases of court case development. Staff interventions are designed to enable the attorneys to negotiate more effectively and to advocate for their clients both in and out of the courtroom. Staff provide information, share resources, prepare reports, and provide both crisis intervention and short-term counseling, as needed. Staff also assess client needs and follow up by locating and making referrals to direct service programs. Such programs frequently include vocational and educational counseling, medical assistance, psychiatric intervention, and addiction services.

Direction and assistance are also provided to those seeking public assistance or public shelter. Staff are sometimes called on by the attorneys for immediate intervention to stabilize a difficult defendant or to help prepare a defendant for court appearances. Staff of DSP also act as liaisons between clients who are being detained, their attorneys, and other Defender Services staff involved in the case.

Written reports are an important part of the job. The written material may be in the form of a letter or memo to the court or a comprehensive psychosocial assessment for referral purposes. Such reports require extensive interviews with the clients, their family, and/or community contacts.

The forensic social worker's clinical evaluation of the client and the worker's ability to professionally convey his or her assessment in court provide additional aid for the defense. The program approach is to develop a casework plan that is client centered and that takes a comprehensive and holistic approach to the defense strategy. This approach acknowledges that psychosocial circumstances impinge on the client and affect his or her responses to the environment. The ultimate goal of using a holistic service plan is to reduce recidivism and criminal activity by providing clients with positive options that address their underlying problems.

Source: Adapted from Legal Aid Society (1998).

---

vices are at the request of attorneys and can occur at any point in the criminal process. The social worker responds but does not initiate the intervention. The focus is on addressing client issues within the context of defense strategies, with social workers functioning as consultants to the attorneys (Legal Aid Society, 1998). The professionals from different disciplines are seen as a team, and each individual is aware of the importance of collaboration to achieve the organization's goals and objectives. However, these goals and objectives are established by the attorney in charge of the case.

In common to social workers employed in school, hospital, criminal justice, or legal settings is the ancillary role of social services. The need for collaboration with other professionals is recognized in all these settings. Similarly, the potential for role ambiguity or role conflict is present in these environments. The people in charge usually represent the major mission of the host setting—educators, attorneys, wardens, physicians, and/or hospital administrators. Although the social work function may be mandated by law, this does not necessarily mean that the function is understood well—or appreciated—by those in charge. Social workers working in host settings may experience ethical conflicts as they seek to carry out their roles according to an ethical code that is distinct from that of the dominant discipline. For instance, social workers encourage self-determination and autonomy, while other professionals may find the practices aligned with these goals to be slow and inefficient. It is important for social workers to understand the values of the professions that dominate the institutions in which they work. Validating the perspectives of other professionals can be an important part of preventing and resolving conflicts. For example, when a social worker validates a parole officer's strong desire for social control and safety, the parole officer may realize that the social worker is an important part of the justice system. He or she may then be more open to the reasons why social workers value empowerment and autonomy. Regardless of the values involved in a particular conflict, it is important for social workers to listen respectfully to and seek to understand the opinions of colleagues whose training and experiences are different from their own.

When Social Work No Longer Dominates

Some organizations maintain close ties with social work out of tradition rather than the current realities of the work environment. Whereas such organizations were once closely associated with social work and staffed by professionally trained social workers, now social work is no longer the dominant profession. Nevertheless, an alliance remains. Two examples of this evolution can be found in the settings of public welfare and Jewish community centers.

Public Welfare

Public welfare organizations are government agencies that provide programs of financial assistance, such as Temporary Assistance to Needy Families, medical assistance (i.e., Medicaid), and food stamps. In the late 1960s and early 1970s, a number of factors, such as the separation of income maintenance (cash assistance) and service provision mandated under the 1967 amendments to the Social Security Act, coalesced to alter the focus of public welfare programs.

During the same time period, the declassification of social service positions had been initiated in public agencies throughout the country. Declassification means the reduction in standards and work-related experience required for public sector jobs (Gibelman, 1995).The end result was that those positions still designated as professional (requiring a BSW or MSW) tended to be found within "soft" service areas, such as child protective services or adoption. Positions related to income maintenance tended to be relegated to a new category of workers and clerks, for whom social work professional qualifications were not required. The service-delivery functions associated with child protection and child welfare were delegated to separate departments or units, such as a division of youth and family services or administration for children's services.

Public welfare agencies, then, were left with the function of determining eligibility for public benefits and monitoring the use of such benefits among those who qualify (Hagen & Wang, 1993).At about the same time, management experts took over the stewardship of these agencies, believing that they were just another kind of business operation like an insurance company or a manufacturing operation.Those in charge of the public welfare systems did not want to hire social workers. MBAs didn't succeed well either, according to the prevailing political definition of success (reducing welfare costs), and the next phase was to bring in public administrators whose expertise was in the "business" of government (Gibelman, 1995).

Today, the majority of employees in public welfare have not studied social work, nor do they hold a degree in this field (Gibelman & Schervish, 1996; Ginsberg, 1983). Nevertheless, the title "social worker" has often been retained based on the position classification rather than the qualifications of those holding the position.

Jewish Community Centers

Jewish community centers (JCCs) were founded, staffed, and maintained by social workers for much of their more than one-hundred-year history (Altman, 1988; Sweifach, 2001). JCCs, in their earliest days, were primarily concerned with the socialization and acculturation of Jewish immigrants.Today, JCCs provide an array of social, recreational, and cultural services.The building of Jewish identity has become recognized as a mission of importance to today's JCC. As the mission has changed, hiring trends have also changed.

As the mission of the JCC has evolved, its workforce needs have also shifted. This shift has been described as a move toward an interdisciplinary structure, with social workers functioning as guests (Sweifach, 2001). Now JCCs hire from the fields of education, recreation, and Jewish studies, among others, to meet the requirements of current programs and services (Altman, 1988; Sweifach, 2001). Consequently, the earlier and integral role of social workers has become more marginalized. Although social workers are still employed within these settings, their job responsibilities may not necessarily be congruent with social work practice.When social workers' skills are inconsistent with program focus, the result may extend from worker dissatisfaction and high turnover rates to ineffectiveness in the delivery of services.

Unique Challenges

The day-to-day interactions between psychologists, psychiatrists, and social workers; between teachers, special educators, and social workers; or between physicians, nurses, and social workers present challenges that go beyond those of practice in a social service organizational setting. First, there is the issue of value orientation. Garland (1995), for example, noted that for social workers in health and mental health care settings, value conflicts abound between social workers and their medically based host settings. Midgley and Sanzenbach (1989) suggest that social workers who are employed by sectarian agencies are confronted with value conflicts between social work and religious teachings.

Ethical conflicts in social work practice may be more apparent in host settings than in human service organizations. These may concern value conflicts, such as that of punishment versus rehabilitation. Social workers' obligations regarding confidentiality and the primacy of clients' needs may also diverge from the procedures set forth by the host institution. In the area of interdisciplinary collaboration, the *Code of Ethics* (National Association of Social Workers, 1999) establishes in Section 2.03 that the "professional and ethical obligations of the interdisciplinary team as a whole and of its individual members should be clearly established" (p. 16). However, implementing this prescription is not typically within the jurisdiction of the social worker.

Another issue is that the social worker may occupy a low status relative to other professionals who dominate the host setting. For example, psychiatrists are often the major players in psychiatric settings. Within the hospital, the administrator in charge of discharge planning may well be the "chief"; increasingly, these positions are held by nurses. Thus, issues of power and status affect the work environment.

The negative manifestations of social work in these settings include value conflicts, burnout, and surrender of professional allegiance. Many social workers feel unwelcome. They may come to identify with the values and practice methodologies of the host settings. Some fight the host system, while others leave for more satisfying work environments. Role strain and role status issues are exacerbated by the reluctance of social workers in host settings to specify their professional contributions or to gather and critically evaluate empirical data on their effectiveness (Auslander, 1996).

Despite the large number of social workers who practice in host settings, many of the issues of practice in these settings remain unresolved. Some of the outstanding questions concern how social work fits with the achievement of organizational goals; whether social work practice can retain its uniqueness if organizational goals are inconsistent with social work values; and whether the tasks social workers assume in such settings are consistent with professional practice standards. Without answers to these questions, the strategies discussed in the remaining chapters may apply less clearly and with more caveats than is the case with social work practice carried out in human service organizations.

Key Points

◆ Host settings are organizations whose missions are something other than the provision of human services.

◆ Host settings in which social workers are employed in ancillary roles include hospitals, medical clinics, schools, religious organizations, correctional facilities, and the criminal justice system.

◆ Working in host organizations involves several challenges, such as role incongruity, role ambiguity, and the lack of social and professional supports.

◆ There may be overt or covert discrepancies between social work values and the dominant values of the host setting.

◆ Available supervision is often administratively rather than professionally oriented, and the supervisor is likely to be a member of a profession other than social work.

◆ Collaboration is an essential aspect of practice in a host setting.

◆ In some settings, such as Jewish community centers and public welfare agencies, social workers were the dominant workforce in the past but no longer are.

◆ Issues of power, status, values, and role are recurrent themes when social workers practice in host organizations.

Suggested Learning Activities and Discussion Questions

1. When you begin employment in a host setting, what steps might you take to clarify role expectations? How would you negotiate any differences in role expectations that you and a non–social worker administrator might have?

2. If you are not currently in field placement or employed in a host setting, think of a social work colleague who works in a hospital, school, community center, or correctional facility. Interview this colleague about his or her perceptions of issues that arise from working in this environment. Inquire about the professional supports available and how he or she addresses the challenges posed by employment in a host setting on a personal and professional level.

3. What strategies might you recommend to Mary (and others in a similar situation) in regard to: (a) interpreting the social work role; (b) enlisting the support and help of school psychologists in expanding her range of assignments; and (c) utilizing professional resources to articulate to the school community what social workers do?

4. Role conflict is one of the major themes that emerge in discussions of work in a host setting. If you work for or might be considering employment in a host setting, what preventive and ameliorative steps might you take to deal with role conflict?

Recommended Readings

Albert, A. R. (Ed.). (1997). *Social work in juvenile and criminal justice settings* (2nd ed.). New York: Charles C Thomas.

Constable, R., Massat, C. R., McDonald, S., & Flynn, J. P. (2006). *School social work: Practice, policy, and research perspectives.* Chicago: Lyceum Books.

Tourse, R. W. C., & Mooney, J. F. (1999). *Collaborative practice: School and human service partnerships.* Westport, CT: Praeger.

van Wormer, K. (2009). Restorative justice as social justice for victims of gendered violence: A standpoint feminist perspective. *Social Work, 54*(2), 107-116.

References

Altman, M. (1988). Competencies required of Jewish community center professionals today and tomorrow. *Journal of Jewish Communal Service, 64*(3), 256-257.

Auslander, G. (1996). Outcome evaluation in host organizations: A research agenda. *Administration in Social Work, 10*(2), 15-27.

Barker, R. L. (1999). *Social work dictionary* (4th ed.). Washington, DC: NASW Press.

Bureau of Justice Statistics. (2005). *Prison statistics: Summary findings.* Available: http://www.ojp.usdoj.gov/bjs/prisons.htm

Compton, B. R., Galaway, B., & Cournoyer, B. R. (2005). *Social work processes* (7th ed.). Belmont, CA: Brooks/Cole.

Corcoran, J., Stephenson, M., Perryman, D., & Allen, S. (2001). Perceptions and utilization of a police-social work crisis intervention approach to domestic violence. *Families in Society, 82*(4), 393-398.

Dane, B. O., & Simon, B. L. (1991). Resident guests: Social workers in host settings. *Social Work, 36*, 208-213.

Dziegielweski, S. (2004). *The changing face of health care social work* (2nd ed.). New York: Springer.

Fabricant, M. (1985). The industrialization of social work practice. *Social Work, 30*(5), 389-395.

Garland, D. (1995). Church social work. In R. L. Edwards (Ed.-in-chief), *Encyclopedia of social work* (19th ed., pp. 475-483). Washington, DC: NASW Press.

Gibelman, M. (1995). *What social workers do.* Washington, DC: NASW Press.

Gibelman, M., & Lens, V. (2002). Entering the debate about school vouchers: A social work perspective. *Children and Schools, 24*(4), 207-221.

Gibelman, M., & Schervish, P. (1996). Social work and public social service practice: A status report (1996). *Families in Society, 77*(2), 117-124.

Gilbert, J., Grimm, R., & Parnham, J. (2001). Applying therapeutic principles to a family-focused juvenile justice model. *Alabama Law Review, 52*, 1153-1219.

Ginsberg, L. H. (1983). *The practice of social work in public welfare.* New York: Free Press.

Goren, S. (1981). The wonderland of social work in the schools: Or how Alice learned to cope. *School Social Work, 6*(1), 19-26.

Hagen, J. L., & Wang, L. (1993). Roles and functions of public welfare workers. *Administration in Social Work, 17*, 81-103.

Huxtable, M. (1998). School social work: An international profession. *Social Work, 20*(22), 95-109.

Kelly, M., & Stone, S. (2009). An analysis of factors shaping interventions used by school social workers. *Children and Schools, 23*(3), 163-176.

Lee, J. M. (2010). The role of medical social work for burn patients and family. *Journal of Korean Burn Society, 13*(1), 10-13.

Legal Aid Society. (1998). *Annual report*. Available http://www.legal-aid.org/ar99/crimd.htm

Midgley, J., & Sanzenbach, P. (1989). Social work, religion, and the global challenge of fundamentalism. *International Social Work, 32*, 273-287.

Miller, J. G. (1995). Criminal justice: Social work roles. In R. L. Edwards (Ed.-in-chief), *Encyclopedia of social work* (19th ed., pp. 653-659). Washington, DC: NASW Press.

National Association of Social Workers. (1999). *Code of ethics*. Washington, DC: Author.

National Association of Social Workers. (2000). Education for children and youths. *Social Work Speaks: National Association of Social Workers Policy Statements, 2000-2003* (5th ed., pp. 89-95). Washington, DC: Author.

Oktay, J. S. (1995). Primary health care. In R. L. Edwards (Ed.-in-chief), *Encyclopedia of social work* (19th ed., pp. 1887-1894). Washington, DC: NASW Press.

Popple, P. R., & Leighninger, L. (1993). *Social work, social welfare, and American society* (2nd ed.). Boston: Allyn & Bacon.

Roberts, A. R., & Rock, M. (2002). An overview of forensic social work and risk assessments with the dually diagnosed. In A. R. Roberts & G. J. Greene (Eds.), *Social workers' desk reference* (pp. 661-668). New York: Oxford University Press.

Ross, J. (1995). Hospital social work. In R. L. Edwards (Ed.-in-chief), *Encyclopedia of social work* (19th ed., pp. 1365-1376). Washington, DC: NASW Press.

Sweifach, J. S. (2001). *The relationship of social work functions to job responsibilities within JCCs*. Unpublished doctoral dissertation. New York: Yeshiva University, Wurzweiler School of Social Work.

Torres, S., Jr. (1996). The status of school social workers in America. *Social Work in Education, 18*, 8-18.

Tower, K. (2000). Image crisis: A study of attitudes about school social workers. *Social Work in Education, 22*, 83-94.

Treger, H. (1995). Police social work. In R. L. Edwards (Ed.-in-chief), *Encyclopedia of social work* (19th ed., pp. 1843-1848). Washington, DC: NASW Press.

van Wormer, K. (2009). Restorative justice as social justice for victims of gendered violence: A standpoint feminist perspective. *Social Work, 54*(2), 107-116.

Chapter 8

Conditions of Work

Conditions of work are the rules, procedures, and operating modes that govern how social workers carry out their responsibilities in the agency. All organizations have operating procedures, though they may not always be in written form. Without such procedures, how work is conducted would be determined by a particular social worker, the supervisor, or whoever is the "boss" at any given time. Because social workers do not necessarily stay in any one job for the duration of their career, the rules associated with how work is carried out must be known and communicated to new staff so that there is continuity and some degree of order. This chapter covers the conditions of work and also provides an overview of unionization in social work, a movement that has at times during organized social welfare's history been a major force in shaping the work environment.

Organizational Policies

As noted in chapter 6, there are both formal and informal environments within an organization. In addition, there are formal and informal rules governing how work is performed. Formal rules detail the conditions of employment—vacation and sick leave, entitlements to benefits, performance appraisal review systems, and the like. In some organizations, there may be an employee handbook as well as an office procedures handbook. The former deals with official policies passed by the board of directors or a similar authority in the case of public or for-profit organizations. Office procedures tend to deal with issues outside of formal policy, such as dress codes, use of the telephone for personal calls, and coffee breaks.

Formal Policies Concerning Employment

The formal rules governing employment are typically found in a personnel policies and procedures handbook (which might also be called the personnel policy manual; see box 8.1), which governs the conditions of work for all employees. In nonprofit organizations, this document is reviewed and approved by the board of directors. In all agencies, the CEO is responsible for carrying out the policies, though he or she may delegate this function. In large organizations, for example, there may be a human resources manager who oversees the implementation of personnel policies. Some agencies decentralize some

---

BOX 8.1
Employee Handbooks

Most handbooks contain:
- ◆ A definition of the employment relationship
- ◆ Policies concerning the work environment, such as an antiharassment policy, antiviolence policy, and no-smoking policy
- ◆ Procedures for handling accidents on the job
- ◆ A statement concerning equal opportunity employment
- ◆ Procedures regarding personnel records and privacy
- ◆ Systems for performance appraisal
- ◆ Reasons for and conditions of employee separation
- ◆ Rules of work, such as attendance, hours, overtime, compensatory time, outside activities and compensation, and reimbursement for authorized expenses
- ◆ Employee benefits, including benefits eligibility, vacations, holidays, sick leave, personal time off, family and medical leave, personal leave of absence, military service, jury duty, time off to vote, and professional development
- ◆ Insurance programs, such as health insurance, life insurance, pension plan, workers' compensation, and professional liability insurance

---

employment functions. In larger agencies in which specific units operate with greater autonomy, program directors are often free to advertise for positions (pending approval from others in the agency), conduct interviews, and do their own hiring. This decentralization can be helpful, as unit directors usually know the needs of their program better than those who work in the central office.

These manuals also provide consistency in expectations, as everyone is covered by and accountable to the same rules. The handbooks set forth the parameters of acceptable behavior in the workplace (Ginsberg, 1997d). Organizations have leeway in some workplace rules, such as employee benefits and insurance programs. However, in regard to many, if not most, rules of employment, legislative or judicial decisions provide the guidelines for formulating agency policies.

Laws Governing Employment

Equal Employment Opportunity

Discrimination in employment based on race, ethnicity, or sex has been explicitly prohibited by law since the passage of the Civil Rights Act in 1964 (P.L. 88–352), and antidiscrimination provisions have been strengthened in subsequent amendments. The 1964 law made all discrimination illegal and, in Title VII, specifically forbade discrimination in employment practices based on race, color, religion, sex, or national origin. The act was amended in 1991, through Title VI, to prohibit discrimination based on gender, race, color, or national origin in any program or activity that receives financial assistance from the federal government (Wells & Idelson, 1995). Most social workers are employed in organizations that receive, directly or indirectly, government funds. In addition, most states have their own laws related to employment issues, including equal employment law (Swaboda, 1996b).

Laws that forbid discrimination often do not go far enough in their protections. This explains why there are also laws that affirm rights. Several examples of protective laws are discussed in the following sections. These include laws regarding salary equity, opportunities for upward mobility for people of color and women, affirmative action, and the rights of people with disabilities.

Salary Protection

Equal pay legislation was first introduced through the Equal Pay Act of 1963 (P.L. 88–38) as an amendment to the Fair Labor Standards Act (52 Stat. 1060). This law requires equal pay for equal work involving equal skill, effort, responsibility, and working conditions (Gunderson, 1994). It has been widely used to equalize pay inequities between men and women.

Despite protective laws, women and people of color still, in general, earn lower salaries than men in the same or similar positions. A recent analysis of Bureau of Labor Statistics data reveals that as the percentage of women in occupational groups increases, weekly salaries decrease (Gibelman, 2002). Conversely, as the proportion of men within the industry increases, so does salary. These patterns in different professions and industries suggest the continued pervasiveness of the problem of salary inequities. Wage disparities continue to this day in various professions (Lalive & Stutzer, 2010).

Within social work, evidence of wage disparities based on gender was documented as early as 1961 (Becker, 1961) and consistently reaffirmed in subsequent investigations (e.g., Fortune & Hanks, 1988; Gibelman & Schervish, 1997; Huber & Orlando, 1995).

Promotional Opportunities

Title II of the Civil Rights Act of 1991 (P.L. 102–166), known as the Glass Ceiling Act of 1991, specifically addressed concerns about the underrepresentation of women and minorities in management and decision-making positions and the need to remove artificial barriers to advancement. It established the Glass Ceiling Commission to study and make recommendations about the elimination of such barriers and the creation of opportunities to move women and minorities into management.

In March 1995, the Department of Labor's Glass Ceiling Commission released the final results of its study of corporate America. The study examined the glass ceiling phenomenon as it relates to five target groups—women of all races and ethnicities and African American, Asian American, Hispanic American, and American Indian men and concluded that "a glass ceiling exists and that it operates substantially to exclude minorities and women from the top levels of management" (Glass Ceiling Commission, 1995, p. 7).

Other studies have also documented the glass ceiling throughout the branches of government (e.g., Bagues & Esteve-Volart, 2010; General Accounting Office, 1995; Guy, 1993; Jennings, 1993; Pincus, 1994; U.S. Merit Systems Protection Board, 1992). A more recent study suggests that the glass ceiling exists even within nonprofit human service organizations, a somewhat surprising finding due to this sector's commitment to fostering civil rights and human well-being (Gibelman, 2000).

Affirmative Action

The policy of affirmative action is, in itself, brief and straightforward. In 1965, President Johnson, through Executive Order 11246, expanded an earlier order by President Kennedy to require that contractors take affirmative steps in hiring women and minorities in all business operations, not just in fulfilling federal contracts (Pecora, 1995). Companies were required to submit the "numerical goals and timetables" used in carrying out their affirmative action plan (Wells & Idelson, 1995). The order did not require specific timetables or quotas (numerical imperatives in absolute or proportionate terms), although, in time, individual businesses, bolstered by the courts, instituted such quantitative measures.

Affirmative action rejects the notion that policies are sufficient if they simply prohibit discrimination against individuals on the basis of gender, race, or ethnic background. Inequities must be reduced and eliminated through active intervention (Gibelman, 1999; Pecora, 1995). However, current political and social views that race- and gender-conscious policies lead to preferential treatment and unfair advantages for some at the expense of others further challenge the advancement of women and people of color (Burstein, 1994; Gibelman, 1999).

Americans with Disabilities Act

In general, civil rights laws have been used with greatest frequency and success by women and people of color. However, there are other forms of discrimination that affect access to the workplace. The Americans with Disabilities Act (ADA) of 1990 (P.L. 101-336) was enacted to remedy some of the deficiencies in and loopholes of prior laws.

The ADA extended broad civil rights protections to about 43 million Americans with disabilities. Some of the purposes of the act are to provide a federal mandate to eliminate discrimination against individuals with disabilities, to provide enforceable standards to address discrimination, to ensure that the federal government plays an active role in enforcing the standards, and to invoke congressional authority to address the major areas of discrimination (Pecora & Wagner, 2000). The employment provisions became effective on July 26, 1992, and apply to employers with twenty-five or more employees. The ADA is an equal opportunity law, not an affirmative action law (Pecora & Wagner, 2000).

How Far Have We Come?

The broad goal of antidiscriminatory and affirmative action policies was to correct the discriminatory practices of the past and to create a balance in the workforce that was reflective of the balance between the races and genders in American society. However, despite these laws, people of color, people with disabilities, and women still face barriers to hiring, advancement, and equal pay (see, for example, Affirmative Action and Diversity Project, 1998). In general, gender and racial equity laws have been poorly enforced, and barriers such as continued sex-role stereotyping and role socialization, fear of repercussions on the part of the affected party, and covert and sometimes overt opposition within the workplace continue (DiNitto & McNeece, 2008). For these reasons, enforcement of organizational policies in regard to antidiscrimination and affirmation of legal rights is very important.

Provisions of agency personnel policies and procedures thus reflect federal, state, and local laws, and organizations are responsible for abiding by these laws. Because state laws can add additional requirements to federal laws, the laws regarding employment vary to some degree from one state to another. For example, Rhode Island law prohibits discrimination on the basis of sexual orientation. New Hampshire voted to bar the use of genetic testing as a condition of employment, membership in a labor organization, or in granting licenses. Maine now prohibits employers from requiring job applicants to submit to HIV tests or reveal if they have ever had such a test (Swaboda, 1996b).

Most personnel policies and procedures manuals include an antidiscrimination clause that reflects federal and state laws. The means for redress are also usually included. Nevertheless, deciding to "call the agency on the carpet" about discriminatory practices takes courage, as illustrated in the vignette in box 8.2.

BOX 8.2
Pay Inequity: Taking Action

Susan worked in a large multiservice agency that employed a staff of about 150. There were three satellite offices, and Susan was the branch director of one of them. The other two branch directors were men. Susan had the same or better qualifications than the other branch directors in regard to education, experience, and longevity within the agency.

In an informal discussion with the chief financial officer of the agency, Susan learned that her annual salary was $6,000 lower than that of the other two branch directors. She had wondered about this issue for some time but was privy only to the overall budget figure for staff salaries, not individual salaries. Salaries were treated as highly confidential; one just didn't ask.

The chief financial officer, a woman, volunteered this information because of her own anger; she felt that she was underpaid compared to senior managers who were men. She felt that Susan would be an ally. Susan reacted to the news with anger and

(continued on next page)

---

thought about resigning. Counseled by her family and friends, she finally decided to take action. She consulted the personnel policies and procedures manual about grievance procedures and then carefully drafted a memo to the executive director, to whom she reported. The memo was worded to avoid accusations or overt emotion; she attempted to stick to the facts and to ask for a salary adjustment on the basis of gender equity. Rather than impersonally sending the memo through interoffice mail, she made an appointment to meet with the executive director. She rehearsed this meeting until she was confident that she could conduct the conversation professionally.

At the meeting with the executive director, Susan was pleased that she was able to articulate the issues as she had planned. She also handed him a copy of the memo. She did not, however, anticipate his negative reaction. He indicated that salaries of other employees were not her business and that if there were salary differences, there must be good reason for them. However, he did not explain what these reasons might be. He cautioned her about "rocking the boat" and did not offer to look into the matter. Susan left his office feeling defeated and scared that there might be retaliation.

Susan gave the matter considerable thought over the next few days. Again counseled by her friends, she decided to seek legal advice. The attorney to whom she was referred was an expert in employment law. The attorney indicated that Susan had every right—even an obligation—to file a complaint with the Equal Employment Opportunity Commission (EEOC). Susan was told that this process could take considerable time, due to the backlog of complaints to the EEOC, and that legal action should wait for a ruling by the EEOC, which would give them standing in court.

Susan carefully considered her options and the potential consequences. She decided that she felt strongly about the inequity—there was no justification for it, and it was morally and legally wrong. Accordingly, she filed the complaint with the EEOC. Within a few weeks, she realized that the executive director as well as her immediate supervisor knew about the complaint. She was getting the cold shoulder from just about everyone. Over the next few weeks, the work environment became increasingly unpleasant. She began to look for another job. Given her skills and experience, she was able to locate a new position within two months, gave appropriate notice, and left the agency hurt, ignored, and intent on pursuing her legal claims.

An affirmative response came from the EEOC a year later. With the EEOC's ruling that she had legal standing to sue, Susan's attorney filed a suit against the agency charging violation of the Civil Rights Act (P.L. 88-352). Eventually, the agency made a financial settlement, and legal proceedings were avoided. The money was not what was important to Susan. She won her victory in the form of an acknowledgment by the agency that it had discriminated against her on the basis of gender.

Even though Susan eventually won her battle, it was a long, emotional, and difficult process. She could not be fired for filing the complaint, as the law expressly forbids retribution. However, the personal costs were high, and she opted to find another job while continuing to seek remedy for the inequity she experienced. Others in a similar situation may have opted to stay silent and remain on the job, albeit angry, and still others may have chosen to find another job but not take any action.

Workplace Rules

An organization's personnel policies and procedures manual details many of the rules of the workplace. One relatively recent addition to many manuals is a prohibition against sexual harassment. This prohibition is spelled out in federal civil rights law and in state law as well. The inclusion of related provisions in organizational policies and procedures is due to a growing awareness about and sensitivity to issues of gender in the workplace and the frequency with which inappropriate sexual behaviors occur. Such policies apply to inappropriate behavior initiated by men toward women, women toward men, men toward men, or women toward women.

The work environment has changed. What was once permissible behavior among coworkers, such as comments on attire or jokes about the dating habits of another employee, are no longer tolerated. Organizations have procedures for handling complaints of sexual harassment, as illustrated in box 8.3.

BOX 8.3
Agency Antiharassment Policy

Metropolitan Mental Health Care Center (MMHCC) is steadfastly opposed to all forms of harassment of or by an employee or individual associated with the agency. Harassment will not be tolerated.

It is the Center's policy to prohibit harassment of an employee by another employee, management representative, or person associated with Metropolitan Mental Health Care Center, including, but not limited to, harassment on the basis of race, color, creed, religion, age, sex, disability, handicap, marital status, nationality, national origin, sexual orientation, ancestry, liability for service in the armed forces of the United States, status as a veteran, political belief, genetic information, possession of atypical hereditary cellular or blood trait, or any other consideration made unlawful by federal, state, or local laws.

Harassment is unlawful. Although it is not easy to define precisely what harassment is, it certainly includes slurs, epithets, threats, derogatory comments, unwelcome jokes, inappropriate teasing, and other similar verbal or physical conduct. In addition, sexual harassment refers to behavior that is unwelcome and offensive and that negatively affects a person's employment, performance, or working environment. Some examples of sexual harassing behaviors include, but are not limited to:

◆ Sexual innuendoes, suggestive comments, and jokes of a sexual nature
◆ Sexual propositions, demands, and threats
◆ Displays of sexually suggestive objects or pictures
◆ Graphic or obscene gestures, suggestive or insulting sounds, leering, and whistling
◆ Physical contact, including touching, pinching, pushing, and brushing against the body
◆ Unwelcome sexual advances

(continued on next page)

If you believe you have been a victim of harassment, you should bring the problem to the immediate attention of your supervisor or any management representative with whom you feel comfortable. If your complaint involves someone in your direct line of supervision, or you are uncomfortable for any reason with discussing such matters with your supervisor, you should report the problem to a management representative. Failure to report claims of harassment hampers MMHCC's ability to take necessary steps to remedy such situations.

The Center will investigate all allegations of harassment promptly and will take all appropriate corrective action. Retaliation in any form against an employee who makes a complaint of sexual harassment or against any employee who participates in the investigation of such a complaint is strictly prohibited. MMHCC will keep the complaint confidential to the maximum extent possible, but effective investigation of such allegations may involve disclosure to the accused individual and to witnesses in order to gather all the facts.

The Center will ensure that all staff work in a professional atmosphere that promotes equal opportunities and prohibits discriminatory practices, including harassment, whether the source of such harassment is coworkers, volunteers, or any other person with whom any employee deals in the scope of his or her employment.

Sexual harassment policies address the changing societal and workplace context. Another area in which organizations have sought to intervene is in the use of drugs and alcohol. As with sexual harassment, organizational policy reflects changing ideas about acceptable behavior. Many organizations now specify in writing that the organization is a drug-free workplace, meaning that the use of drugs on the premises is forbidden. An example of such a policy is given in box 8.4.

BOX 8.4
Drug-Free Workplace

Portland Mental Health Association (PMHA) is committed to maintaining a drug-free workplace, in keeping with the spirit and intent of the Drug-Free Workplace Act of 1988 (P.L. 100–690). The use of controlled substances is inconsistent with the behavior expected of PMHA employees, subjects all employees and visitors to our facility to unacceptable safety risks, and undermines the Association's ability to operate effectively and efficiently. For these reasons, the unlawful manufacture, distribution, dispensation, possession, sale, or use of a controlled substance in the workplace or while engaged in PMHA business off agency premises is strictly prohibited.

Employees are to be aware of the dangers of substance abuse, PMHA policy regarding drugs, the penalties that shall be imposed on employees for drug abuse violations occurring in the workplace, and any available drug counseling and rehabilitation programs. Employees convicted of controlled substance—related violations, including pleas of nolo contendere (i.e., no contest), must inform the PMHA within five days of

(*continued on next page*)

such conviction or plea. Violations of this policy may lead to disciplinary action up to and including immediate termination of employment and/or require satisfactory participation in a substance abuse rehabilitation or treatment program as a condition of continued employment. Such violations also have legal consequences.

Employees with questions about this policy or issues related to drug or alcohol use in the workplace should raise their concerns with their supervisor without fear of reprisal.

Some organizations also have an antiviolence policy, an unfortunate necessity given the well-publicized and horrific incidents of violence that have occurred in recent years. Although certainly not commonplace, acts of violence do occur in the workplace, particularly when employees are under extreme stress and there is an absence of mechanisms to detect and address such stress before a tragic event has occurred. Box 8.5 gives an example of such a policy.

BOX 8.5
No Violence Here

Hillside Hospital will not tolerate any conduct injurious to security, personal safety, employee welfare, and the hospital's operations. Hillside Hospital strictly prohibits any type of verbal or physical threats of abuse or abuse directed at supervisors, coworkers, subordinates, and others. Hillside Hospital also strictly prohibits possession of firearms, explosives, knives, or other weapons on agency property and/or while employees are engaged in agency business. A violation of this policy will result in disciplinary action, including termination.

Hillside Hospital encourages all employees who know or suspect that another employee has threatened or discussed committing any act of violence to immediately report such information directly to his or her supervisor or another management representative. Prompt reporting will assist management to maintain a safe workplace. Hillside Hospital will take such reports seriously and promptly investigate all reports. It will take appropriate remedial actions against violators, including termination, if an investigation establishes that corrective action is warranted.

Conflicts of Interest

All employees are expected to devote their best efforts to the interests of the organization that employs them. In general, human service organizations recognize the right of employees to engage in activities outside their employment that are of a private nature and unrelated to agency business, provided such activities do not affect job performance or pose a conflict of interest.

A sizable number of human service professionals who work in agencies also have a small solo or group private practice (Gibelman & Schervish, 1997). Private practice not only augments agency income but may also provide opportunity for more intensive or specialized practice than that afforded in an agency. However, there is a potential for a conflict of interest, as the vignette in box 8.6 shows.

BOX 8.6
A Conflict of Interest?

Jennifer is the director of professional services at the local YM/YWCA. In addition to recreational programs, the Y also offers an array of social services, such as programs for senior citizens, Meals on Wheels, information and referral, and a small counseling program. Jennifer has a solid professional reputation both at the Y and in the community, and she is often delegated responsibility for speaking at public forums about the Y and its programs.

In addition to her work at the Y, Jennifer maintains a private practice in which she provides psychotherapeutic services to individuals and families. With some frequency, community residents approach her after the speaking engagements and ask about counseling services for themselves or a family member.

Jennifer refers them to her private practice. Her rationale is that these clients approached her as an individual, not as a representative of the Y. Furthermore, the type of counseling she provides is different from that provided at the Y; the Y limits its services to short-term interventions. Jennifer also feels that the Y's services are primarily oriented to low-income people in the community who need the sliding fee scale offered by the Y. There is a waiting list for the Y's counseling service, and Jennifer further reasons that she can respond immediately to clients' needs, whereas the Y cannot.

All employees of the Y are required to sign a conflict of interest statement once a year, revealing any actual or potential conflicts between themselves and the organization. Jennifer has always indicated on this form that there is no area of conflict. Do you agree?

As this vignette illustrates, there may not always be consensus about what constitutes a conflict of interest. When the situation is not clear or diverse views about the situation are expressed, it is important to obtain clarification from the agency's administration.

Dress

What is appropriate business attire? Years ago, "appropriate" meant a suit and tie for men, and a dress or suit for women. Then changes were introduced. First it was casual Friday, when employees were allowed to dress down, within limits. No jeans. No short tops. No sneakers. Today, dressing down has become the norm rather than the exception for people who work in offices. A relaxed work environment is believed to be one factor in attracting new employees and fostering morale among existing employees (Swaboda, 1996a).

How employees dress affects the public image of the organization. When a social woker meets with a client, for example, what message might be communicated if the worker is dressed for a baseball game? What would you wear if you were representing your agency at a coalition meeting of agencies to draft a position statement? As an agency representative, you need to look your best—"anything" does not go!

It is also important to remember that different cultural groups have different expectations and norms concerning dress. For instance, many years ago I worked as a clinical social worker in the Puerto Rican community in Philadelphia. After several weeks, it became very apparent that professionals were expected to dress more formally than I prefer to dress. It was important for me to respect the cultural norms of my clients. As such, I learned to become comfortable with carefully pressed khakis (my first experience with an iron) and a tie.

It is also important for human service workers to take into account the nature of their role when they decide how to dress. Those conducting home visits will not want to dress in a manner that will draw undue attention to themselves. When in doubt, discuss the issue of dress with your supervisor and other workers.

Big Brother Is Watching

Technology has revolutionized how we work. Record keeping, for example, has been greatly simplified by computer programs. Computer workstations at every desk, or easy access to a computer, have also brought new workplace concerns. Surfing the Web for the latest sales may be a big temptation to some employees. E-mail and text messaging are also temptations that impinge upon time and energy in the workplace. In days past, supervisors focused on restricting the use of the office telephone for personal calls; now e-mail offers an easy means to keep in touch with friends and family—on work time!

Some organizations have sought to limit the personal use of computers through workplace rules. Others have gone further. Computer programs such as Silent Watch allow the boss to monitor computer use. Such programs provide information about who is logged on to what website and for how long. Organizations may inform employees of the use of such software; others may simply monitor computer time without informing staff.

Staff may feel that the monitoring of computer usage is a form of Big Brother looking over their shoulders. However, the equipment belongs to the organization; the time spent on it is time away from work responsibilities.

Although such monitoring practices have been confined, in general, to large corporate organizations and those in which employees spend considerable time online, the growing use of technology in the workplace suggests that the use of monitoring systems may become more common in the future.

At-Will Employment

Perhaps in response to a growing number of wrongful termination suits against employers, many human service organizations, depending on state law, provide a statement about the at-will nature of employment. At-will employment means that both you and the organization have the right to terminate the employment relationship at any time with or without cause.

At-will employment does not mean that an agency can fire you because someone doesn't like you, or because you are a woman or person of color, or in retaliation for such actions as whistle-blowing, or because you have filed a sexual harassment complaint. Federal and state laws protect against such firings. However, at-will employment does mean that, within the law, the agency can terminate employment because of budget cuts, program changes, staff retrenchment, or staff reorganization; the job is not guaranteed even when performance has been assessed positively.

To enforce the at-will nature of employment, organizations' personnel policies and procedures handbooks usually refer to "regular" rather than "permanent" employees. Employers avoid implying long-term employment commitments, both in writing and verbally (Himmelberg, 1996).

As long as the organization follows its own policies and procedures, and such policies are consistent with federal, state, and local laws, employment can be terminated. Being consistent with policies and procedures means, for example, that the organization provides the specified notification time for termination, provides severance pay if the policies allow for it, and/or follows grievance procedures as they are set forth. Because the personnel manual is a rule book, this document is extremely important, and it is wise to be familiar with its contents.

A personnel handbook often serves as an employee's introduction to an organization—and to its culture. It alerts workers to the rules and regulations of the organization and, in general, sets the tone for what the employer expects of workers. If workers don't pay close attention to the manual, they risk being uninformed about the guidelines that govern their employment (Ginsberg, 1997d).

Job Benefits

In recent years, the job market has been highly favorable for employees. In the final years of the twentieth century, the national rate of unemployment was at an all-time low. With a booming economy, more and more jobs were created, and there was growth within the human services workforce. The start of the new millennium saw a reversal of circumstances, with waves of job cuts raising the nation's unemployment rate (Brick, 2001). This trend continued through the recession of 2007/2009, in which unemployment reached 10 percent.

Even when the economy was fairly strong, this strength was not necessarily associated with decreased national investment in human services. Prosperity often means more money for human services, even though it is often associated with a decrease in poverty-related social problems. Charitable giving, for example, increases when the economy is strong. When human service organizations are in a position to expand their programs and services, they hire new staff and retain existing staff. The quality and quantity of services offered depend upon a stable and skilled workforce. When there is low unemployment and a shortage of skilled personnel, workers have the incentive to change jobs. To build workforce stability, the organization's management must make special efforts to counter this trend (Umiker, 1999).

At such times, organizations may consider improving the working conditions for their employees. The rationale is that if life can be made easier for employees, there will be less absence or lateness, more productivity, and greater longevity on the job. Findings of a study conducted of changing practices in regard to fringe benefits revealed that there has been a substantial increase in recent years in the number of organizations providing child care. More employers are allowing employees time off to care for dependents; paid time-off programs, which allow employees to combine and use vacation, sick, and personal days, are on the rise; and flexible work hours are becoming more common (Moore, 1998).

Some organizations are extending medical benefits to domestic or nontraditional partners (Ginsberg, 1997b). Other organizations are increasing the amount of flexibility workers may exercise over the use of vacation time, such as trading pay for more time off or selling back unused vacation time to the agency (Ginsberg, 1997a). The operating premise is that agencies can compensate employees without increasing their own expenses, thus enhancing staff morale and increasing staff loyalty.

Job sharing is another accommodation to the needs of employees. In job sharing, two employees split the time and duties of one position. This enables employees to balance the need to earn an income with the need or desire to attend to family responsibilities, and thus it is considered to be a family-oriented policy (Ginsberg, 1997c).

Job sharing is usually left to the employees to arrange, and each situation may have to be negotiated separately, as each situation is unique. Another complication is the need for the job-sharing partners to achieve a high level of cooperation over a long period of time. For these reasons, employers may be hesitant to offer job sharing as an option (Ginsberg, 1997c).

During times of low unemployment, organizations find that they must address an increasing array of workplace concerns and employee needs. As noted, these range from flexible benefits and work-time arrangements to child care provisions. Workers are attracted to organizations that offer substantial benefits in addition to salary; it is not unusual for the level of benefits to be the deciding factor for a worker taking a job and staying in it.

Unions

Some organizations that employ social workers are "union shops," where union contracts govern the conditions of work. Disputes between management and workers usually occur when the labor contract is about to expire and agreement has not been reached over the terms of a new contract. At such times, negotiations become more intense, and often an arbitrator is brought in to facilitate the process. When these efforts fail, a strike may result.

Unionization of human service professional employees occurs less frequently than with other occupational groups, such as airline pilots, hospital support staff, and teachers. Nevertheless, its origins go back to the earliest days of the profession. In the late 1800s, social workers such as Jane Addams and Lillian Wald supported the formation of unions and facilitated alliances between social work and unions (Kolko-Phillips & Straussner, 1988).

Further impetus for social workers to unionize occurred during the Great Depression, primarily as a way to improve working conditions (Rosenberg, 1999). In 1933, for example, a group of Chicago-based public welfare workers joined together to form the Social Service Workers Union. Their concerns included salaries, benefits, working conditions, training, and supervision (Karger, 1989). Social reform issues affecting the larger society were also part of the agenda of social workers' early participation in unions.

The popularity of unions among social workers has waxed and waned. During the 1960s, there was a resurgence of interest in unionization, brought on in part by progressive social programs that emphasized empowerment and political action. This movement was seen as empowering not only client groups but also workers. It was during this decade that public social welfare workers formed their own national union, the National Federation of Social Service Employees. Local unions, such as the Social Service Employees Union in New York, the Independent Union of Public Aid Employees in Chicago, and the Welfare Employees Union in Detroit, experienced a high level of member participation and sought improved working conditions, better training, and better quality of services to clients (Rosenberg, 1999). Most recently, in 1998, the Clinical Social Work Federation became affiliated with the Office and Professional Employees International Union, AFL-CIO. This affiliation was caused by the threat posed to the profession by managed care organizations and a desire for more political clout (Krackow, 1998). Unions have been touted as a powerful means to help social workers maintain professional standards of care and protect working conditions, including wages and job security (Fisher & Karger, 1997). In 2004, 20 percent of the 562,000 social workers in the United States were members of a union, usually through their place of employment (U.S. Bureau of Labor Statistics, 2006).

Although unionization of social workers in select settings has been, to some extent, successful, it remains a controversial issue within the profession. Questions center around the compatibility of professional values and union membership (Kelly, 1992). The primary obligation of a professional is to the client. Collective bargaining, on the other hand, concerns the work conditions that primarily affect the worker (though not exclusively, as when union contracts specify caseload size). Unions have also been seen as introducing an additional level of bureaucracy and creating an adversarial relationship with administrators (Fisher & Karger, 1997).

Despite such concerns, the *Code of Ethics* (National Association of Social Workers, 1999) acknowledges and supports the involvement of social workers in unions: "Social workers may engage in organized action, including the formation of and participation in labor unions, to improve the services to clients and working conditions" (p. 22). However, this acknowledgment is also accompanied by an admonition:

> The action of social workers who are involved in labor-management disputes, job actions, or labor strikes should be guided by the professional's values, ethical principles, and ethical standards. Reasonable differences of opinion exist among social workers concerning their primary obligation as professionals during an actual or threatened labor strike or job action. Social workers should carefully examine relevant issues and their possible impact on clients before deciding on a course of action. (National Association of Social Workers, 1999, p. 22)

Areas of common ground certainly exist between organized labor and professional social work practice. Unions can be an important medium for empowering both client and worker and for focusing public attention on social issues (Fisher & Karger, 1997).

Key Points

- ◆ Workplace rules ensure both uniformity and continuity in how the work of the organization is carried out.
- ◆ Formal conditions of work are set forth in a personnel policies and procedures manual.
- ◆ Despite protective laws, discrimination on the basis of race and gender in regard to promotion and salary persists.
- ◆ As new social problems and concerns emerge, organizations have adapted their policies to address such workplace issues as violence, drug use and abuse, and sexual harassment.
- ◆ The work environment has grown more relaxed in terms of dress codes; however, workers' attire can send important messages to clients.
- ◆ Many states now have at-will employment, which negates the notion of permanent employment.
- ◆ When unemployment is low, organizations take a harder look at benefit packages to attract workers and retain their workforce.
- ◆ An increasing number of organizations are offering flexible time arrangements, child care assistance, job sharing, and extension of benefits to nontraditional partners.

◆ Some human service organizations are union shops; union contracts govern the conditions of work.

◆ The popularity of unions among social workers has waxed and waned, and unionization remains a controversial issue.

Suggested Learning Activities and Discussion Questions

1. Locate and read your organization's personnel policies and procedures manual. In a paragraph or two, give an overview of the key policies governing your employment. Are there any provisions that surprise you? Are there provisions that you consider unfair?

2. Review the case vignette in box 8.6 concerning conflict of interest. Do you agree with Jennifer's justifications? What ethical issues can you identify? What would you do if you were in Jennifer's place? What would you do if you were Jennifer's supervisor?

3. If you found out that your salary was lower than that of another staff member for what you considered comparable work responsibilities, what recourse would you have? What would you do?

4. What do you see as the benefits and limitations of unionization of social workers? Would you support unionization in your place of employment? If so, what do you think a union could accomplish?

Recommended Readings

Brody, R. (2005). *Effectively managing human service organizations* (3rd ed.). Thousand Oaks, CA: Sage Publications.

Burstein, P. (Ed.). (1994). *Equal employment opportunity: Labor market discrimination and public policy*. New York: Aldine de Gruyter.

Glass Ceiling Commission. (1995). *Good for business: Making full sense of the nation's human capital*. Washington, DC: U.S. Department of Labor.

Odendahl, T., & O'Neill, M. (Eds.). (1994). *Women and power in the nonprofit sector*. San Francisco: Jossey-Bass.

Skrentny, J. D. (Ed.). (1998). *Affirmative action: Dynamics of policy development*. Thousand Oaks, CA: Sage Publications.

U.S. Equal Employment Opportunity Commission. (1991). *The Americans with Disabilities Act: Your responsibilities as an employer*. Washington, DC: Author.

References

Affirmative Action and Diversity Project. (1998). Available: http://ucsb.edu/projects/aa/pages/news.html

Bagues, M. F., & Esteve-Volart, B. (2010). Can gender parity break the glass ceiling: Evidence from a repeated randomized experiment. *The Review of Economic Studies, 77*(4), 1301–1328.

Becker, R. (1961). *Study of salaries of NASW members*. New York: National Association of Social Workers.

Brick, M. (2001, September 7). Unemployment rate rises to four-year high in August. *New York Times*. Available: http://www.nytimes.com/2001/09/07/business/07CND-ECON.html

Burstein, P. (Ed.). (1994). *Equal employment opportunity*. New York: Aldine de Gruyter.

DiNitto, D. M., & McNeece, C.A. (2008). *Social work: Issues and opportunities in a challenging profession* (3rd ed.) Chicago: Lyceum Books.

Fisher, R., & Karger, H. J. (1997). *Social work and community in a private world: Getting out in public*. New York: Addison-Wesley Longman.

Fortune, A. E., & Hanks, L. L. (1988). Gender inequities in early social work careers. *Social Work, 33*, 221-226.

General Accounting Office. (1995). *Equal opportunity employment: Women and minority representation at Interior, Agriculture, Navy, and State*. Document #GGD-95-211. Washington, DC: U.S. Government Printing Office.

Gibelman, M. (1999). Taking a stand on affirmative action: A social justice perspective. *Journal of Sociology and Social Welfare, 27*(1), 153-174.

Gibelman, M. (2000). The nonprofit sector and gender discrimination: A preliminary investigation into the glass ceiling. *Journal of Nonprofit Management & Leadership, 10*(3), 251-269.

Gibelman, M. (2002). So how far have we come? The pestilent and persistent gender gap in pay. *Affilia: Journal of Women and Social Work, 17*(3), 279-298.

Gibelman, M., & Schervish, P. H. (1997). *Who we are: A second look*. Washington, DC: NASW Press.

Ginsberg, S. (1997a, July 6). In today's quest for compensation, money isn't everything; companies find that flexible benefits, stock and other alternatives to pay raises can keep employee morale up, expenses down. *Washington Post*, p. H5.

Ginsberg, S. (1997b, August 14). More companies reaching out with gay-friendly policies; domestic partners gain momentum in light labor markets. *Washington Post*, p. H4.

Ginsberg, S. (1997c, October 26). When half a job is better than one; despite some problems, employees with family needs choose to share duties to increase flexibility. *Washington Post*, p. H4.

Ginsberg, S. (1997d, November 30). To know the rules of work, a little manual dexterity is crucial. *Washington Post*, p. H4.

Glass Ceiling Commission. (1995). *Good for business: Making full sense of the nation's human capital*. Washington, DC: U.S. Department of Labor.

Gunderson, M. (1994). Male-female wage differentials and policy responses. In P. Burstein (Ed.), *Equal employment opportunity: Labor market discrimination and public policy* (pp. 207-227). New York: Aldine de Gruyter.

Guy, M. E. (1993). Three steps forward, two steps backward: The status of women's integration into public management. *Public Administration Review, 53*(4), 285-293.

Himmelberg, M. (1996, February 18). The finer points of firing. *Washington Post*, p. H4.

Huber, R., & Orlando, B. P. (1995). Persisting gender differences in social workers' incomes: Does the profession really care? *Social Work, 40*(5), 585-591.

Jennings, V.T. (1993, May 5). NIH director concedes discrimination at agency. *Washington Post*, p. A7.

Karger, H. J. (1989). The common and conflicting goals of labor and social work. *Administration in Social Work, 13*(1), 1-17.

Kelly, M. (1992). Are union membership and professional social work compatible? In E. Gambrill & R. Pruger (Eds.), *Controversial issues in social work* (pp. 13-26). Needham Heights, MA: Allyn & Bacon.

Kolko-Phillips, N., & Straussner, L.A. (1988).The relationship between social work and labor unions:A history of strife and cooperation. *Journal of Sociology & Social Welfare, 15,* 105-118.

Krackow, H. H. (1998). Clinical social work joins the national guild of medical providers. *The Clinician, 29*(2), 1, 11.

Lalive, R., & Stutzer,A. (2010).Approval of equal rights and gender differences in well-being. *Journal of Population Economics, 23*(3), 933-962.

Moore, K. (1998, February 15).The value of benefits. *Washington Post*, p. H7.

National Association of Social Workers. (1996). *Code of ethics.*Washington, DC:Author.

Pecora, P. J. (1995). Personnel management. In R. L. Edwards (Ed.-in-chief). *Encyclopedia of social work* (19th ed., pp. 1828-1836).Washington, DC: NASW Press.

Pecora, P. J., & Wagner, M. (2000). Managing personnel. In R. J. Patti (Ed.), *The handbook of social welfare management* (pp. 395-423).Thousand Oaks, CA: Sage Publications.

Pincus, W. (1994, September 9). CIA and the "glass ceiling" secret. *Washington Post*, p. A25.

Rosenberg, J. (1999). *An investigation of the participation of social workers in unions.* Unpublished manuscript. New York:Yeshiva University,Wurzweiler School of Social Work.

Swaboda, F. (1996a, January 28). More managers are discovering that a casual dress code can improve morale and attract employees. *Washington Post*, p. H4.

Swaboda, F. (1996b, March 10). States, not Congress, pioneer new directions in labor law. *Washington Post*, p. H5.

Umiker, W. (1999). Principles of workforce stability. *Health Care Management, 18*(2), 58-64.

U.S. Bureau of Labor Statistics. (2006). *Social workers.*Available: http://www.bls.gov/oco/ocos060.htm

U.S. Merit Systems Protection Board. (1992). *A question of equity:Women and the glass ceiling in the federal government.*Washington, DC: U.S. Government Printing Office.

Wells, R. M., & Idelson, H. (1995, March 18). Panel will examine effects of affirmative action. *Congressional Quarterly, 53*(11), 819-820.

Chapter 9

The Changing Environment of Organizations

Some of the internal dynamics that can affect the organizational environment have been identified in previous chapters. Finances, for example, can be a potent force in determining the scope of work of an organization, as well as the conditions under which work is carried out. In this chapter, some of the external forces affecting the work of human service organizations are discussed.

Just as the organization defines the boundaries of social work practice, the larger sociopolitical and economic environment influences the role and functions of the organization. These roles and functions change over time. Because of the volatility of the external environment, there are few constants in organizational life.

The Organization as an Open System

The organization's environment has a significant influence on how it functions, what it does, who it serves, and what services it provides. The external environment is all the conditions outside the organization that affect its functioning (Schmid, 2000). Relevant players include funding sources, policy makers, volunteers, clients, and the community (Burke, 2011; Weiner, 1990). The strength of such influence varies along a continuum and may be molded by different factors. For example, the for-profit sector is subject to the influences of the marketplace and consumer choice. Public agencies are particularly vulnerable to changes in public priorities and social policy.

All human service organizations must be responsive to their environment if they are to survive and flourish. Organizations often have little control over many of the external conditions that affect them, such as technological change, culture, the economy, the labor market, and prevailing sociopolitical viewpoints and priorities (Schmid, 2000).

Demands on human service organizations from the external environment include cost controls, the use of time-limited outcome-oriented interventions, and accountability to various constituent groups and the general public for quality, effectiveness, and efficiency of services. A human service agency that remains steadfast in its commitment to the provision of long-term psychotherapeutically oriented services and that has not instituted accountability measures or quality controls, for example, is going to find itself at odds with its environment. This may result in loss of clients and revenue and may threaten the continuation of agency operations. At times, agencies consciously assume such risks in order to adhere to their core values. Social workers and social work supervisors are encouraged to engage others in their agency in open and supportive dialogues about these serious dilemmas. While maintaining, expanding, or changing the mission of an organization is often viewed as the role of the board of directors or the CEO, this is not necessarily the case. Social workers are often the ones who have the most contact with the agency's clients and communities and are important players in the evolving role of the organization. For this reason, organizations that have open collaborative systems of communication and management may be able to adapt more quickly to environmental changes (Lewis, Packard, & Lewis, 2007). Listening to and valuing the views of those closest to clients has long been recognized as important to the success of many different types of organizations and may be particularly important in a rapidly changing global arena (Furman, 2010; Prigoff, 2000).

Changing Public Policies

Public policies have a substantial influence on the scope of the services provided by human service organizations. Each time a new law concerning human well-being is passed or an existing law is reauthorized, human service organizations are affected. Federal and state legislation has prompted not only new programs but also the creation of new organizations to address such problems and issues as domestic violence, refugee resettlement, homelessness, and reintegration of institutionalized persons into the community. Changing public policies can also mean the end of an organization. For example, because of deinstitutionalization, many residential facilities were closed. The external environment thus provides the legitimacy and resources an organization requires to maintain itself (Burke, 2011; Schmid, 2000).

Social policies may lead to the establishment of programs to meet the needs of specific populations. For example, the enactment of such national social welfare legislation as the Adoption Assistance and Child Welfare Act of 1980 (P.L. 96-272) encouraged permanency planning and family preservation. The Stewart B. McKinney Homeless Assistance Act of 1987 (P.L. 100-77) was the first major federal initiative to address the problem of homelessness as not just a need for housing but also a need for services ranging from mental health to substance abuse treatment. The Americans with Disabilities Act of 1990 (P.L. 101-336) furthered the rights of people with disabilities. These acts resulted in new and expanded roles for human service organizations. Laws such as these targeted specific areas of social need, often extending the reach of government-sponsored programs to previously unserved or underserved populations.

Two examples of the changing nature of social policies are welfare reform and the most recent child welfare law.

Welfare Reform

The economic recession of the early 1990s resulted in more people joining the ranks of the poor and more people on welfare; the welfare rolls grew by 25 percent during this period (Lens, 2000). The abolishment of Aid to Families with Dependent Children (AFDC) in 1996 and its replacement with Temporary Assistance for Needy Families (TANF), subsumed under the Personal Responsibility and Work Opportunity Reconciliation Act of 1996 (P.L. 104–193), turned welfare into a highly restrictive block-grant program that limited aid to five years, required states to place recipients in the workforce, and mandated penalties against states and recipients for noncompliance (National Association of Social Workers, 1999; Super, Parrott, Steinmetz, & Mann, 1996).

Welfare reform holds many implications for the work of human service organizations. *Entitlement* is no longer the operative word for the public welfare system. States are free to redesign their service systems to reflect local conditions and preferences. Public welfare agencies have had to revamp their procedures and operations to administer an entirely different program, with new rules for eligibility determination, duration of benefits, and enforcement of work provisions and sanctions. In the long term, such public agencies are likely to curtail some of their operations as the number of TANF recipients drops.

Nonprofit agencies that have provided programs of service to welfare recipients, such as job training, day care, counseling, and financial management, have also had to alter their programs to meet the mandates of welfare reform. Emphasis is almost exclusively on reducing dependency by helping people to become self-sufficient through employment. This means initiating or expanding welfare-to-work programs. Kilborn (1996) noted: "For the children of penalized parents, Congress has a last resort: an unlimited budget to put them in foster homes" (p. E3). The consequences of welfare reform may well lead to new socioeconomic needs among clients of human service organizations.

Child Welfare

The Adoption and Safe Families Act of 1997 (ASFA; P.L. 105–89) modified the landmark Adoption Assistance and Child Welfare Act of 1980 (AACWA; P.L. 96–272). The AACWA spurred the permanency planning movement, the goal of which was to return children in foster care to their natural families or free them for adoption if families were unable to assume care within a reasonable period of time (Brissett-Chapman, 1995). No definition was provided of "reasonable effort" to achieve permanency. This act substantially altered the way child welfare organizations provided services to children and families, with permanency planning replacing the more open-ended reunification goals of the past. Programs were redesigned to reflect this new emphasis.

The ASFA was enacted in response to the perceived weaknesses of the AACWA. Under the new law, reasonable efforts are no longer required under certain circumstances, such as when the separation of a child from the family has occurred because of abandonment, torture, chronic abuse, or sexual abuse

(Blanchard, 1999).The new goal is the promotion of adoption of children in foster care; a main tenet of the law is the primacy of the child's health and safety. The change of goals once again created a need to change the focus of organizational programs.

ASFA, like welfare reform, affords the states substantial latitude. For example, it is largely up to each state to define "reasonable efforts." The definition used by each state, in turn, affects the way in which organizations approach the scope of work involved in carrying out ASFA mandates. Depending on the definition used, organizations providing services under ASFA may require varying numbers of family contact hours and duration and intensity of services and may have different benchmarks to measure the outcomes of interventions.

ASFA also reduced the time frame for the first permanency hearing from eighteen months under AACWA to fifteen of the previous twenty-two months to move children in foster care more quickly into permanent homes, specifically adoptive homes (Blanchard, 1999). One implication is that practitioners of organizations providing foster care services need to work faster to achieve reunification or to substantiate the legal termination of parental rights.Time limits intensify worker contact with all involved in the case to ensure rapid implementation of the case plan.

Human service organizations that contract with state agencies to implement foster care programs must "buy in" to the time limitations involved, even if they run counter to what may be considered the best interests of the child and family.Agencies, in fact, may be encouraged to seek an adoptive placement for a child concurrent with the efforts to reunite a child with the natural family (Blanchard, 1999). Ethical dilemmas such as these affect the provision of services and how they are "lived" by social workers.

Impact of Policy Shifts

Each public policy shift alters the nature of the tasks and responsibilities delegated to human service organizations. Public agencies and for-profit or nonprofit organizations under contract are also subject to annual legislative budget allocations, which may forestall or enhance the types of resources available to serve client populations.Within this climate, agency staff may be unsure about the goals and priorities of their work.Appointed officials, such as commissioners or, in the case of nonprofits, CEOs, may have their own agenda. Long-term employees, on the other hand, are a powerful force in organizational maintenance and protecting the status quo. Often it is the workers who determine the extent to which new ways of operating and new program priorities are realized.

Managed Care

Managed care has become a central philosophy and organizing theme for the delivery of health and human services. Managed care has been defined by the U.S. Department of Health and Human Services as an organized system of care that attempts to balance access, quality, and cost effectiveness by using intensive case management, provider selection, and cost containment methodologies (Moss, 1995). Managed care is an attempt to control what has come to be perceived as uncontrollable health care and service costs.

Managed care has spawned a new type of organization—the managed care organization, which manages and controls the cost and quality of health and mental health care. MCOs include health maintenance organizations, preferred provider organizations, competitive medical plans, and managed indemnity-insurance programs. Some of these are nonprofit organizations; others are for-profit. While much has been made in political arenas about the Obama administration's health care policies, in truth very little about the structural nature of health care will change. While legislation that expands health care coverage should mean that more poor Americans can obtain coverage, the actual nature of health care organizations is unlikely to change. In fact, many of these newly covered people will have their care provided for by various types of MCOs (Barr, 2011). Additionally, states and the federal government must find ways of paying for this expansion, a tough task given the lack of political will during an election year and continued concern over the economy and the growing national debt.

Adaptations by Health and Human Service Organizations

Health and human service organizations and the social workers within them have had to learn quickly the business of managed care, including its technicalities, reimbursement systems, and legal and regulatory requirements. Organizations have had to train personnel to understand the complexities of managed care, to maintain case records to meet MCO record-keeping procedures, and to modify interventions to comply with a short-term behavioral-oriented treatment focus. Such organizational retooling involves significant costs to the organization and the potential for deviation from agency mission (Meezan & McBeath, 2011; Siskind, 1997).

Intervention methods are dictated by limits on reimbursable care, such as limitations on the number of visits that are covered. In addition, some MCOs have introduced standardized preferred practice guidelines and protocols that indicate the preferred practices or interventions to use to address a particular client problem (Mitchell, 1998), effectively limiting the freedom of agency staff to tailor services. The agency must balance these external requirements against the needs of the clients served (Gibelman & Whiting, 1999).

Another effect of managed care is the increased competition among agencies for access to the few available slots on provider panels. Human service agencies must apply for provider status, which sometimes includes all eligible employees by category (e.g., those who have an MSW and are licensed) if permitted by the MCO or may be on an employee-by-employee basis. When the MCO provider panels are full—that is, when the MCO has enough practitioners to whom to refer clients—new applicants are closed out.

Focus on Results

Managed care has brought with it heightened demands for accountability, with particular emphasis on documenting the successful outcomes of service. Requirements to demonstrate the effectiveness of treatment and achievement of planned outcomes are now a component of most MCO contracts, as these companies look for results-oriented data. Human service organizations, as part of the culture of the helping professions, have traditionally been oriented to understanding and describing process rather than documenting goals and outcomes. Now, human service organizations must be able to document that the services provided result in achievement of the goals detailed in the service plan, with a positive effect on client well-being, circumstances, self-management, and/or recovery.

These demands require the staff to acquire new skills, including negotiating with MCOs to become approved service providers, maintaining record-keeping systems, and measuring intervention outcomes. Expertise in conflict resolution is also a required skill, particularly in mediating conflicts between the client and the MCO (Galambos, 1999; Strom-Gottfried, 1998).

The two sides of the power equation in the relationship between MCOs and human service organizations are far from equal. Insurance companies and MCOs have formal authority and resource power (Strom-Gottfried, 1998). If agencies do not offer what the MCO seeks, the MCO will simply go elsewhere. A number of studies have addressed means of organizational survival within the managed care environment (see, for example, Corcoran & Vandiver, 1996; Emenhiser, Barker, & DeWoody, 1995).

Despite the many vocal critics of managed care and the likelihood that Congress will at some time act to curtail some of the most flagrant flaws in the system, the importance of cost containment is not likely to abate. We have already begun to witness the extension of managed care models into new service arenas, such as family and child welfare (Feild, 1996). Experiments with capitation (a uniform fee) for foster and group home care, intended to motivate more rapid permanency planning, have been implemented on a selective basis (Petr & Johnson, 1999). This suggests that a growing number and types of human service organizations will be working with managed care companies.

Changing Patterns of Service Delivery

Individual responsibility, privatization, local control, and smaller government are dominant themes that provide the framework for the social service delivery system of the new millennium. In combination, they suggest the magnitude of the accommodations demanded on the part of human service organizations (Lens & Gibelman, 2000).

These themes have been actualized primarily through two primary means. The first is cash transfers from the federal government to state and local governments to implement programs, which allow states to design programs to meet specific local needs and preferences. In this devolution process, the federal government maintains some fiscal responsibility but may demand that states contribute higher levels of funds. This is particularly problematic as states struggle to balance their budgets in the current economic context. In 2011, the vast majority of states had to cut their budgets in response to the global economic downturn. The second means is the use of the private marketplace to deliver human services, commonly known as privatization. Privatization is an all-encompassing term with many variations, from total abdication of a government role to heavy government financial subsidization of the private sector (Gibelman, 1998). Privatization is predicated on the widespread belief that the private sector can do things better (qualitatively), at lesser cost, and more efficiently than the public sector (Steen & Duran, 2010).

An intermediary step in privatization widely used within the human services is purchase of service. Here, the government retains a primary role in service funding but delegates, through contracting, service delivery responsibility to the private sector (Gibelman, 1995).

Promoting Competition

For many years, nonprofit organizations held a virtual monopoly in the delivery of contracted services. For-profits were largely out of the running, because of statutory limitations and because many businesses did not believe that there was a profit to be made. Nonprofit organizations have a long contractual history with public agencies, and their track record in delivering publicly funded services has both positive and negative aspects. The positive aspect is their long history and experience with delivering services. The negative aspect is that nonprofit organizations have tended to take on some of the bureaucratic features that typify the public agencies. Gradually, for-profits have been entering the human services market as legislative restrictions have been removed.

The 1996 welfare reform act was a major impetus to the burgeoning role of for-profits in the human services. Through successful lobbying, for-profit representatives were able to influence a one-word change in the sweeping welfare reform legislation; this was the deletion of the word *nonprofit* in regard to eligible providers of service. For-profits instantly became eligible for the billions of dollars spent annually for services to children, including mental health services such as residential and outpatient care (Bernstein, 1997). The expansion of for-profit organizations' involvement in human services is part of a larger global movement toward privatization. Leading international organizations such as the International Monetary Fund and the World Bank encourage all nations to engage in what is known as "structural adjustment"—the privatization of most government services (Shandra, Shircliff, & London, 2011). As one of the principal sources of financing for these organizations, the United States government, perhaps paradoxically, is part of a global movement toward privatization and a diminished role of government in human services.

Competition between nonprofit and for-profit organizations for the same contracts has put pressure on nonprofits to become more entrepreneurial. One result has been a growing number of mergers and nonprofit and for-profit partnerships. Not all nonprofits have been able to compete successfully. For-profits, in general, have more operating capital and a greater ability to expand their service offerings quickly to meet demand.

For public agencies, the large-scale entrance of for-profits in the human service business has created a greatly expanded number and type of potential service deliverers from which to choose, while nonprofits faced uncertain competition from these new providers. At the same time, the independence of for-profit agencies has decreased, because a lower proportion of their revenues comes solely from fee-for-service and a higher proportion comes from government funding.

Reductions in Government Funding

The history of U.S. social welfare policy shows a consistent pattern of ambivalence about long-term commitments to social programs for vulnerable populations. Threats and the actuality of funding cuts and program retrenchment are not new to human service agencies, their personnel, and their clients. Because the vast majority of human service organizations receive a portion of their funding from government grants and contracts, they are subject to the changing tides of public policy priorities and shifting budget allocations.

The decrease in federal dollars for contracting, the increase in state decision making about fiscal expenditures, the decline of state revenues due to the recession of 2007/2009, the move to privatization, and the evolution of a cost containment philosophy actualized through managed care have combined to create a substantially different environment for human service organizations. These conditions of change suggest uncertainty and insecurity among all levels of personnel regarding organizational stability, and they entail modifications in the primary service focus, types of programs offered, operating mode, and management style of human service organizations.

Consumerism

With growing momentum, the word *consumerism* has crept into the business world, including the business of human services. Consumerism is "a social movement and orientation designed to advocate for and protect the interests of people in their roles as users of services or commodities and to scrutinize the activities, skills, training, effectiveness, outcomes, and products of those who provide these goods or services" (Barker, 1999, p. 101).

Consumerism has its roots in the social movements of the 1960s when groups representing people with mental illness and disabilities, women, older adults, people receiving public benefits such as welfare, and others began to challenge the systems designed to serve them. Rejecting paternalism, in which professionals identified client needs and the services to respond to them, the consumer movement advocated the rights of individuals and groups to self-determination and independence. In social work, this movement led to more consumer-oriented services. Barker (1999) defines consumer-centered social work as "an orientation by social work practitioners that places a high value on the self-determination of the client and emphasizes those intervention strategies that encourage client independence, self-advocacy, and self-judgment in negotiating the social services of the welfare system" (p. 101).

Having a consumer orientation means that a human service organization must constantly evaluate the needs of the community and of actual and potential clients. Client needs—needs of individuals, families, and groups—guide the organization in the design and delivery of its services. The agency must be open and responsive to changes in community needs, as shown in some examples of operating principles and performance standards listed in box 9.1.

BOX 9.1
Consumerism: Principles and Practice

Operating Principle	*The Principle in Action*
The defined purpose of the agency is to be responsive to the needs of individuals, families, and groups in its community.	The agency's written mission or purpose statement is formally reviewed at least every four years in light of changing community needs.
Planning and community collaboration are continually refocused to center on the needs and desires of current and potential consumers.	The agency provides both formal and informal opportunities for consumer input in designing and reshaping existing services to better meet consumer needs.
Potential consumers, referral sources, and cooperating organizations understand the agency's capacities, availability, and the means required or available to pay for those services.	Consumers are provided with information about the agency's services that enables them to make an informed choice about the use of the service and the right to receive service in a noncoercive manner that protects their right to self-determination.
The services of the agency are offered promptly and responsively, taking into account client needs and demands.	Every effort is made to provide or refer for service at the point the person seeks help through the agency.
Consumers are able to obtain services without encountering discrimination, insensitivity to cultural differences, and physical or other barriers.	Outreach, intake, and service delivery processes are periodically reexamined to ensure the absence of barriers that prevent access to services; the agency is proactive in providing or arranging for assistance in communication for people with special needs.
The agency works in partnership with consumers and the community to achieve access to education, intervention, work opportunities, economic security, transportation, housing, and other community supports, as these affect and are needed by significant numbers of those served.	Case-and-cause advocacy are built into all programs and services of the agency.

Source: Adapted from Council on Accreditation of Services for Families and Children (1997).

Accountability

Public demand for accountability continues to grow, and public and nonprofit organizations delivering human services have not been exempt from these demands. Accountability is defined broadly as "the extent to which an organization is answerable to its community, the consumers of service, and/or to governing bodies, such as a board of directors, for its processes and outcomes" (Council on Accreditation, 1997, p. 5).

The emphasis on accountability can be seen in the increased importance that funding bodies are placing on demonstrating the outcomes of services. Government, private foundations, and managed care companies are demanding greater performance accountability (Martin, 2000). Human service organizations are being called on to document and prove the quality and cost effectiveness of the services they provide and to demonstrate that these services are changing the lives of people. Performance accountability is now codified in the Government Performance & Results Act of 1993 (P.L. 103–62), and states also have their own sets of administrative procedures (Melkers & Willoughby, 1998). Nonprofit organizations, too, have recognized the need to reinvent themselves to increase productivity, enhance services, manage costs, and improve performance.

As the call for accountability has gained momentum, human service organizations have had to develop measurement systems and procedures (Herman & Renz, 1999; Martin & Kettner, 1996; Mullen & Magnabosco, 1997; Poole, Davis, Reisman, & Nelson, 2001). Managed care companies have been helpful in providing protocols for measuring outcomes and have development procedures that service-providing agencies are expected to follow. Such procedures are sometimes greeted by direct service workers with mixed feelings. Clearly, more paperwork is involved. Workers may feel that some requirements are unnecessary and not useful. At the same time, human service professionals recognize the importance of assessing the extent to which interventions produce desired results.

Under the best of circumstances, accountability is a complex concept and, in practice, difficult to achieve. In addition to the issues inherent in establishing accountability systems, including the development of performance measures, accountability demands come from different sources, each with its own requirements.

Consider the relationship of nonprofit organizations to government. A nonprofit agency may receive funding to serve clients eligible under Medicaid and Medicare. Some clients may receive their Medicaid or Medicare benefits through managed care companies, each of which has its own reporting requirements. The same nonprofit agency may have contracts to serve targeted populations through the state human service agency, Housing and Urban Development, the State Office of Education, and the Department of Justice. Each funding source may demand its own form of accountability for services provided and money spent. Multiple funding streams mean multiple accountability systems.

Other funding sources for nonprofits, such as United Way, individual contributors, foundations, and third-party payers, have different expectations and demands. Public agencies are accountable to the local, state, or federal legislative bodies and to citizens, whose taxes fund their work. For-profit agencies are accountable to their stockholders.

Accountability goes beyond the financial realm. Nonprofit organizations are accountable to their respective boards of directors in regard to achieving organizational goals and, in the process, complying with established program priorities. The Internal Revenue Service has its own set of rules and regulations. In addition, watchdog agencies, such as the Better Business Bureau, also have standards of performance for charitable organizations. Substantial time and effort must be devoted by the organization to meeting these accountability demands.

One of the hallmarks of the past decade is the growing trend of litigating disputes and grievances and the increasing involvement of the courts and state and federal legislatures in how and how well human services are organized, delivered, and evaluated (Tremper, 1994). Within the context of a litigious society, human service organizations are increasing vulnerable to charges such as negligence, breach of duty through acts of omission or commission, conflict of interest, failure to uphold confidentiality, abrogation of privileged communication, violation of informed consent, poor quality of service, and unorthodox treatment (Besharov, 1985; Gelman, 1995; Gibelman, Gelman, & Pollack, 1997).

Human service organizations have responded to the demands for increasing accountability and decreasing liability by instituting risk management procedures. Risk management refers to the policies, procedures, and processes of an organization designed to reduce the chances of liability exposure. In order to manage risk, the organization must conduct its business according to sound financial practices and applicable laws, regulations, and professional requirements (Gibelman & Gelman, 1999). When risk management strategies are successful, the organization is more accountable to its various stockholders.

Quality Control

Under the rubric of accountability is the process of quality improvement. Recently, while visiting a chocolate factory in Switzerland, I observed what I considered to be the ultimate in quality control: a man sat at the end of the automated assembly line and checked each bar of chocolate for imperfections. Any chocolate bar that was not perfectly shaped or that contained any markings was discarded. Similar controls exist in most industries that produce goods, from automobiles to T-shirts. We often see a product marked "imperfect" or "second," meaning that it has not met the standards of the manufacturer, and we can buy it at a reduced cost.

Checking for imperfections in chocolate bars or a set of linens now has its equivalent processes in the human services. These are known as continuous quality improvement processes. Through such processes, human service organizations evaluate the effectiveness and efficiency of the services provided, determine whether these services meet predetermined expectations about quality and outcomes, and, with this information, correct any deficiencies identified (Council on Accreditation, 1997).

What exactly is quality improvement? The Council on Accreditation (1997) defines quality improvement as an ongoing process in which the organization:

◆ Allocates appropriate resources, equipment, and personnel to accomplish the purposes stated in its mission

◆ Has clearly defined policies and procedures to guide staff responsible for service provision

◆ Has a well defined plan for anticipating, correcting, and ameliorating problems (p. 6)

Quality improvement is predicated on a clear delineation by the organization of the desired expectations and service outcomes for each of its programs. An organization's approach to continuous quality improvement is usually expressed in a set of procedures or plans that detail the objectives and scope of the activity, the methods of monitoring and reporting the results, and follow-up mechanisms, as well as the person, position, or committee responsible for these efforts. Box 9.2 illustrates one agency's approach to continuous quality improvement.

The Inevitability of Change

The only certainty for human service organizations today is that the external environment will continue to change, with consequent pressure to adapt operating modes and program emphases. To adapt to external demands, the organization must operate as an open system, aware of and sensitive to the implications of legislative, judicial, and budgetary change, as well as changes in consumer needs and desires. An organization that is attuned to sociopolitical currents is in a better position to anticipate change and to prepare for it. Such an organization will also be better situated to influence the course of change.

A positive spin on the impact of external change is that the organization, because of its need to adapt, is stimulated to learn, which in turn may result in greater innovations (Schmid, 2000). The degree to which creativity and innovation result from ongoing adaptations depends, in part, on the intensity of the external demands for change. Organizations, in general, are better able to innovate when it comes to initiating or expanding programs of service, rather than reorienting or terminating programs.

Many of the external influences are felt throughout the organization in programs, funding, rules and regulations for how services are carried out, and even the type of people who are hired to do the organization's work. These externally induced changes are a product of the changing context of human services, and they are ongoing. Human service organizations accommodate

BOX 9.2
Sample Quality Improvement Plan

Purpose

To ensure the quality of service provided by Hollywood Mental Health Clinic (HMHC), the agency establishes and maintains a continuous quality improvement process that is anticipatory and prospective and that emphasizes the ongoing involvement of persons served (through consumer satisfaction surveys or other means), the board of directors, and all personnel. The purpose of this process is to systematically:
 ◆ Evaluate the effectiveness and efficiency of the services provided
 ◆ Determine whether the services meet predetermined expectations about quality and outcome
 ◆ Correct any identified deficiencies

   To ensure that the quality assurance function is carried out in a comprehensive, agency-wide, and ongoing manner, HMHC utilizes several distinct but interrelated components and multiple sources of information. The quality improvement process is designed and implemented with input from consumers of service, the board of directors, personnel, and, as applicable, volunteers. Case review and monitoring of services are carried out by those involved in the delivery of the service, while utilization review is the responsibility of management. The overall quality assurance program is under the jurisdiction of the board of directors.

Delegation of Responsibility

To accomplish these purposes, the board of directors designates responsibility to a Quality Assurance Committee composed of:
 ◆ Three members of the board's Professional Services Committee
 ◆ The executive director and/or a senior staff designee

Roles and Responsibilities

The Quality Assurance Committee is responsible for carrying out and coordinating quality improvement process activities, including:
 ◆ Objectives and scope of the activity
 ◆ Methods of monitoring
 ◆ Reporting of results
 ◆ Follow-up mechanisms

The Committee devises means to monitor and considers findings related to:
 ◆ The degree to which the organization's services continue to be relevant and needed by consumers
 ◆ The existing services provided by others in the community to meet those needs that are related to achieving the purposes of the organization
 ◆ Gaps in the array of services needed by the defined community

(continued on next page)

◆ Changing demographics and the needs of new or differing cultural groups, increased community need, overutilization or underutilization, and other reasons indicating a need for a redirection, elimination, and/or expansion of service
◆ Analysis of data collected to determine the organization's responsiveness to community needs and optimal future directions

The Committee conducts the following review processes and integrates the findings into the overall quality improvement process:
◆ Review of research safeguards, when research is carried out by the organization
◆ Review of the use of treatment modalities, with particular scrutiny of those that involve risk or limit freedom of choice
◆ Review of grievances or incidents involving persons served or personnel

The Quality Assurance Committee is further responsible for overseeing, coordinating, and, as appropriate, participating in external reviews conducted by state and county agencies with whom HMHC is contracted.

The Quality Assurance Committee meets on a quarterly basis. In carrying out these committee responsibilities, personnel and board responsibilities are further clarified, as follows.

Professional Services Committee

The committee is composed of three to four members of the board of directors, elected by the board and/or designated by the board president. The responsibilities of this committee are to:
◆ Represent the board of directors on the Quality Assurance Committee and participate fully therein
◆ Review all policies governing the agency's programs and services and make recommendations to the board regarding changes in policies and procedures that will ensure the agency's responsiveness to client and community needs
◆ Review staff- or board-initiated recommendations concerning new programs or special projects and recommend policies to govern their administration and operation
◆ Review the agencies fee policies and structures and make recommendations to the board when changes in the fee structure are considered appropriate
◆ Receive and review utilization reports from personnel and make recommendations for improvements, as needed
◆ Hear grievances of clients not resolved at the staff/management level of review

The Professional Services Committee, on an annual basis or as necessary and appropriate, reports to the full board of directors on the process and outcomes of its work and provides input to the board on its strategic planning regarding:
◆ Short-term goals that support the achievement of the agency's mission and purposes and that allow the organization to flexibly respond to changing needs and adapt to outcome information that requires a corrective response within a time frame of one to two years

(continued on next page)

◆ Long-term goals for the overall continual improvement of the organization's operations and service outcomes

Personnel Responsibilities

The executive director shall, in consultation with the Professional Services Committee, designate personnel to be members of the Utilization Review Committee. The committee shall, at a minimum, be composed of a consulting psychiatrist, the director of Professional Services, the director of Resettlement Services, the director of Older Adult Services, and two members who shall rotate on an annual basis.

Utilization review focuses on:
◆ Appropriateness and effectiveness of services
◆ Necessity and cost effectiveness of continued service to persons served

The internal Utilization Review Committee is responsible for:
◆ Delineating the desired expectations and service outcomes for each of its programs, with a plan on how to achieve them
◆ Developing and implementing objective measurement criteria for admission, for referral, for extended treatment or service, and for changes in status or level of need presented by the person served
◆ Developing measurement systems to track consumers' level of satisfaction with services received and clients' progress toward achievement of service goals
◆ Determining benchmarks or standards for service delivery against which performance levels can be monitored

To accomplish these purposes, the committee establishes a formal planning process with input from all personnel and consumers of service with regard to:
◆ Purpose of the utilization review process
◆ Methods of assessment
◆ Tasks to be carried out
◆ Schedule
◆ Participants in each identified task

This committee will meet at least once quarterly and engage in:
◆ Reviewing the agency's key programs: clinical, older adult, job search, and resettlement
◆ Reviewing procedures for review of individual client care
◆ Ensuring that, in any and all review processes of the agency, such processes are carried out in accord with agency policies and procedures with regard to confidentiality
◆ Ensuring that a utilization review is conducted so that no person involved in the review is in a position of conflict of interest, and all professional disciplines involved in the provision of a service are represented in the review process
◆ Preparing required reports, annually or as often as specified, for the United Way of America

The Utilization Review Committee will maintain written minutes of its meetings and report its findings to the Quality Assurance Committee for review, discussion, and possible action.

external influences through such means as initiating new fund-raising strategies, eliminating some programs and inaugurating others, retraining staff, downsizing operations, and reducing staff size. Externally induced change has a domino effect—it reverberates throughout the organization and stimulates internal changes.

Key Points

- ◆ The human service organization is an open system that is affected by and exerts influence on its external environment.
- ◆ Players in the external environment includes funders, policy makers, clients, and the community.
- ◆ External factors affecting the organization include new or modified social policies, levels and sources of funding, managed care requirements, and accountability demands.
- ◆ Cost containment is the major theme of managed care.
- ◆ MCOs impose restrictions on organizations in regard to the length and type of services that can be provided, with an emphasis on short-term behavior-oriented interventions.
- ◆ MCOs demand that organizations measure and document the outcomes of services, requiring the development of new practitioner skills and organizational procedures.
- ◆ Human service organizations face increasing levels and types of accountability demands from many sources.
- ◆ Outcome measurement processes and tools are relatively undeveloped.
- ◆ Many states have opted to privatize their service systems, relying on nonprofit and, increasingly, for-profit organizations to deliver publicly funded services.
- ◆ Government funding of human services vacillates; in periods of fiscal retrenchment, nonprofit organizations face substantial uncertainty and insecurity.
- ◆ Over the past half century, a consumer orientation has become a potent force in the planning, provision, and evaluation of human services.
- ◆ Human service organizations have instituted quality control procedures to monitor, on an ongoing basis, the effectiveness and efficiency of the services they provide.
- ◆ External change is a constant and ongoing adaptation on the part of human service organizations.

Suggested Learning Activities and Discussion Questions

1. Budget cuts can result when Congress or the state legislature fails to appropriate funds at the requested and expected level. Are you aware of any such budget cuts that have affected the programs of your agency? If you are unsure, ask your supervisor. If budget cuts have affected the

programs run by your agency, what steps were taken to either identify alternative funding or scale back the services provided? What were the implications for the professional staff? For the clients of the agency?
2. Find out if your agency contracts with managed care companies. If the answer is yes, try to obtain information about the contract provisions—how many visits are authorized, what types of services are allowed, what types of records the managed care company requires, and so forth. What are your thoughts—both positive and negative—about these provisions?
3. The people who receive services from human service organizations may be referred to as "clients," "patients," or "consumers." In what way do these terms imply different mind-sets about the people served?
4. You want to know if the services you provide meet standards of quality. For one of the specific services you provide, give a definition of "quality" and identify indicators that would help you, your supervisor, and the agency know that the standard has been reached.

Recommended Readings

Baum, J.A. C., & Singh, J. V. (Eds.). (1994). *Evolutionary dynamics of organizations*. New York: Oxford University Press.

Bryson, J. M. (2011). *Strategic planning for public and nonprofit organizations: A guide to strengthening and sustaining organizational achievement*. New York: John Wiley and Sons.

Corcoran, K., & Vandiver, V. (1996). *Maneuvering the maze of managed care: Skills for mental health practitioners*. New York: Free Press.

Emenhiser, D., Barker, R., & DeWoody, M. (1995). *Managed care: An agency guide to surviving and thriving*. Washington, DC: Child Welfare League of America.

Hatry, H. P. (1999). *Performance measurement: Getting results*. Washington, DC: Urban Institute Press.

Karger, H. J., & Stoesz, D. (1998). *American social welfare policy: A pluralistic approach* (3rd ed.). New York: Longman.

Oster, S. M. (1995). *Strategic management for nonprofit organizations*. New York: Oxford University Press.

Schamess, G., & Lightburn, A. (Eds.). (1998). *Humane managed care?* Washington, DC: NASW Press.

Scott, W. R. (1992). *Organizations, rational, natural, and open systems*. Englewood Cliffs, NJ: Prentice Hall.

References

Barker, R. L. (1999). *Social work dictionary* (4th ed.). Washington, DC: NASW Press.

Barr, D.A. (2011). *Introduction to US health policy: The organization, financing, and delivery of health care in America* (3rd ed.). Baltimore, MD: Johns Hopkins University Press.

Bernstein, N. (1997, May 4). Deletion of word in welfare bill opens foster care to big business. *New York Times*, pp. 1, 26.

Besharov, D. (1985). *The vulnerable social worker*. Silver Spring, MD: National Association of Social Workers.

Blanchard, C. (1999). *Relationship of services and family reunification in New Jersey*. Unpublished Ph.D. dissertation. New York: Yeshiva University, Wurzweiler School of Social Work.

Brissett-Chapman, S. (1995). Child abuse and neglect: Direct practice. In R. L. Edwards (Ed.-in-chief), *Encyclopedia of social work* (19th ed., pp. 353–366). Washington, DC: NASW Press.

Burke, W. W. (2011). *Organizational change: Theory and practice* (3rd ed.). Thousand Oaks, CA: Sage.

Corcoran, K., & Vandiver, V. (1996). *Maneuvering the maze of managed care: Skills for mental health practitioners*. New York: Free Press.

Council on Accreditation of Services to Families and Children. (1997). *1997 standards for behavioral health care services and community support and education services* (U.S. ed.). New York: Author.

Emenhiser, D., Barker, R., & DeWoody, M. (1995). *Managed care: An agency guide to surviving and thriving*. Washington, DC: Child Welfare League of America.

Feild, T. (1996). Managed care and child welfare: Will it work? *Public Welfare, 54*(3), 4–10.

Furman, R. (2010). *Social work practice with men at risk*. New York: Columbia University Press.

Galambos, C. (1999). Resolving ethical conflicts in a managed care environment. *Health & Social Work, 24*(3), 191–197.

Gelman, S. R. (1995). Boards of directors. In R. L. Edwards (Ed.-in-chief), *Encyclopedia of social work* (19th ed., pp. 305–312). Washington, DC: NASW Press.

Gibelman, M. (1995). Purchasing social services. In R. L. Edwards (Ed.-in-chief), *Encyclopedia of social work* (19th ed., pp. 1998–2007). Washington, DC: NASW Press.

Gibelman, M. (1998). Theory, practice, and experience in the purchase of services. In M. Gibelman & H. W. Demone, Jr. (Eds.), *The privatization of human services: Policy and practice issues* (pp. 1–51). New York: Springer.

Gibelman, M., & Gelman, S. R. (1999). Safeguarding the nonprofit agency: The role of the board of directors in risk management. *Journal of Residential Treatment for Children and Youth, 16*(4), 19–37.

Gibelman, M., Gelman, S.R., & Pollack, D. (1997). The credibility of nonprofit boards: A view from the 1990s. *Administration in Social Work, 21*(2), 29–40.

Gibelman, M., & Whiting, L. (1999). Negotiating and contracting in a managed care environment: Considerations for practitioners. *Health & Social Work, 24*(3), 180–190.

Herman, R. D., & Renz, D. O. (1999). Theses on nonprofit organizational effectiveness. *Nonprofit and Voluntary Sector Quarterly, 28*(2), 107–126.

Kilborn, P. (1996, December 8). Welfare all over the map. *New York Times*, p. E3.

Lens, V. (2000). *Welfare reform and the media*. Unpublished Ph.D. dissertation. New York: Yeshiva University, Wurzweiler School of Social Work.

Lens, V., & Gibelman, M. (2000). Advocacy be not forsaken! Retrospective lessons from welfare reform. *Families in Society, 81*(6), 611–620.

Lewis, J.A., Packard, T. R., & Lewis, M. D. (2007). *Management of human service programs* (4th ed.). Belmont, CA: Brooks/Cole.

Martin, L. L. (2000). The environmental context of social welfare administration. In R. J. Patti (Ed.), *The handbook of social welfare management* (pp. 55–67). Thousand Oaks, CA: Sage Publications.

Martin, L. L., & Kettner, P. M. (1996). *Measuring the performance of human service programs*. Thousand Oaks, CA: Sage Publications.

Meezan, W., & McBeath, B. (2011). Moving toward performance-based, managed care contracting in child welfare: Perspectives on staffing, financial management, and information technology. *Administration in Social Work, 35*(2), 180–206.

Melkers, J., & Willoughby, K. (1998). The state of the states: Performance budgeting requirements in 47 out of 50 states. *Public Administration Review, 58*, 66–73.

Mitchell, C. G. (1998). Perceptions of empathy and client satisfaction with managed behavioral health care. *Social Work, 43*(5), 404–411.

Moss, S. (1995). *Purchasing managed care services for alcohol and other drug treatment.* Technical assistance publication series, No. 16, Vol. III. Publication No. (SMA) 95-3040. Rockville, MD: U.S. Department of Health and Human Services.

Mullen, E. J., & Magnabosco, J. L. (Eds.). (1997). *Outcome measurement in the human services: Cross-cutting issues and methods.* Washington, DC: NASW Press.

National Association of Social Workers. (1996, August 27). *Personal Responsibility and Work Opportunity Reconciliation Act of 1996: Summary of provisions.* Government Relations Update. Washington, DC: Author.

Petr, C. G., & Johnson, I. C. (1999). Privatization of foster care in Kansas: A cautionary tale. *Social Work, 44*(3), 263–267.

Poole, D. L., Davis, J. K., Reisman, J., & Nelson, J. E. (2001). Improving the quality of outcome evaluation plans. *Nonprofit Management & Leadership, 11*(4), 405–421.

Prigoff, A. (2000). *Economics for social workers: Social outcomes of economic globalization with strategies for community action.* Belmont, CA: Brooks/Cole.

Schmid, H. (2000). Agency-environment relations: Understanding task environments. In R. J. Patti (Ed.), *The handbook of social welfare management* (pp. 133–154). Thousand Oaks, CA: Sage Publications.

Shandra, J. M., Shircliff, E., & London, B. (2011). The International Monetary Fund, World Bank, and structural adjustment: A cross-national analysis of forest loss. *Social Science Research, 40*(1), 210–225.

Siskind, A. (1997). Agency mission, social work practice, and professional training in a managed care environment. *Smith College Studies in Social Work, 67*, 16–19.

Steen, J. A., & Duran, L. (2010). Attitudes toward privatization policy within the human service arena. *Journal of Policy Practice, 10*(1), 51–64.

Strom-Gottfried, K. (1998). Applying a conflict resolution framework to disputes in managed care. *Social Work, 43*(5), 393–401.

Super, D. A., Parrott, S., Steinmetz, S., & Mann, C. (1996, August 14). *The new welfare law.* Washington, DC: Center on Budget and Policy Priorities.

Tremper, C. (1994). Risk management. In R. D. Herman & Associates (Eds.), *The Jossey-Bass handbook of nonprofit leadership and management* (pp. 485–508). San Francisco: Jossey-Bass.

Weiner, M. E. (1990). *Human services management: Analysis and applications* (2nd ed.). Belmont, CA: Wadsworth.

Chapter 10

Internal Sources of Organizational Change

This chapter focuses on some of the internal situations that stimulate an organization to change. Examples include the departure of the chief executive officer, reorganization, downsizing or outsourcing of staff, budget shortfalls that affect the scope and breadth of programs, a changing client base, relocation of the agency's offices, and entering into arrangements with managed care companies. Change may also be initiated because of a purposeful process to improve agency programs and/or better respond to community needs. At the core of successful organizational adaptation is planning—anticipating change, having the procedures in place to implement change, and monitoring the change process in a way that provides ongoing feedback for further adaptations.

The organization's elected leadership (its board of directors) and management (the CEO and senior-level staff) are constantly looking for ways to make services more relevant to the needs of the community. Responsiveness to the community, operating efficiencies, and cost are among the internal concerns of an organization that motivate—and sometimes necessitate—organizational change.

Organizational change is both a process and an outcome. Process refers to the identification of the need for change and the actions taken to achieve it. Change, such as the decision to promote efficiency through the use of text messaging and database management systems, may span a relatively short period of time. Once the decision has been made, it can be acted on quickly; the appropriate equipment can be purchased, and staff can participate in one or two training sessions. Implementing other organizational changes may take a much longer period of time. For example, feedback from the community may indicate that the agency should consider instituting services for older adults. Consideration of a new program initiative, however, involves a thorough needs assessment, a cost analysis, exploration of potential funding sources, and a marketing plan, and agency priorities must be revisited. These activities may take a few months or even a few years.

Although a voicemail system may have some organizational impact, such as negative consumer feedback about there not being a real person to answer the phone and the depersonalization of this form of consumer-agency contact, it is unlikely that severe long-term consequences will result. On the other hand, the initiation of a range of services oriented to a population that had not earlier been a target of the agency's services significantly alters the composition of the agency's constituency. These services, in fact, may affect the ability of the organization to carry out its primary mission, as a shift in program priorities and the reallocation of resources may be involved. Depending, in part, on the pace of change—how quickly the organization puts in place a new program and to what extent it replaces rather than augments existing programs—transformation may be evolutionary or radical. In either event, ultimately, the organization's leadership may need to amend its mission so that its programs of service and its purpose are in alignment.

Thus, change is a matter of degree and kind. Change may be small or broadly based, short term or long term (Perlmutter & Gummer, 1994; Trivedi, Grebla, & Wright, 2011), depending on the degree of structural change involved and the impact on mission. An organization may opt to change its name—for example, from Ravenwood Mental Health Center to Community Services of Ravenwood County. If the change is in name alone, and it is felt that the new name more accurately reflects the image and purpose of the agency, then it is a change of rather small scale. If, however, the name change comes about due to the merger of two agencies or the transformation of the agency from a nonprofit to a for-profit entity, then the transformation is of much larger significance. Change—both large and small—has become a constant in the lives of organizations.

Management Turnover

Change at the top management level ushers in a period of uncertainty for most organizations. The uncertainty is accentuated when the departure of the CEO is abrupt and/or unexpected. In other instances, turnover is the norm. For example, in the public sector, the election of a new mayor or governor means that the agency chiefs are out of a job.

Under any circumstance, the departure of the CEO creates a vacuum in the organization. The board of directors of the nonprofit organization diverts its energies from policy making, planning, and fund-raising to finding a new CEO. In public and for-profit organizations, the search process may be less visible but nevertheless involves the time and energy of key players, such as elected officials or shareholders.

Uncertainty at the top can have a ripple effect throughout the organization, cause employees to feel insecure about their jobs, and heighten normal stress levels (Ginsberg, 1997b; Hernandez & Leslie, 2001). Staff reactions may range from feelings of uneasiness about who the replacement will be or even feelings of anger and betrayal about the exit of the former CEO. The scenario in box 10.1 illustrates some of the reactions that may be anticipated when a CEO departs.

BOX 10.1
The Departure of the CEO

When Mr. Phillips resigned from his position as CEO of a nonprofit nursing home, the agency was struggling. Mr. Phillips had been at the helm for only three years, and the board now sought a new leader who would be able to turn the agency around—and also one who would stick around.

The board was uncertain about the future direction and hired an outside firm to help conduct a thorough review of operations after Mr. Phillips left. Anxiety ran deep among employees. Underlying the anxiety was disappointment about Mr. Phillips's decision to leave (some staff even felt that they had been betrayed), concerns about who might take his place, and fear about what recommendations might be made by the outside firm that might affect their jobs.

The associate director, Ms. Greene, was appointed as interim CEO, and most staff were of the opinion that she should get the job. However, a search committee was appointed, and rumors about the board's desire to go outside the agency to find someone with stature in the nursing home industry abounded. It also became apparent that no decision would be made in the short term. The decision to appoint a search committee meant that the job would have to be advertised, resumes screened, and first and perhaps second or third interviews set up. Then, if someone other than Ms. Greene was selected, the new CEO would likely need to give notice at his or her current job. It looked like the period of uncertainty might last six or more months.

Sometimes there is an internal candidate who is recognized as the logical replacement. Ms. Greene had the backing of staff, but the search committee wanted to explore all options. Typically, human service organizations opt to open the search process to include external candidates; the search committee or those responsible for selection of the final candidate want to be sure that they are making the best possible choice for the organization.

Search processes vary in length. Often, the search process takes several months or even a year or more. Even if the time between the departure of one CEO and the start of a new CEO is relatively short, the interim period is one of uncertainty for all key stakeholders of the organization. The uncertainty itself may constitute a period of change for the organization. At a minimum, the interim period is one in which change is waiting to happen.

A New Boss

In the spring of 2000, the Child Welfare League of America (CWLA) hired a new executive director, Shay Bilchik, the eighth director in the eighty-year history of this national organization. In an interview, he was asked about his short-term and long-term goals for CWLA. He responded:

> In the short term, I want to look at our organizational structure, staffing patterns, and how we operate as a team within the organization. Are we as efficient as we can be? Are we staffed as we need to be? We're also continuing work on a strategic

plan—and the field will have input on that. Then, I want to take the information I receive during this first one hundred days and look at the long-term vision of the organization. It could be that it remains much the same as what it has been, because obviously we've done pretty well over the past eighty years. But it might also evolve in a way that allows us to create an even stronger national presence on our issues and a stronger ability to effectuate change. ("Shay Bilchik," 2000)

Mr. Bilchik expressed his intent to examine the organization to assess what it does well and what it might do better. A reexamination of agency priorities and operating modes is to be expected when there is a new CEO. The hiring of a new executive means a fresh perspective is brought to bear on how the organization accomplishes its mission. The new CEO is likely to have conceptions and preferences about how the organization should run and is usually given wide latitude by the governing body to implement changes, even if the old way of doing business had been quite successful. The case of Carl in box 10.2 illustrates some of the changes a new CEO may seek to institute.

BOX 10.2
Taking the Helm

When Carl was hired as the new CEO of a child and family mental health agency, he made it clear to the board that the first order of business was to talk with key stakeholders—community representatives, board members, and staff—to learn about and evaluate how the agency runs and the strengths and weaknesses associated with current operations. In negotiations before he accepted this new position, he had shared with the search committee and board of directors his belief that some reorganizing of staff and operations would probably be in order; this assumption on his part was based on the information already provided to him about the status of the agency.

True to his word, Carl spent the first month on the job meeting and talking with staff, board members, committee chairs, representatives of other community agencies, and funders about their perceptions of the agency and what worked well and not so well. At his first meeting with the board as CEO, Carl presented a summary of his findings. He then detailed the first steps in a plan to address some of the issues that had been identified in his fact-finding efforts. He presented a plan in stages, the first steps of which were relatively minor: to move staff offices around so that people in the same departments would be near each other. The second stage was more complex: a revised organizational chart that reflected a restructuring plan.

The director of clinical services had been with the agency for twenty years. In the proposed restructuring plan, this position was downgraded and a new position, chief operating officer, was created to oversee the various program areas. Traditionally, therapeutic services had been the major focus of agency services. However, there had been a gradual but steady decrease in the client population requesting and utilizing these services. In the restructuring plan, such services were placed on equal footing, in terms of people and financial resources, with services to older adults, job training services, and foster care services. Thus, the restructuring plan had far-reaching implications in regard to the staffing needs and patterns of the agency and program priorities. Ultimately, the very mission of the agency was subject to reexamination.

Change in top management can mean small or large changes for the organization in the months and years ahead. Change is a given, even if only in the personality of the new CEO, which influences the climate of the organization. A new CEO can be the precipitating factor for major structural, financial, and technological change as well, depending on the status of the organization at the time the new person comes on board. The opportunity to institute such changes is typically greatest when the CEO is expected to invigorate the agency and set a more energetic, change-oriented agenda. Opposition to change may be less intense during the initial months after the new CEO takes the helm.

Facing a Financial Crunch

When an organization faces a budget deficit, the CEO, in consultation with the board of directors (if the organization is a nonprofit agency) will examine all possible options. Options may include streamlining operations, cutting back or curtailing unprofitable programs, and reducing operating expenses. Cost cutting tends to occur in conjunction with expanded efforts to identify new sources of revenue.

Because personnel is the single largest budget category for most human service organizations, it is not uncommon for budget cuts to be made in this area. This may mean downsizing of staff. Agencies often face serious dilemmas during lean times. For instance, should the agency invest in needed infrastructure or business services (such as accounting or development) or in maintaining or increasing the number of direct service providers? When agencies must make these difficult choices, it is helpful for administrators to seek feedback from various constituents. Direct service workers often have a difficult time appreciating how difficult these decisions are, since they are confronted every day by the pressing needs of their clients.

Downsizing

In the 1970s and 1980s many industries were forced to downsize as an economic strategy and/or because of changing workforce needs (Pearlstein, 1993). During the 1980s, for example, there were substantial budget cuts in the area of human services. In this same time frame, the medical establishment experienced the impact of cost containment strategies. Sometimes entire divisions of agencies or institutions were eliminated, such as the social work departments of hospitals. Outplacement services were often offered to help employees deal with their emotions and provide practical help in locating new jobs. Those not downsized experienced their own share of anger and frustration, which affected morale. The need for outplacement services decreased in the 1990s due to the booming economy. Still, some organizations continued to offer outplacement services, and some firms extended their services to include career management (Ginsberg, 1997a). This trend has increased during the latest recession, with agencies and organizations downsizing even further in the name of being more "efficient." Employers have no legal obligation to provide downsized workers with a severance package, including outplacement services, unless the workers are covered by a bargaining agreement or another kind of contract, but they often do it voluntarily (Grimsley, 2000).

Contracting Out

Human service organizations have followed in the footsteps of corporate America in regard to a growing reliance on the use of part-time or temporary personnel. A variation on this theme concerns the selective contracting out or, as this phenomenon is also known, outsourcing of functions that the organization previously handled internally. Rather than hiring staff to perform certain tasks within the physical boundaries of the organization, the functions are instead performed off-site by people (or companies) contracted to provide a very specific service. Contracting out, then, is a variation of downsizing and serves to reduce direct personnel costs.

The types of organizational activities that may be contracted out are varied. For example, an organization that provides information to consumers about Medicare benefits may decide to contract out for the writing, production, and distribution of pamphlets rather than maintaining full- or part-time staff to fulfill this function. Payment is likely to be on a product basis rather than per hour. Similarly, public relations activities, such as preparing press releases about major organizational events (fund-raisers or initiation of new programs), may be outsourced. In fact, the entire fund-raising function of an agency may be contracted out.

In recent years, we have seen an increase in the number of for-profit and nonprofit concerns that provide contracted services to augment those provided by other human service organizations (O'Neill, 2000; Stolt, Blomqvist, & Winblad, 2011). For example, a family service agency that provides family counseling services may not have the capacity to conduct case assessments that determine an older adult's ability to live independently. Rather than increasing the agency's capacity to provide a case assessment service, the organization may elect to contract out this function.

The decision to outsource agency functions may have unintended consequences. When specific functions are contracted out, such as assessments of the ability of an individual to live independently, the service performed is extremely limited. There may be no provisions for follow-up, other than preparation of a report, and continuity of services may be affected. When the assessment function is handled as part of a continuum of services, practitioners have the opportunity to make immediate recommendations to families about the type of service and levels of care their elderly family members need. Agencies may also be able to assist in making the care arrangements or ensuring that they are made through other agencies.

From the agency's point of view, outsourcing has appeal because direct personnel costs are reduced, while the organization is still able to carry out its obligations to its clients through outside sources. A mediating factor, however, is the possibility that the agency will lose in-house expertise. At some future time, the agency may need to redevelop its internal capabilities, which can involve significant expense.

Another potential consequence of either downsizing or contracting out is diminished employee loyalty to the organization, stemming from the perception that the agency no longer has a sense of loyalty to employees (Ginsberg, 1997a). Both scenarios—downsizing and contracting out—may create periods of disequilibrium within the organization with potential impact on practitioners and clients. On the other hand, these steps may help reduce the organization's costs in a way that protects its core programs.

Managed Care

The topic of managed care has emerged in several chapters of this book. It represents one of the more profound changes in the external environment of human service organizations in recent decades. The impact of managed care also affects the internal workings of the organization, as it influences who the organization serves, the methodologies employed in working with clients, the length of treatment, the level of expertise needed by practitioners employed by the agency, and the level and types of accountability demanded.

The decision of an organization to enter into arrangements with a managed care company to provide services to its enrolled consumers requires reorientation of staff to the new way of doing business. This reorientation goes beyond the client-worker relationship (length and type of service) and affects documentation and record-keeping requirements, billing and payment procedures, and methods for resolving disputes in regard to such matters as diagnosis and treatment needs and length and intensity of service (Gibelman & Whiting, 1999).

Managed care companies demand accurate accounts of the units of service provided, timely submission of paperwork, and compliance with reimbursement procedures. Staff members may not have the skills needed to fulfill these activities. To meet the requirements of managed care contracts, agencies may find it necessary to help staff retool through staff development and training to meet the new task demands.

Doing business with MCOs may also pose a new set of financial challenges to the human service organization. The MCO exercises the prerogative of negotiating payment terms with each provider and determining what, in its view, constitutes usual, customary, and reasonable payment for services. To obtain the managed care contract or get on the list of preferred providers, the organization must be willing to negotiate its fees. Most often, this means lowering fees in order to be competitive. By forcing providers to compete with each other for contracts, MCOs influence, if not control, the market. MCOs often offer capitation contracts, in which providers are paid a fixed and predetermined amount per client or caseload, no matter what the length of treatment. The agency is paid the same amount whether the social worker never sees the client, sees the client only a few times, or sees the client over a longer period

of time (Gibelman & Whiting, 1999). Financial necessity may push the organization to provide shorter-term services, even if client need suggests otherwise.

As MCOs become more significant players in mediating between clients
and human service organizations, we are likely to see them gain a stronger voice
in the internal professional and business practices of the agency. Beyond business operations and programs of service, there is an increasing array of ethical
concerns that confront the human service organization engaged in contracting
with MCOs, some of which are explored in this book.

A Changing Client Base

The majority of human service organizations are based in communities and seek
to serve the needs of that community. The needs of communities are not constant. Demographics change. Economic conditions change. Accordingly, community-based agencies need to periodically reexamine their mission and programs to ensure responsiveness to the needs of those within the community.
Planning and community collaboration are ongoing organizational processes to
design, reshape, and redefine existing programs and services to better meet the
needs of clients and potential consumers (Council on Accreditation, 1997).

One challenge to the community-based organization is when the client base
served by the organization ceases to need the service.

The introduction of new programs meets a number of organizational mandates, including responsiveness to the community and generating new sources
of revenue. As the case in box 10.3 suggests, demographic changes in a com-

---

BOX 10.3
Changing Community Needs

The Resettlement, Employment, and Guidance Center (REGC) has been serving
its community for over ten years. When the Center was established, this community
was largely composed of Orthodox Jews, and the agency's services were oriented to
meet the needs of this population. However, over the last decade, there has been a
significant change in the demographics of the community so that it is now composed
primarily of African American and Hispanic residents. Because of these shifting demographics, the client census and financial base of the agency have been hit hard.

REGC utilized a variety of mechanisms to determine its current and future place
in the community. First, the board established a committee to conduct a needs assessment of the community. Several staff members were asked to join this initiative
and lend their expertise. Second, the president of the board and the executive director made appointments to talk with key community leaders, including church and
elected officials. Other board members were asked to confer with nonprofit managers in neighborhoods that had undergone similar demographic changes to see how
they had responded.

(continued on next page)

These processes led to the identification of potential new programs to better serve the community, one of which was a forensic program for those who have been involved in the criminal justice system. The target population is multicultural and bilingual and includes those suffering from multiple social and psychological disorders, as well as those with a history of minor or major criminal offenses. This population is under the supervision of the criminal justice system—on parole, probation, or alternative sentencing. Many have a history of substance abuse and exhibit significant emotional, social, and cognitive problems.

At issue for the board of directors was how the proposed programs would be financed. Another concern was the impact of the proposed program direction on the mission of the agency. Also under consideration of the board was the impact of new program initiatives on the staffing needs of the agency. Existing staff would need to be retrained to carry out the new programs and/or new staff would need to be hired. Many of the existing staff were Orthodox Jews who were committed to carrying out the original purposes of the agency and serving the community as it had previously existed. Now, expertise would be needed in different areas, including hiring bilingual staff who had expertise in forensic services and in substance abuse treatment.

The funding problems were resolved more easily than personnel and mission concerns. The city and state public agencies were in short supply of agencies with which they could contract and were eager to enter into negotiations with REGC. Several board members were resistant to reorienting the agency services in this manner and threatened to resign from the board. Others felt that there was little choice; the agency either had to adapt and modify its program of services or cease operations altogether. Clearly, the changes proposed had major and long-term implications for REGC.

munity necessitate reexamination of the services traditionally offered and assessment of the needs of new community residents.

As this case also illustrates, reorientation of the agency's programs may meet with resistance from key players within the organization—management, board members, and staff. Some board members may feel that the mission of the organization has been compromised to the breaking point. Dissension within the board means the potential loss of some members. This does not mean that changes should not be initiated. However, consequences should be anticipated.

Staff may not be happy about these changes. Social workers, for example, who may have both a preference for and expertise in working within the Orthodox Jewish community may find themselves out of a job or needing to develop new skills to work with different populations who have different types of problems. Staff, understandably, fear that their jobs may be in jeopardy. At a minimum, as an organization revisits its programs, staff are likely to feel insecure and uncertain about their future.

Some organizations may assist their employees in coping with change through staff development and training to prepare staff to assume new roles. Several studies have shown that employees are more receptive to change when they receive training in the new procedures, programs, and services (Kreitner

& Kinicki, 1995). Unions may provide assistance to their members in dealing with change by negotiating for their interests with management. Staff, too, may take matters into their own hands by advocating on their own behalf or on behalf of their clients, forming alliances with staff of other organizations around areas of common concern, or providing informal emotional and practical support in coping with change.

Relocation

Relocation may be motivated by several factors. An agency may seek to purchase a building of its own rather than rent, or the agency may seek to find a cheaper rental. An agency may also want to relocate when it believes that a new location will better position it—physically—to serve its target population. In the scenario in box 10.4, the relocation was motivated by the opportunity to purchase a building.

BOX 10.4
A Nonprofit Buys a Building

Baywood Family Services, a multiservice agency serving a largely white, middle-class community, had been in operation for twenty years. It was located in the town center of a large county located adjacent to a major metropolitan area. Through the generosity of a benefactor, the agency received a bequest that was earmarked to assist in the purchase of a building.

The board of directors was thrilled about this opportunity and, in collaboration with the agency's CEO, began to investigate real estate options. After several months of visits to various properties by members of the committee assigned to look at real estate, the board voted to bid on a building located in a neighboring town. The building was located on a main street, was accessible to public transportation, and, because of its size, offered the possibility that unused space could be rented out, which would cover a portion of the monthly mortgage and overhead costs. All signs were "go," and the building was purchased.

After a year in the new building, the CEO brought to the attention of the board the fact that the client census was down—the agency was serving a significantly lower number of people than it had a year ago. Board members speculated about why this might be the case. Consideration was given to the impact of the move on the client population, and some assumptions were reexamined. For example, in discussing the relocation before the fact, the board had thought that clients from the town in which the agency was originally located would have no trouble getting to the new location. What they had not done, however, was ask clients whether they would be willing to travel to the next town or, more generally, how the move might affect them.

(continued on next page)

> With hindsight, the board also questioned some of its other assumptions. For example, although the building was located on a busy street, the neighborhood was considered to be less safe than the locale of the rental site, and clients were reluctant to come to the agency for evening appointments. Access of the new building to public transportation, initially seen as an advantage, was found to be, at best, a neutral point, because most clients in the suburban area had cars. Finally, and perhaps most important, the agency had not carefully explored the needs of the potential client population in its new neighborhood or assessed the competition the agency might experience from other service providers located in the new community. Thus, despite the time and effort expended in exploring the best possible real estate option, the agency neglected to consider all the implications of its relocation.

As this case illustrates, an agency's relocation can have a number of unanticipated consequences. The focus on finding the best facility was shortsighted. The move was motivated primarily by the opportunity to buy a building. Although the agency carefully considered its real estate options, it failed to thoroughly assess the consequences of the move in regard to its client population or the needs of the community in which it would now be located. Thus, the planning process was incomplete.

Planning Processes

A key factor in an organization's ability to respond effectively to external or internal change stimuli lies in its ability to anticipate change demands. For an organization to exercise control, it must manage rather than be managed by change (Perlmutter & Gummer, 1994).

All organizations, if they are to survive, must engage in some type of planning activities, although these may vary significantly in terms of frequency, scope, and breadth. There are different types of planning processes. Short-term planning is focused on the immediate future; virtually all organizations engage in short-term planning through the process of developing annual program plans and budgets. Projecting program growth and expansion and the potential costs involved over a five-year period would be considered long-range planning. What is different in long-range planning is the time horizon.

Planning is the act of examining the future and deciding on certain actions to provide for the future. Strategic planning is the process of deciding on the goals of the organization and on the strategies to be used to achieve these goals (Elkin, 1987). It has also been defined as "a disciplined effort to produce fundamental decisions and actions that shape and guide what an organization (or other entity) is, what it does, and why it does it" (Bryson, 1988, p. 5). The process involves a number of steps, including development and/or clarification of the organization's mission and values and an assessment of the external and internal opportunities and threats confronting the organization. Thus, information is the basis on which strategic issues are identified and strategies are developed (Bryson, 1994). Analogous to the casework relationship, organizational change is predicated on a thorough assessment of the situation, which forms the basis for diagnosis and, ultimately, the change intervention.

Strategic planning is not an annual activity; it occurs less frequently than other types of planning activities. This is primarily because strategic planning, by definition, is a more intensive, long-range process that involves time and money. Typically, an organization will engage in this process every five years. Although all levels of the organization may be involved in the process to some degree, decisions are made at the very highest levels. However, as we have already stated, it is important for organizations to take into account the voices and visions of their direct service staff, clients, and the community. Including these voices in the planning process can help agencies avoid developing strategic plans that are abstract and detached from the day-to-day realities of practice. The outcome of strategic planning is a set of long-range goals and strategies. In a strategic planning system, there is an orderly, gradual process of commitment to certain strategic alternatives (Mulhare, 1999).

Strategic planning is different from long-term planning, although the two may be interrelated. Strategic planning deals with strategizing about the future of the organization (the condition, position, or attributes the organization seeks to obtain) and how that future will be realized; the end result is agreement not only about goals, but also about goal attainment. Strategic planning is proactive: it involves not only anticipating the environmental forces that will affect the organization but also seeking to define and influence those forces.

In response to internal or external stimuli, the organization may decide to engage in either short- or long-term planning, or sometimes both. In the latter instance, short-term planning would constitute the immediate stopgap response to an unanticipated event, such as the departure of the CEO. In such an instance, a transition committee might be formed to address selection of an interim CEO, public relations issues, and staff morale. As discussed earlier, the departure of the CEO may also provide the stimulus for the organization to review its priorities and procedures. Long-term planning might be initiated to ensure the relevancy and quality of an agency's services or to project what its future position in the human services market might be and whether the agency is equipped to meet the demands of that market. The scope of the long-term planning initiative is less encompassing than that of strategic planning.

Whether short or long term, planning can be a response to or stimulus for organizational change. Because change of some type is an expected outcome of the planning process, decisions about the players involved in the planning effort are extremely important. The involvement of all key players in the organization's environment (e.g., community representatives, board members, clients, management, and staff) is essential, particularly in regard to the later "buy in" of these same key players to the decisions that culminate from the planning process (Perlmutter, 2000).

Obstacles to Change

When an organization fails to plan and thus anticipate and manage its future, environmental and internal issues are approached on an ad hoc basis, from one crisis situation to another (Anheier & Cunningham, 1994). Even when agencies use the best of planning processes that anticipate and address change, there are factors that may impede effective response to change stimuli. Organizations develop their own ways of doing business that may not always meet the requirements of efficiency and effectiveness. Each organization has a set of stakeholders—people who have a vested interest in maintaining the status quo. Interests may range from job security to fear of the uncertainty that results from the process of change. Inertia may also come into play, as designing and implementing change strategies involves initiative, energy, and risk (Perlmutter, 2000). Resistance may be based on professional judgments about good practice. For example, social workers may oppose new managed care rules that interfere with client treatment. Thus, there are inhibitors to change that vary in degree and intensity but pose challenges to the successful growth and adaptation of organizations.

In the next chapter, the role of social workers in initiating and promoting strategies to achieve constructive organizational change is explored.

Key Points

- ◆ Conditions internal to the organization, such as the departure of a CEO or a budget shortfall, may stimulate organizational change.
- ◆ Organizational change may range on a continuum from small to large scale.
- ◆ The process of change may span a short period (weeks or months) or a few years.
- ◆ The departure of a CEO almost always leads to a period of uncertainty and transition for the organization.
- ◆ Organizations that face unexpected budget deficits may need to consider downsizing, because personnel make up the largest category of expense.
- ◆ One means that is increasingly used to keep the organization's direct personnel costs down is contracting out or outsourcing specific functions.
- ◆ The requirements of managed care companies have stimulated the revamping of organizational procedures.
- ◆ Organizations may find that they need to retrain staff to meet the requirements of MCOs.
- ◆ To ensure responsiveness to the needs of the community, human service organizations need to periodically review the relevance of their programs of service.
- ◆ Demographic and economic changes are among the factors that influence community needs.

- ◆ Altering the programs of service in response to changing community needs may also involve reexamination of the organization's mission.
- ◆ Systematic planning processes help organizations to anticipate change demands.
- ◆ Short-term planning deals with an immediate agenda, such as annual program planning and budgeting.
- ◆ Long-term planning is undertaken to address such core issues as the type, quality, or quantity of services vis-à-vis community need and/or long-range fund-raising strategies.
- ◆ Strategic planning addresses the future of the organization and how conditions, positions, or attributes can be attained; it is proactive rather than reactive.
- ◆ All key stakeholders should be involved in planning processes.
- ◆ Obstacles to change include vested interests and comfort level with the status quo.

Suggested Learning Activities and Discussion Questions

1. Talk to one of your more senior colleagues—either someone within your organization or a social worker employed elsewhere—about his or her recollections regarding the departure of a CEO. What were the circumstances surrounding the departure? What was the impact on the organization—staff responses, morale, organizational climate, funding, and services?
2. Suppose you are the CEO of an agency that has lost a major contract and is expecting a substantial budget shortfall. Provide three different realistic options that should be considered in deciding how to deal with the budget deficit.
3. Draw up a list of questions you would want senior management and the board of directors to consider in regard to a possible relocation. How would you propose that the answers to these questions be ascertained?
4. Provide examples of a short-term, long-term, and strategic planning process in which your agency has engaged. What motivated the planning initiative? What were the outcomes of the planning? Who was involved? If your agency has not engaged in these planning processes, identify situations in which planning would have been appropriate.

Recommended Readings

Bolman, L. E., & Deal, T. E. (2008). *Reframing organizations* (4th ed.). San Francisco: Jossey-Bass.

Cohen, R., & Cohen, J. (1999). *Chiseled in sand: Perspectives on change in human services organizations*. Pacific Grove, CA: Brooks/Cole.

Fetterman, D. M., Wandersman, A., & Kaftarian, S. J. (Eds.). (1995). *Empowerment evaluation: Knowledge and tools for self-assessment and accountability*. Newbury Park, CA: Sage Publications.

Harrison, M. I., & Shirom,A. (1998). *Organizational diagnosis and assessment: Bridging theory and practice*. Newbury Park, CA: Sage Publications.

Ingraham, P. W.,Thompson,J. R., & Sanders, R. P. (Eds.). (1995). *Transforming government*. San Francisco: Jossey-Bass.

Proehl, R.A. (2001). *Organizational change in the human services*.Thousand Oaks, CA: Sage Publications.

References

Anheier, H. K., & Cunningham, K. (1994). Internationalization of the nonprofit sector. In R. D. Herman & Associates (Eds.), *The Jossey-Bass handbook of nonprofit leadership and management* (pp. 100–116). San Francisco: Jossey-Bass.

Bryson, J. M. (1988). *Strategic planning for public and nonprofit organizations: A guide to strengthening and sustaining organizational achievement*. San Francisco: Jossey-Bass.

Bryson, J. M. (1994). Strategic planning and action planning for nonprofit organizations. In R. D. Herman & Associates (Eds.), *The Jossey-Bass handbook of nonprofit leadership and management* (pp. 154–183). San Francisco: Jossey-Bass.

Council on Accreditation of Services to Families and Children. (1997). *1997 standards for behavioral health care services and community support and education services* (U.S. ed.). New York: Author.

Elkin, R. (1987). Financial management. In A. Minahan (Ed.-in-chief), *Encyclopedia of social work* (18th ed., pp. 618–627). Silver Spring, MD: National Association of Social Workers.

Gibelman, M., & Whiting, L. (1999). Negotiating and contracting in a managed care environment: Considerations for practitioners. *Health & Social Work, 24*(3), 180–190.

Ginsberg, S. (1997a, June 22). From catapult to counseling: The downsizers' new deal. *Washington Post*, p. H4.

Ginsberg, S. (1997b, August 24). When departure produces uncertainty; chief executives are being replaced more frequently than before, causing anxiety among employees at all levels. *Washington Post*, p. H4.

Grimsley, K. D. (2000, March 22). Outsourced? Prepare to bargain. *Washington Post*, p. E1.

Hernandez, C. M., & Leslie, D. R. (2001). Charismatic leadership: The aftermath. *Nonprofit Management & Leadership, 11*(4), 493–497.

Kreitner, R., & Kinicki,A. (1995). *Organizational behavior*. Chicago: Richard D. Irwin.

Mulhare, E. M. (1999). Mindful of the future: Strategic planning ideology and the culture of nonprofit management. *Human Organization, 58*(3), 323–330.

O'Neill, J. V. (2000, October). Social workers risk running businesses. *NASW News*, p. 3.

Pearlstein, S. (1993, October 16). Layoffs become a lasting reality. *Washington Post*, pp. A1, A10.

Perlmutter, F. D. (2000). Initiating and implementing change. In R. J. Patti (Ed.), *The handbook of social welfare management* (pp. 445–457). Thousand Oaks, CA: Sage Publications.

Perlmutter, F. D., & Gummer, B. (1994). Managing organizational transformations. In R. D. Herman & Associates (Eds.), *The Jossey-Bass handbook of nonprofit leadership and management* (pp. 227–246). San Francisco: Jossey-Bass.

"Shay Bilchik." (2000, May). *Children's Voice*, pp. 16–19.

Stolt, R., Blomqvist, P., & Winblad, U. (2011). Privatization of social services: Quality differences in Swedish elderly care. *Social Science and Medicine, 72*(4), 560–567.

Trivedi,A. N., Grebla, R. C., & Wright, S. M. (2011). Despite improved quality of care in the Veterans Affairs Health System, racial disparity persists for important clinical outcomes. *Health Affairs, 30*(8), 1430–1438.

Chapter 11

Coping with Change

Previous chapters have sought to familiarize readers with how human service organizations operate, why they are the way they are, and how external and internal events and circumstances result in the need for ongoing and continuous adaptation and change. Many challenges are posed by the organizational context of practice. Some may be beyond the control of management, the board, and staff, such as when the federal government enacts far-reaching budget cuts in the health and human services. However, many of the external and internal forces that influence the organizational context of work can be mediated.

In this chapter, the potential contributions of the staff of human service organizations to facilitate organizational adaptation and change are explored. Several practice principles that may be adapted by social workers to promote and facilitate organizational change, including the strengths perspective, advocacy, and empowerment, are highlighted. A contract is not renewed, the boss quits, the caseloads increase, or a foundation requests a fiscal review of a grant-funded program. What do you do?

The Strengths Perspective

The strengths perspective, as applied to practice, is an about-face from the historical focus of the helping professions on pathology, problems, deficits, disorders, and illness and, concomitantly, diagnoses, labels, and medication. The strengths perspective looks to the power of people to overcome and surmount adversity (Rapp, 1998; Saleebey, 1999). This concept can be applied to addressing the challenges that arise for practitioners within their organizational setting of practice.

The vocabulary associated with the strengths perspective includes competence, membership, empowerment, vision, assets, growth, potential, and responsibility (Compton, Galaway, & Cournoyer, 2005; Rapp, 1998; Saleebey, 1999). These are positive words that help create a mind-set in which improvement in how we function within organizations and how organizations function to help people is possible. Compton et al. (2005) provide a concise explanation of the principles underlying the strengths perspective. These principles can be adapted and applied to organizations in the following ways:

- ◆ Every organization has strengths, assets, and resources. Every social worker employed in the organization, similarly, has strengths, assets, and resources to contribute to the well-being of the organization and, thus, to the ability to provide effective services with positive client outcomes.

- Like individuals, organizations can be assessed, diagnosed, and "treated."
- Organizations may be dysfunctional in some or even many respects. However, rather than giving up on the organization, board members (as applicable), managers, and practitioners can work together to devise strategies to improve organizational functioning.
- Organizations, like people, desire to remain in existence—to be preserved. There are many stakeholders who feel this way about the organization—the community, clients, employees, and board members.
- The ability of the organization to adapt and change in positive directions is unknown and cannot be determined until change strategies are devised and implemented.
- Viewing the organization as "terminal" (so problematic that nothing can help it) will ensure that this is the case.
- No matter what the identified problems are within the organization, there are also actual or potential assets and resources.
- The strengths, resources, and capacities of organizations (and the people who work within them) can be summoned to better meet the needs of the people served and to accomplish the organization's mission.
- Problems can be turned into possibilities. (Pp. 16–17)

Several theories and perspectives from the organizational literature are similar to the strengths perspective and offer powerful insight into working in organizations. As Raelin (2006) observed,

> There is a growing fascination in this new century with collaborative models of decision making and especially with collaborative leadership. The reason seems to be an appreciation for the need to unblock the capacity for all people to contribute. Rather than rely on a coterie of subordinates to await their marching orders from detached bosses, organizations need to empower anyone who is capable and who has the willingness to assume leadership. (P. 152)

Empowerment

The strengths perspective is closely associated with the concept of empowerment. Power is defined by Barker (1999) as the possession of resources that enable an individual to do something independently or to exercise influence and control over others. Empowerment refers to seizing, gaining, or granting power to an individual or individuals who heretofore have not been in a power position. When one is empowered, one is able to choose among alternatives, influence decision making, and exercise control over events (Clifton & Dahms, 1993). Empowerment has also been described as the collective effect of leadership, manifest, in part, when people feel significant and that what they are doing is important (Bennis, 1989).

Some commentators cite powerlessness as the cause of many of the psychosocial problems experienced by people today (Van Den Tillaart, Kurtz, &

Cash, 2009). Etzioni (1991), for example, voiced concern about the large segments of citizens in contemporary industrial societies who "feel powerless and excluded, and are uninformed about the societal and political processes which govern their lives" (p. 177). Empowerment is the process of overcoming the condition of powerlessness.

Various social movements have embraced the concept of empowerment. The War on Poverty is an important example of societal intervention to overcome alienation through empowerment using such means as maximum participation of groups in the sociopolitical processes and decision making affecting them. The feminist movement has embraced the concept of empowerment, as have AIDS activists (Haney, 1988). These activists have made sure that empowering clients is part of the continuing dialogue (Icard & Schilling, 1992; Wachter, 1992). Power is seen as an enabling force that is noncoercive and oriented to liberating the strength of victimized or disenfranchised groups (DiNitto & McNeece, 2008; Strawn, 1994). Within professional social work practice, empowerment has also been emphasized as an essential tool to enable clients to focus on strengths rather than deficits (Lee, 2001; Mondros & Wilson, 1994; Simon, 1994). Research on the provision of health services to the elderly found that patients who feel a sense of control over their own care and treatment experience better physical health (Levine & Greenlick, 1991). Family empowerment has been identified as a strategy, along with the development of social support networks, to reduce the level and extent of chronic neglect of children (DiLeonardi, 1993; Hegar & Hunzeker, 1988).

The strengths perspective provides the framework by which empowerment may be realized. The same principles that social workers use to facilitate empowerment among individuals, groups, and communities can be applied and used by social workers practicing in an organizational setting. When employees focus on their capacities to suggest and implement strategies to address problems within the organization and are clear about the goals they wish to achieve, change becomes possible. This change may be oriented to policies and procedures affecting workers, clients, or both. Change may also be oriented toward the climate and conditions of work within their organization.

Hollinger-Smith and Ortigara (2004) observed that research on staff empowerment in nursing has found the following factors important to the development of empowerment: commitment to and trust in the organization, autonomy, participation in organizational decision making, job satisfaction, and leadership style. Several of these factors have been explored previously yet warrant further exploration. The expression of the value of professional autonomy within organizations is complex and difficult. Social workers are trained to operate as autonomous workers who use their professional skills, knowledge, values, and practice wisdom to provide services to their clients (Goldstein. 1990). Yet the day-to-day realities of organizational life may challenge autonomy. Supervisors and organizations must find ways to value the perspectives of diverse groups of social workers, each of whom possesses a different set of skills and preferred methods and theories. By doing so, organizations can help maximize their own resources and capacities.

Empowerment suggests a state of mind, an energy, and a readiness to take action. It involves the assumption of power or authority, whether bequeathed by others or acquired. Empowerment also suggests an enabling orientation (Rees, 1997). Once empowered, people are able to utilize their knowledge and skills to achieve desired ends. Such skills include needs assessment, program planning, advocacy, grant writing, fund-raising, mediating, brokering, and community organizing, all of which can be employed to influence both internal and external conditions. Even though social workers possess these skills, their use to promote the cause of the organization, its mission and goals, and its personnel involves a conceptual reorientation of practice principles. The use of social workers' skills to influence events reinforces power and influence, the end result of empowerment.

Social workers practicing within an organizational setting have choices: they can complain about conditions that adversely affect their work with clients, working conditions, or morale. Alternatively, they can choose to exert some influence over the course of events that influence the work environment. The importance of mind-set toward one's role within the organization is evident in the two scenarios in boxes 11.1 and 11.2.

BOX 11.1
It's Not Our Problem

The CEO called a staff meeting to inform staff that the outcome of a major fund-raising campaign had been disappointing and that revenues from a mail solicitation and fund-raising dinner were far below projections. The CEO informed staff that the board's fund development committee was carefully reviewing what went wrong in order to avoid repeating the same mistakes in the future. However, in the interim, revised budget projections suggested that there would be a cash flow problem in a matter of months. Some type of immediate action was necessary to avoid the possibility of program retrenchment and even staff layoffs. The CEO asked staff for their ideas about how this problem could be addressed.

This news was greeted with silence. The CEO waited expectantly. She prodded: "Put yourself in the place of the board, the clients, me—what would you do? As staff, what role might you play?" The CEO had a clear notion of what she wanted to come out of the meeting—motivation and commitment among staff manifest and a willingness to spend some time searching for new funding sources or writing grant proposals. This didn't happen.

A few staff members finally spoke up. "How could the board and CEO have allowed this to happen?" Staff were busy—they already had too much work. How could they be expected to do more? Fund-raising was the responsibility of the board, not the staff.

(continued on next page)

The CEO was frustrated. She reminded those attending the meeting about the unexpected bequest that the agency received two years ago. At that time, staff had been consulted about how the funds might best be put to use. There had been substantial enthusiasm and many suggestions for initiation of new programs and expansion of others. Staff had also volunteered their thoughts on improvements to the building. Now that the tables were turned and staff were expected to help solve a problem, they did not feel that it was their problem.

BOX 11.2
Brainstorming Strategies

The CEO called a staff meeting to inform staff that the outcome of a major fund-raising campaign had been disappointing and that revenues from a mail solicitation and fund-raising dinner were far below projections. The CEO informed staff that the board's fund development committee was carefully reviewing what went wrong in order to avoid repeating the same mistakes in the future. However, in the interim, revised budget projections suggested that there would be a cash flow problem in a matter of months. Some type of immediate action was necessary to avoid the possibility of program retrenchment and even staff layoffs. The CEO asked staff for their ideas about how this problem could be addressed.

The initial reaction was one of stunned silence. Then a few questions were asked—exactly what was the size of the expected budget shortfall? How much time was there before the situation would be considered a crisis? What was the board doing?

After the CEO responded—straightforwardly—to these questions, staff began to brainstorm. Lucy, a senior clinical social worker, offered to review all requests for proposals that had been received in the office in the last few weeks to see if there were any to which the agency might respond. Monica, a supervisor, offered to work with the board's resource development committee to explore ways to develop a more diversified and secure funding base. Louise, a program manager, signed up to work with the CEO and, as needed, the budget and finance committee, to look at the organization's programs and identify those that were not producing revenue; the initial thought was that some of these programs might be put on hiatus until they could be properly subsidized. Staff were in general agreement that the purchase of long-awaited computer equipment could be put on hold until the financial situation was more positive.

The heightened energy in the room as ideas were proposed was palpable. The CEO indicated that she would propose that the entire board, many of whom were well connected in the business community, engage in face-to-face fund-raising with their associates to seek contributions. Perhaps a "challenge" program could be set up, with each board member responsible for soliciting contributions of $25,000. At the conclusion of the meeting, the general sentiment was that the following weeks and months would require the active participation of the board and staff.

As these two scenarios suggest, when faced with an identical situation, different individuals and groups respond in very different ways. Many factors account for these different responses: past history, morale within the organization, level of commitment, education, experience of the staff, and the CEO's leadership ability. In the first scenario, professional staff understood the situation confronting the organization but considered problem solving to be someone else's job. This is often a symptom of low morale and low commitment to the organization. Staff are passive, feeling themselves to be victims of forces over which they have no control. The passivity translates to an unwillingness to assume any responsibility for their own future, their clients, or the organization. Staff, in this instance, acquiesce to and perpetuate their state of powerlessness.

In the second scenario, staff rose to the occasion. The situation was the same, only the responses were significantly different. In both cases, staff were encouraged to seize authority and influence. However, only in the second instance did they accept the use of power. They evidenced an identification with and commitment to the organization and considered themselves to be stakeholders with responsibility for the organization's future. Participation in problem solving was viewed by staff as a given, and they were eager to offer suggestions and work with other stakeholders to help the organization surmount the hurdles confronting it. The organization's problems were not the responsibility of others but the responsibility of everyone. There was concern for the future, not casting blame about how the situation arose.

In reality, efforts to involve staff in problem solving may produce mixed results. Some staff simply have a greater commitment to the organization than others and a broader perception of their role and responsibilities. Under the best of circumstances, employee commitment and loyalty are difficult to achieve and maintain. This is particularly the case when the job market is such that employees can opt to go elsewhere rather than work to improve situations related to their current job. Managers must cultivate employee loyalty (Rhodes, 1989), which involves leading by example, encouraging and facilitating staff participation, acknowledging and rewarding such participation, and maintaining ongoing systems of communication.

Loyalty can be encouraged by a climate in which employees feel valued and empowered. Although management may have the most influence on setting the tone, working style, and climate of the organization, it is not a one-way street. Staff, too, have a responsibility to contribute their knowledge, skills, time, and energy to organizational problem solving. The more positive the organizational climate, the more willing staff are to contribute and to see their work within the organization as part of a team effort. Improving the organizational environment involves an orientation to possibilities, goals, solutions, and strengths.

Directing Power Resources

Staff empowerment is essential for mobilizing to address organizational issues and problems or to initiate planned change that will improve conditions for staff, clients, and the organization.The foundation for empowerment of staff can come from a collective sense of purpose or from the leadership and influence of a few key players within the organization.When staff constitute a cohesive group and are acculturated to teamwork, the potential for employee initiative is enhanced (Byron, 1985). Enthusiasm can be contagious, just as low morale can be.

Power resources may be personal, collective, or institutional. Personal power resources include intelligence, self-confidence, courage, and motivation. Collective resources may include cohesiveness, loyalty, and talent. Institutional power may include leadership, access to resources and information, authority, and continuity.

Organizations have deeply entrenched interests and ways of doing business. Resistance to change is to be expected. However, we know from personal and professional experience that suggestions or requests are likely to be received more enthusiastically when they are stated positively, backed by hard facts, and realistic within the context of the specific agency setting.A litany of complaints about what is wrong is less likely to be warmly received than a statement of a problem backed by data and with suggestions about how the problem might be solved. Transparency, and the perception of it, is essential to healthy organizational change.

Compton et al. (2005) advise that the change process is difficult for many clients: "But as they decide and act, as they identify multiple strategies for achieving outcomes, they are encouraged to put their assets, resources, and resiliences to work" (p. 22).The organization can be considered analogous to the client.The same process of creating possibilities for change by identifying strategies and bolstering resources applies. Perhaps the critical thing to consider is that transparency should be the most important value and guiding principle.

Small-Scale Change

The values and normative behavior that derive from the organization's culture and climate exert pressure on workers to behave in certain conforming ways (Glisson, 2000). Depending on the organizational environment, efforts to institute small changes in incremental stages may be more effective than taking on large-scale initiatives.The incremental approach takes into account and reflects the difficulty of overcoming the comfort of the familiar and the tendency of the organization's members to protect and perpetuate the status quo.

Large-scale change is frequently motivated by change in the external environment or significant internal situations, such as a budget crisis, challenges to the organization's standing in the community, or a purposeful decision to change the organization's mission. Small-scale change, on the other hand, may be motivated by the desire or recognized need to improve the response time to client inquiries, initiate a more efficient intake system, or reorganize task assignments to better reflect practitioners' areas of expertise. Unlike large-scale change, which involves the board and top management in decision making, smaller changes may be instituted under the authority of middle managers.

A focus on short-term change has the added advantage of enhancing the likelihood of timely and concrete results. Short-term goals, such as modifying intake procedures so that clients are seen more quickly and are thus more likely to begin and continue in service, can be achieved in a relatively short time frame—say a year. The achievement of this goal may increase the willingness of staff to go on to the next change venue or even to initiate the next change. Instituting these changes tests the agency's ability to be flexible and responsive in the ongoing quest to improve operations and, thereby, services (Perlmutter, 2000).

Employee Input

Sometimes organizations are very receptive to receiving employee suggestions. A prime example is the suggestion box that can be found in many settings, through which employees are encouraged to communicate their ideas about how operations, climate, or other factors affecting the work of the organization can be improved. The suggestion box can provide a place for staff to make anonymous suggestions without risk. Some organizations have computerized suggestion boxes. Although contributors are not anonymous, rewards, such as a bonus, extra day off, or gift, are offered when the suggestion is adopted (Ginsberg, 1998). The rationale is that staff are in the best position to know what processes or systems need to be improved and have a different perspective than managers about how improvements can be made. While suggestion boxes can be beneficial, it is important for agencies to create various mechanisms to get the input of their human service workers. Taking into consideration the opinions of line-level workers makes them feel empowered, which can prevent burnout and other problems. One method that has been found useful is periodic brainstorming sessions that bring together workers from different levels of the organization to explore potential solutions to various problems and concerns. It is important for social workers to take advantage of opportunities to participate in the management and leadership of their programs. Teamwork and collaboration are important methods for distributing power and can be important to the provision of quality services to clients (Drinka & Clark, 2000; Grumbach & Bodenheimer, 2004).

Whether it is a suggestion box or access to management, the common denominator is a system of communication between management and staff that works. Whether formal or informal, the two-way flow of communication is essential. Staff must feel that management cares about their values, perceptions, and assessments.

Collaboration

Collaboration—actualized through teamwork—is a major factor that can affect the success of the change effort. Teamwork is a straightforward concept—it involves a group of people working together as a unit. It has become increasingly common for managers, supervisors, and direct service staff in many organizations to lead or work in teams to problem solve, coordinate, improve quality, and achieve high levels of consumer satisfaction. It is one means of getting things done (Rees, 1997).

Teamwork is predicated on clear directives and purposes. Creating and charging a team to "look into different computer software" is far different from directing the team to "identify three software packages that will handle this nonprofit agency's financial management and client case record-keeping needs and provide cost and training details on each."The former charge will leave the team floundering to define a purpose that may not reflect the real agenda, whereas the latter provides specific guidelines.

It is not a given that a group of professionals will be able to work effectively together. Studies of teamwork in the organizational setting reveal mixed results, ranging from substantial productivity to ineffectiveness, and show that the most important factors associated with the success of a team approach are how the teams are managed and whether the organization provides them the support they need ("Why Some Teams Succeed," 2000).

The ingredients for a successful team include an open organizational culture with easy access to task-relevant information and to senior management. The team must perceive that it has the authority to make decisions about how to reach its goals based on a clearly established set of objectives.The very act, by management, of encouraging the use of teams suggests an orientation to delegating power downward so that decisions can be made and strategies can be implemented with the commitment and involvement of those who must make them work (Rees, 1997). Good group work skills can also be a factor in the success of teams. Lamentably, group work skills have become less of a focus than they have been historically (Ephross, 2005). It is important for human service workers to develop the ability to take various roles within groups. Good group work skills, such as being empathic, empowering others, drawing connections between different constituents, and validating others, are essential in facilitating teamwork (Toseland & Rivas, 2005). Social workers should encourage their supervisors to use some of their supervision time to work on group facilitation and teamwork skills.

Teams have the advantage of sharing the work that needs to be done and infusing the process with creativity and the talents of members of the team. A team can build and maintain both spirit and momentum in a dynamic process that is results oriented.

Persuading through Hard Facts

Not all stakeholders within an organization will recognize an issue or problem that needs to be addressed. Even if there is consensus that a problem exists, agreement may not extend to the definition of the problem, its causes, or its consequences. Practitioners can play an important role in problem identification by utilizing their data collection and research skills. Fact finding is the beginning point for identifying the problem and defining its scope and impact.

Assessing the Situation

The conceptual base of the strengths perspective and the strategies associated with empowerment suggest a beginning point for the social work practitioner seeking to effect change within the organization. In work with clients, practitioners begin with an assessment of the situation. The same first step holds true when the "client" is the organization. The practitioner seeks to engage with the organization's representatives—usually the supervisor or unit director, or even, as appropriate, the executive director—around an area of mutual interest or concern. Collaboration in the assessment process gives all stakeholders an opportunity for input. It is during this time that the agenda is focused on exploring the discrepancies between how the organization functions—what it does and how well it does it—and expectations of what it should be doing and the outcomes it should be achieving.

Assessment of the problem—its cause, scope, and impact—is the precursor for developing an action plan. Hard facts are persuasive. There are many ways to collect, record, and analyze information in the course of a regular workday. How many clients have complained that they cannot manage or dislike using the voicemail system? What factors account for a decrease in the client census? In the first instance—the voicemail system—it is easy to collect data simply by jotting down the number of times this issue is raised and the type of experience reported by clients. In regard to a decrease in the client census, a survey of clients who have dropped out of a program might be undertaken. Frontline social workers can count the number of people coming to soup kitchens and the number who are turned away from shelters because they are filled. This information can be provided to decision makers. Social workers can also vocalize the human impacts of fiscal cutbacks or the frustrations experienced by families who get the runaround from an agency to which they have come for help.

The needs assessment process can be undertaken by an individual within the organization, but this is both unusual and less effective than a team approach. The involvement of the entire staff in this exploration process allows for the articulation of different perspectives and eventual clarity and consensus about the areas of organizational functioning that can be improved. This process also includes identifying what works well (organizational strengths), as well as what doesn't work so well (areas of dysfunction).

Next Steps

Identifying the problem is the first step of a multistage process. There is no one formula for how a change process can be initiated and completed. In general, however, the elements of the process include those delineated in box 11.3.

BOX 11.3
Elements of the Change Process

- ◆ Define the problem (one outcome of the needs assessment).
- ◆ Define the desired future state—how things should look when the change process is completed.
- ◆ Identify the level and degree of change required to move from the current state to the desired state.
- ◆ Identify the supporters of change and their influence and those who have a stake in maintaining the status quo.
- ◆ Consider the organization's culture and how the culture supports or inhibits change.
- ◆ Define the people and financial, programmatic, and procedural resources of the organization that must be garnered to achieve change.
- ◆ Evaluate the choices involved for bringing about change.
- ◆ Plan and implement the action steps necessary to achieve change.
- ◆ Manage the transition.
- ◆ Monitor, evaluate, and stabilize the change.

*Source:*Adapted from Mink, Esterhuysen, Mink, & Owen (1993).

Some of these stages in the change process may be undertaken concurrently. The sequencing of steps in the process is also subject to variation—depending on the nature of the change initiative. When the component tasks are divided and delegated to subgroups of teams, the work may be accomplished more efficiently and may utilize the expertise and talents of different staff. Clearly, another advantage lies in the involvement of many staff members in the process; their stake in the change efforts rises exponentially. Teams may need to be formed at different stages of the process.

The Importance of Outcomes

Among the changes affecting the work of the organization is the increased demand for accountability, as discussed in chapter 9. In the face of increasing demands for accountability and quality improvement, organizations are required to demonstrate the effectiveness of the services they provide (Auslander, 1996). This external demand on the organization translates into internal demands made on practitioners.

In today's environment, human service organizations need to reorient their focus from "doing" to "doing with what results?" It is not just a matter of answering this question for funders or board members. The organization must be able to determine how well it is achieving its mission. Social workers, too, want to know if what they do makes a difference.

The measurement of outcomes involves planning and implementing systematic evaluation processes. The information needed to measure outcomes must be clearly articulated from the outset, and appropriate methods to obtain such data identified.

While it is important to keep outcomes in mind, it is also important to remember that the way human service managers and leaders go about their business is important to the culture of an organization (Chen, Kirkman, Kanfer, Allen, & Rosen, 2007). For instance, when community members and paraprofessional workers are part of the process of deciding on appropriate outcomes and selecting good sources of information and measures, the process has a positive influence on organizational change. This attention to process, in conjunction with working toward the achievement of goals, is extremely important for human service workers to remember. How we treat others is always as important as the work that we do (Furman & Collins, 2005). Empowerment and collaboration should be deeply embedded in all our activities as human service workers.

Sources of Information

Deciding what data to collect, how often, from whom, and how is a complex process. Relevant factors include the scope of the agency's programs and the nature of the demands on the organization to produce certain types of outcome data. There is no "one size fits all" model. However, there is some consensus about how to get information, as shown in box 11.4.

BOX 11.4
Getting the Information You Need

- ◆ Information gathering should make use of a number of different methods, including self-administered surveys, interviews, standardized questionnaires, and focus groups.
- ◆ Information should be gathered from multiple sources, such as clients, direct service practitioners, board members, and potential users of services, such as community residents.
- ◆ In addition to outcome data, information should be collected about who is served and what services are provided.
- ◆ Information about the services of other community organizations should be collected in order to identify potential overlap or duplication of services and to provide potential linkages to other service providers to augment the services an agency provides.
- ◆ Interpretation of results should include multiple stakeholders within the organization.
- ◆ Those within the organization who are expected to use the outcome information should be trained to understand the uses and limits of outcome measures.
- ◆ Collecting information for its own sake is not productive; outcome data should be incorporated into a plan to improve organizational processes.

Source: Adapted from Epstein, Hernandez, & Manderscheid (1996).

The measurement of outcomes is predicated on clearly articulated organizational goals and objectives. Outcomes are the measurable conditions that denote how and to what extent program or service objectives have been achieved. The outcome to be measured, in many instances, is the flip side of the objective. For example, if the objective is to achieve the goals in the individual's service plan within a specified time frame, then the outcome to be measured is twofold: (1) whether and to what extent the service plan goals have been achieved and (2) whether they have been achieved within the specified time frame. The assessment of outcomes, in this case, may also seek to identify what barriers may have prevented achievement of some or all of the goals delineated in the service plan.

Types of Measurements

A number of means may be used by the organization to measure outcomes. These range from standardized assessment tools administered at defined intervals and at case closing to exit interviews, consumer satisfaction surveys, and collateral interviews with other agencies involved in the case, such as job training programs.

Virtually all outcome measures involve collection of data relevant to the objective. Data collection occurs both at a single point in time, such as at the time of service termination, or at time intervals, for example, every six months. Measures of outcomes of an individual case provide important information with which to assess progress toward the specific goals set forth in the service plan, such as whether and to what extent a client has successfully completed a job training program, secured employment, overcome symptoms of depression, or ceased to use drugs or alcohol.

Analysis of aggregate data, on the other hand, provides an overview of the results of specific types of interventions or programs of service and permits the identification of themes and trends that assist in long-range planning to better meet the needs of the clients. Issues of concern here are the quality of care provided, responsiveness of services to the needs of the population being served, and consumer satisfaction with services.

The information derived from the measurement of outcomes is a major source of input into potential organizational change, as it helps to identify issues and problems, such as discrepancies between service goals and the outcomes achieved. Outcome measures can provide the essential information for organizational innovation and improvement. Such innovations span the gamut of organizational concerns—structure, finances, leadership, staff, interorganizational relationships, programs, target populations, and services.

Key Points

- ◆ Practice principles used by practitioners in their work with clients, such as the strengths perspective, empowerment, and advocacy, can be adapted to promote and facilitate organizational growth and change.

♦ Empowerment involves a proactive mind-set, an energy, and a readiness to take action.

♦ Attitude is an important dimension in whether and to what extent staff involve themselves in organizational problem solving.

♦ When the initiative comes from staff, proposals for incremental change are less likely to meet with resistance from management than are more broad-based proposals.

♦ Small-scale changes may lead to rapid and visible results, which reinforce staff empowerment.

♦ A two-way flow of communication between managers and staff is essential to address organizational concerns effectively.

♦ When staff are cohesive and are used to working collaboratively in teams, they are more likely to assume responsibility and initiative for organizational problem solving.

♦ Successful teamwork is based on clear purpose and direction.

♦ Problem assessment is the basis for constructing an action plan for change.

♦ Documentation of the outcomes of services is an essential part of accountability.

♦ Measuring outcomes requires clearly stated program and/or service objectives, and these objectives must be measurable.

Suggested Learning Activities and Discussion Questions

1. Consider your organization as the client. Prepare a list of five organizational assets or strengths. Then prepare a second list identifying five areas of organizational functioning in need of improvement.

2. Of the five areas listed as in need of improvement, which of these do you consider to be amenable to change? Why?

3. It's time to initiate some new programs that are more responsive to the needs of the community served. Identify the types of information you will need and the strategies you might use to gather information to support a new program initiative.

4. Assume that you have been assigned to work on a team to plan a new program of service for your organization. Outline the sequential steps you think would be involved in this effort. How would you address the allocation of tasks, time frames for completion of tasks, and accountability?

5. You are given the responsibility to develop a plan to measure the outcomes of a new program designed to promote intergenerational linkages between senior citizens and adolescents. Outline a plan for completing this task.

Recommended Readings

Gordon, A. L. (1999). *Outcome initiatives in child welfare.* Washington, DC: Child Welfare League of America Press.

Harrison, M. I., & Shirom, A. (1998). *Organizational diagnosis and assessment: Bridging theory and practice.* Newbury Park, CA: Sage Publications.

Kinzey, R. E. (2000). *Using public relations strategies to promote your nonprofit organization*. Binghamton, NY: Haworth Press.

Lee, J. (2001). *The empowerment approach to social work practice* (2nd ed.). New York: Columbia University Press.

Morley, E., Vinson, E., & Hatry, H. (2001). *Outcome measurement in nonprofit organizations: Current practices and recommendations.* Washington, DC: Independent Sector and the Urban Institute.

Parker, G., McAdams, J., & Zielinski, D. (2000). *Rewarding teams: Lessons from the trenches.* San Francisco: Jossey-Bass.

Saleebey, D. (1999). *The strengths perspective in social work practice* (3rd ed.). New York: Longman.

References

Auslander, G. K. (1996). Outcome evaluation in host organizations: A research agenda. *Administration in Social Work, 20*(2), 15–20.

Barker, R. L. (1999). *Social work dictionary* (4th ed.). Washington, DC: NASW Press.

Bennis, W. (1989). *Why leaders can't lead.* San Francisco: Jossey-Bass.

Byron, W. J. (1985). The workplace as a community: Promoting employee satisfaction. *Health Progress, 66*(2), 24–27.

Chen, G., Kirkman, B. L., Kanfer, R., Allen, D., & Rosen, B. (2007). A multilevel study of leadership, empowerment, and performance teams. *Journal of Applied Psychology, 92*(2), 331–346.

Clifton, R. L., & Dahms, A. M. (1993). *Grassroots organizations* (2nd ed.). Prospect Heights, IL: Waveland Press.

Compton, B. R., Galaway, B., & Cournoyer, B. R. (2005). *Social work processes* (7th ed.). Belmont, CA: Brooks/Cole.

DiLeonardi, J. W. (1993). Families in poverty and chronic neglect of children. *Families in Society, 74,* 557–562.

DiNitto, D. M., & McNeece, C. A. (2008). *Social work: Issues and opportunities in a challenging profession* (3rd ed.). Chicago: Lyceum Books.

Drinka, T., & Clark, P. G. (2000). *Health care teamwork: Interdisciplinary practice and teaching.* Westport, CT: Auburn House.

Ephross, P. H. (2005). Social work with groups: Practice principles. In G. L. Greif & P. H. Ephross (Eds.), *Group work with populations at risk* (2nd ed., pp. 1–14). New York: Oxford University Press.

Epstein, I., Hernandez, M., & Manderscheid, R. (1996, October 22). *Outcome roundtable for child services: Conference paper.* Tampa: University of South Florida.

Etzioni, A. (1991). *A responsive society.* San Francisco: Jossey-Bass.

Furman, R., & Collins, K. (2005). Culturally sensitive practices and crisis management: Social constructionism as an integrative model. *Journal of Police Crisis Negotiation, 5*(2), 47–57.

Ginsberg, S. (1998, January 25). High marks for the lowly suggestion box; it's making a comeback as better-educated and managerial-minded employees find that feedback can bring rewards. *Washington Post,* p. H4.

Glisson, C. (2000). Organizational climate and culture. In R. J. Patti (Ed.), *The handbook of social welfare management* (pp. 195–218). Thousand Oaks, CA: Sage Publications.

Goldstein, H. (1990). The limits and art of understanding in social work practice. *Families in Society, 80*(4), 385–395.

Grumbach, K., & Bodenheimer, T. (2004). Can healthcare teams improve primary care practice? *Journal of the American Medical Association, 291*, 1246-1251.

Haney, P. (1988). Providing empowerment to the person with AIDS. *Social Work, 33*, 251-253.

Hegar, R. L., & Hunzeker, J. M. (1988). Moving toward empowerment-based practice in public child welfare. *Social Work, 33*, 499-502.

Hollinger-Smith, L., & Ortigara, A. (2004). Long-term care workforce. *Alzheimer's Care Quarterly, 5*(1), 60-71.

Icard, L. D., & Schilling, R. F. (1992). Preventing AIDS among black gay men and black gay and heterosexual male intravenous drug users. *Social Work, 37*, 440-445.

Lee, J. A. B. (2001). *The empowerment approach to social work practice* (2nd ed.). New York: Columbia University Press.

Levine, S., & Greenlick, M. (1991). Removing barriers to the empowerment of the elderly in health programs. *Gerontologist, 31*, 581-582.

Mink, O. G., Esterhuysen, P. W., Mink, B. P., & Owen, K. W. (1993). *Change at work: A comprehensive management process for transforming organizations.* San Francisco: Jossey-Bass.

Mondros, J. B., & Wilson, S. M. (1994). *Organizing for power and empowerment.* New York: Columbia University Press.

Perlmutter, F. D. (2000). Initiating and implementing change. In R. J. Patti (Ed.), *The handbook of social welfare management* (pp. 445-457). Thousand Oaks, CA: Sage Publications.

Raelin, J. (2006). Does action learning promote collaborative leadership? *Academy of Management Learning & Education, 5*(2), 152-168.

Rapp, C. A. (1998). *The strengths model: Case management with people suffering from severe and persistent mental illness.* New York: Oxford University Press.

Rees, F. (1997). *Teamwork from start to finish.* San Francisco: Jossey-Bass.

Rhodes, D. W. (1989). Employee loyalty is an attainable goal. *Journal of Business Strategy, 10*(6), 51-53.

Saleebey, D. (Ed.). (1999). *The strengths perspective in social work practice* (3rd ed.). New York: Longman.

Simon, B. L. (1994). *The empowerment tradition in American social work.* New York: Columbia University Press.

Strawn, C. (1994). Beyond the buzz word: Empowerment in community outreach and education. *Journal of Applied Behavioral Science, 30*, 159-174.

Toseland, R. W., & Rivas, R. F. (2005). *An introduction to group practice* (5th ed.). Boston: Allyn & Bacon.

Van Den Tillaart, S., Kurtz, D., & Cash, P. (2009). Powerlessness, marginalized identity, and silencing of health concerns: Voiced realities of women living with mental diagnosis. *International Journal of Mental Health Nursing, 18*(3), 153-163.

Wachter, R. M. (1992, January 9). AIDS, activism, and the politics of health. *New England Journal of Medicine, 326*, 128-133.

"Why some teams succeed (and so many don't)." (2000, October). *Harvard Management Update*, pp. 7-9.

Chapter 12

Lending a Helping Hand: Making Your Organization Better

In this chapter, we turn our attention to how our knowledge about organizations can be put to use to enhance professional practice, quality services, and the work environment. The individual choices practitioners face in addressing the challenges of employment in an organizational setting are explored, including when and under what circumstances to take action, how mentoring can positively influence one's attitude and position within the organization, and deciding when it is time to move on.

Selecting Your Battles

Taking on the organization about every matter of concern is not likely to be a successful strategy in dealing with the stresses and strains of agency-based practice. Tackling each and every source of dissatisfaction related to the workplace is neither realistic nor productive. Thus, individually and collectively, practitioners must determine which organizational issues are high priority and, of these, which are most amenable to change.

There are several reasons why you cannot act on every concern you have or turn every concern that you feel is major into a battle. First, you will quickly burn out if you expend too much energy fighting every perceived injustice or problem. Second, there may be good reasons for why things are the way they are; we cannot be right all of the time. Third, spending too much time on organizational dynamics actually means we are spending less time working with clients. Last, people who complain about multiple issues more frequently than their colleagues are quickly discounted and are not taken seriously when they do bring up issues that truly need to be resolved. It is important to not be perceived as Chicken Little—make sure the sky is indeed falling before you suggest that it is.

It is important that you reflect upon the actual importance of the issue you are bringing up, the timing, and how you will be perceived. Being a reflective practitioner who is aware of how you are most likely to be perceived is a key aspect to being an effective change agent. Every social worker must develop the ability to know when and how to pick his or her battles.

When an issue is so important that you decide you need to take action, there are official lines of authority that need to be followed. If there is a workload problem, the first person to talk to is your supervisor. If a worker skips this step and goes directly to the program director, this may annoy or anger the supervisor, who has been passed over in the chain of command. The program director can be expected to route the practitioner back to the supervisor to ensure that the appropriate procedures are followed. At this point, the supervisor is likely to be less sympathetic to the complaint or issue.

It is important to cultivate relationships with those in the organization who command the respect of the majority of employees (Garthwait, 2011). This person may not be the CEO or another administrator. It may be a member of the support staff who knows how to get things done, where things are, and whom to approach about what. The assistance of informal leaders may facilitate resolution of some workplace problems, particularly at the interpersonal level.

Dealing with Difficult Colleagues

There are difficult people in every workplace: the clock watcher who does only what can be done within the set hours; the whiner; the gossiper; the constant complainer; the goof-off who takes two-hour lunches but signs out for only one hour; the space cadet who constantly misplaces case records and forgets to make a note of times for meetings and appointments, even with clients; the antagonist who is rude and unpleasant; the victim, who externalizes responsibility for his or her own deficiencies; and the worrier, who constantly frets about matters large and small. The list goes on.

Social workers have an ethical responsibility to their colleagues. The National Association of Social Workers (2008) *Code of Ethics* stipulates that:

> Social workers should treat colleagues with respect and should represent accurately and fairly the qualifications, views, and obligations of colleagues.
>
> Social workers should avoid unwarranted negative criticism of colleagues in communications with clients or with other professionals. Unwarranted negative criticism may include demeaning comments that refer to colleagues' level of competence or to individuals' attributes such as race, ethnicity, national origin, color, sex, sexual orientation, age, marital status, political belief, religion, and mental or physical disability. (P. 15)

The interpersonal aspects of the work environment are almost always complex and difficult (Bredemeier, 2001). At the same time, a spirit of collegiality and goodwill among the organization's employees makes for a pleasant environment. Such a spirit can be fostered through the individual and collective efforts of staff. On the individual level, one can avoid condoning and encouraging whining or gossiping by walking away from it. Gossip usually pertains to purely personal matters, such as the style of dress of another worker, who is getting a divorce, who is unpopular with whom. It is distinguished from professional banter relating to the work of the agency, such as who is getting promoted or hired and what new policies are being discussed. Such dialogue, although not always accurate, is not mean spirited. Gossip, on the other hand, pits one employee against another and can result in an unpleasant environment in which distrust can fester. Engaging in people bashing, even by being a bystander when it is occurring, may cause others to view you as unprofessional and untrustworthy (Garthwait, 2011).

It is easy to blame coworkers, the boss, the board, or the state of the world for the problems that beset an organization. Externalizing the problem tends to promote a passive stance; whatever is wrong is outside the control of staff. There is nowhere to go with blaming, except to feel powerless, the very antithesis of constructive organizational behavior. It is important to have good boundaries and a good understanding of what your "stuff" is and is not. You must also have a good understanding of what you can and cannot control. It is useful to remember the wisdom of twelve-step self-help programs when you confront agency problems—you should strive for the serenity to accept the things you cannot change, the courage to change the things you can, and the wisdom to know the difference.

The informal environment of an organization can be an important mediating factor in resolving small problems before they become systemic. This is especially true in day-to-day annoyances that gnaw at morale and make the workplace uncomfortable. The workplace can be improved if employees show concern and respect for coworkers. Relationships with colleagues are a potent influence on one's attitude toward the job. Positive relationships can make the difference, as demonstrated in the situation described in box 12.1.

BOX 12.1
Who's Been in the Refrigerator?

Michelle, a clinical social worker, has noticed that some really annoying incidents have been occurring at the mental health clinic where she has worked for two years. Chief among the annoyances is the refrigerator thief. Stealing from the refrigerator is something that just didn't used to happen.

The agency provides a refrigerator that is used by about thirty employees. Michelle likes half-and-half in her coffee. She has put a carton in the refrigerator with her name on it numerous times, only to come in the next day to find the carton nearly empty. Other items disappear even when labeled.

Michelle has become so angry that one day she purposely put spoiled milk in the container. Obviously someone went for it, because the next morning when she came to work, the container was in the trash.

Michelle's situation is an example of a common workplace issue that can serve as an irritant, adversely affecting collegial relationships and morale. Some of the problem-solving skills associated with social work practice can be applied to workplace situations such as that faced by Michelle.

Michelle has the option of acting on her own behalf. She can keep the cream in a thermos at her desk; she can hide the cream in the refrigerator by pouring it into a clean container that normally holds another liquid, such as vinegar; or she can post a sign on the refrigerator door in the hope that she can embarrass the guilty party into ceasing this behavior.

There are larger opportunities to influence the workplace that can be identified from this simple situation. This presents an opportunity to build esprit de corps. Surely Michelle is not the only victim of the refrigerator thief. Michelle might publicly raise the issue at a staff meeting and ask whether there is a better way to safeguard refrigerated items. Chances are good that other staff members will be eager to cooperate, and one source of workplace irritation can be eliminated.

Clearly, interpersonal issues among staff are not always resolvable on a collegial level. There may be times when the type of issue affecting staff relations demands the intervention of management. For example, if money disappears from people's wallets and it is clearly the work of an insider, then the seriousness of the situation calls for strong managerial intervention. In some cases, managers can promote problem resolution by participating with staff in discussions and decision making. Efforts to promote community in the workplace can provide personal satisfaction.

No Organization Is Perfect

Realistic expectations about the organizational setting of practice can be important in determining the degree to which work is personally fulfilling. Like people, organizations are complex. They need to be understood for what they are—a formal system designed to accomplish a specific purpose. Organizations differ in the extent to which their culture, climate, and processes facilitate or inhibit the accomplishment of these purposes.

The attitude a practitioner brings to the job is crucial in determining the fit between the practitioner and the organization. Similarly, how the practitioner relates to the organization, its management, colleagues, and clients affects the overall culture and climate, in what can be termed a cyclical and interconnected process. Enthusiasm, commitment, and a willingness to pitch in—the ingredients of empowerment—can reverberate from one staff person to the next, creating and reinforcing a more positive environment.

Social workers need to think "outside the box" about how the work of the organization can be made more effective. This involves a broad conception of one's role within the organization, initiative, and a willingness to apply what one knows about people and systems to one's own work environment. The perception that an issue or problem within the organization is the concern of others, not oneself, or that the issue is outside the purview of one's job creates a "do nothing" mind-set. In turn, this minimalist perception of one's role can breed discontent with and disengagement from the organization.

The *Code of Ethics* (National Association of Social Workers, 2008) sets forth the obligations of practitioners to the employing organization, as well as to colleagues. The ethical obligations detailed in the *Code* include working to improve the employing organizations' policies and procedures and the efficiency and effectiveness of services. The fulfillment of this obligation involves a commitment to the agency. This commitment is manifest in an attitude of collaboration and cooperation and an orientation to positive change. By contributing to the effectiveness of the organization, practitioners improve their ability to carry out their professional roles.

A central theme throughout this book has been that the expertise social workers bring to their work with clients can be applied to their own work within the organization. Examples of the knowledge and skills social workers can apply to organizational growth and development include advocacy, open communication, fact finding, needs assessment, evaluation, negotiating and mediating, and team problem solving. The perspective of practitioners about how the organization can be improved can help managers make the right decisions.

The boundaries of one's role within the organization are established not only by the organization but also by the aspirations and initiative of staff. Self-advocacy is one way to increase job satisfaction within the agency context, as the scenario in box 12.2 suggests.

BOX 12.2
Speak Up!

You want to try something new at work—you want more responsibility. Or you have been working at the agency for a couple of years and you think it's time for a raise. Or you think you're not getting credit for the work you've done. However, you don't know what to do about it. You teach your clients about empowerment, yet you fail to apply the same skills yourself.

When you're at a restaurant and you don't like the meal you've been served, you ask for the waiter to return it, right? If you buy something that doesn't fit, you take it back to the store and ask the salesperson for another size. But at work, you don't behave assertively, perhaps because you don't want your supervisor to think you're ungrateful, or pushy, or demanding, or whiny. But there are things you can do.

Prepare   You have to prepare yourself before you ask for a raise, added responsibility, or a different job assignment.

Get informed   Save yourself the embarrassment of asking for more money when the board minutes you just read indicate that your agency is running a large deficit. Don't ask for added responsibility until you know that your supervisor likes the work you do now.

(continued on next page)

> ***Talk to colleagues***   Find out what they think about your asking for more responsibility. Do they think your boss would go for it? What do your coworkers think of your idea?
>
> ***Rehearse***   Before you meet with your boss to discuss what you want, do a dress rehearsal with a friend. Practice what you want to say to your boss, and get your friend's feedback—do you sound whiny, powerful, confident? Then make an appointment—don't just drop in and chance catching your supervisor at a bad time, unless there is a stated open-door policy.
>
> ***Have realistic expectations***   Resistance should be expected. Be ready with answers to your supervisor's doubts. Anticipate the problems or questions you will be asked, and strategize about the answers.

Practitioners who wait for their supervisor to initiate discussions about job performance, expectations, or career opportunities within the organization may be missing possibilities (Joyce, 1999). Feedback about your performance and career development need not rest solely between you and your supervisor. Many organizations initiate mentoring programs to facilitate the socialization of new employees to the agency and to guide their career development.

Mentoring

Mentoring has been identified as a major factor in promoting a positive attitude and achieving success on the job. Mentoring has also been shown to provide the guidance and role modeling by which employees can develop career paths that reflect the commonly accepted indicators of success (position title, scope of responsibilities, salary, benefits) (Donovan, 1990; Murrell, Crosby, & Ely, 1999; Segal, 2000; Teixeira, 1999; Walsh & Borkowski, 1999).

The term *mentoring* has been used for a vast array of activities and attributes. Mentoring here refers to a process characterized by a cooperative and nurturing relationship between an experienced person and a less experienced person with the goal of helping the less experienced person develop in some specified capacity (Schlee, 2000). Usually, this relationship occurs between a senior staff person and a new staff member and may be focused on the adjustment of new practitioners to the organization and, later, on their career development within the setting (Jowers & Herr, 1990).

There is no one formula for successful mentoring. Because it occurs within the context of a relationship, the focus may be idiosyncratic to the people involved—the experience and background of the mentee, as well as the position within the organization held by the mentor. Box 12.3 details some of the benefits of mentoring for the social worker and for the organization.

If the organization does not have and is not able to initiate a formal mentoring program, find yourself a mentor anyway! Approach a colleague or manager

---

BOX 12.3
Benefits of Mentoring

Benefits for the social worker:

◆ Gains more knowledge about how the organization works, the informal and formal centers of power, the most efficient and effective ways to get work done, and "potholes" to be avoided
◆ Learns about the organization faster and more effectively
◆ Has a senior staff person monitor and provide feedback about his or her work
◆ Has a senior staff person advocate for his or her interests
◆ Gains skill and knowledge in developing and managing organizational and personal priorities
◆ Develops specific knowledge and skills through a tutorial arrangement
◆ Has access to a road map of the roles of, and relationships between, volunteers, management, and staff

Benefits for the organization:

◆ Provides faster and more efficient socialization of new staff to the agency
◆ Provides a mechanism by which to increase staff loyalty
◆ Provides new staff with information about career development opportunities within the agency
◆ Promotes morale and a positive work climate through a stronger informal organizational environment
◆ Augments the agency's formal orientation and in-service training
◆ Augments the normal supervisory processes of the agency
◆ Creates a more politically savvy and astute staff
◆ Develops a cadre of staff who may be motivated and prepared to assume management positions

---

in the organization who has been there awhile, knows the ropes, and is respected. Ask the person if he or she would be willing to be an informal mentor to you.

Professional Development

One of the best ways to prevent burnout is to work continuously on developing your personal capacities and professional skills. Social work is a profession in which we are the tool; as such, there is often a fine line between our personal issues and our professional work. When social workers realize their buttons are being pushed and that their work is bringing up painful emotional issues, it is important to find mechanisms for personal growth and change. Many social workers find counseling or therapy valuable. Not only does therapy allow human service workers a safe place to sort out how their personal histories affect their work, but they may develop an increased capacity for empathy.

Understanding what it feels like to be a client can help social workers understand just how hard the process of change actually is.

In addition to seeking help for personal issues and deficits, it is important for social workers to continue to develop their existing strengths. By working to develop areas of excellence, social workers simultaneously add value to their agencies, work toward the betterment of client services, and prepare themselves for the future. Starting a skills journal is an excellent way to work on developing your skills. A skills journal offers human service workers a place to write about their currents skills and explore ways in which they can increase and maximize these strengths. For instance, a human service worker who is a good writer might learn grant-writing skills. A social worker who is highly organized and good at developing treatment plans might work on getting involved in the long-term planning processes of his or her agency. Continuing to develop skills helps human service workers feel hopeful, excitement, and energized.

Self-Care

To be successful in your agency, you have to take good care of yourself. It is important for human service workers to take vacations that make them feel rested and rejuvenated. Agencies often do not give human service workers a great deal of time off from their jobs, typically two to four weeks a year. The work that we do is often taxing, and taking time off is important.

The idea of "mental health days" is a bit controversial. Different agencies have different policies about what constitutes a sick day. While it may stretch the strict guidelines of what is permitted by agency policy, at times it may be a good idea for social workers to take a day off for their own emotional well-being. For instance, if a human service worker experiences the loss of a relationship, he or she may not be able to attend to the needs of clients the following day. Of course, it is essential to remember the needs of our clients and our responsibilities as professionals. These responsibilities must be balanced with the need for self-care. An emotionally volatile worker is of little use to clients. While it is true that workers must learn to put on a happy face and go on, there are days when this is hard to do.

Looking toward Your Future

The emphasis throughout this book has been on the organization as viewed from the vantage point of the practitioner. Much of the literature about human service organizations is top down—viewing purposes, processes, and environment from the perspective of the organization's elected and appointed leadership. Viewing the organization from the perspective of the direct service worker can empower staff to understand and act more effectively to shape their work world. It is through empowerment that practitioners can become active players in their organization rather than passive recipients of decisions made by others.

The more knowledgeable staff are about how organizations function, the better positioned they are to identify and implement more effective ways to carry out the organization's work. Organizational effectiveness lends itself to and is a component of a positive work environment.

Career Decision Making

How do you know that it's time to leave? Conversely, how do you know when you should stay put? There is no one answer. Just as there are individual preferences involved in the selection of a job, as discussed in chapter 1, there are a variety of factors affecting the decision to stay or leave.

Some practitioners stay with their employing agency because it offers a comfortable environment. The nature of the work fits their interests. Others appreciate the philosophy of the current management, employee treatment, and work rewards. If you stay with your agency, you may be promoted at a younger age, allowed to try new things, and encouraged to take on bigger and better responsibilities (Joyce, 2000). Organizations that offer training, development, and advancement opportunities are likely to have a stable professional staff.

Data suggest, however, that it is unlikely that a practitioner will spend his or her career in one organization (Gibelman & Schervish, 1997). Career mobility in social work is the rule rather than the exception and may be motivated by a number of factors. The concept of lifetime employment in a single organization no longer exists in any sector of the labor market (Joyce, 2000).

Early in a worker's career, mobility may be afforded only by moving on to another organization. This is because many human service organizations are small, and career opportunities within them may be limited. Hierarchical movement— for example, from direct service to supervision or middle management—may not be possible within one's organization because these positions are few in number. Practitioners may decide that their current job in foster care or in adult day care may not be the area of practice they wish to pursue; their preference may lie in the field of health or mental health. In such instances, the practitioner may make a lateral move to an agency that offers the types of programs more in line with his or her current interests. Some practitioners may be motivated to leave by financial considerations. Changing jobs is often the best way to increase one's salary, particularly when the job market is favorable to employees.

Developing Skills for Your Agency and Yourself

As we have frequently asserted, all human service workers engage in leadership each and every day. Additionally, the vast majority of human service workers will find themselves at some point taking on formal management positions.

Therefore, it is essential that human service workers systematically develop their leadership skills. This not only prepares them for future administrative roles but increases the overall social capital and function of human service agencies. The more line-level workers who are able to increase their capacity for leadership, the more likely human service agencies will improve their overall function and adapt to changing contexts. Also, developing marketing skills makes one increasingly more marketable.

Leading through Difficult Times

As we have discussed, during the last several years the country has undergone an economic downturn the likes of which we have not seen since the Great Depression. For leaders and managers, times of global fiscal stress have profound implications for the type of skills they need. Many of these skills are the same as those discussed throughout the book, but they are highlighted and accentuated by the nature of the times. Other skills are ones that managers may not need as frequently. Difficult economic times, therefore, demand that leaders and workers alike develop new skills and continue to improve skills that are frequently important, but which take new importance during times of stress and crisis.

Line-Level Leadership Skills and Difficult Times

A theme in this book is the important contributions that line-level human service workers make toward the leadership of organizations. This is especially true during difficult times. When times are hard, it often feels as though your agency is falling apart. At times, these perceptions are exaggerated, yet sometimes they may be accurate. When it feels like an organization is falling apart, workers often engage in several types of destructive behavior: 1) competing with coworkers; 2) engaging in sabotage of administrator's actions; and 3) acting out behavior that the workers attribute to factors other than the real cause. It is important to watch for these three tendencies in your own behavior. During hard times, it is important to become more collaborative and increasingly invested in the well-being of others. So too, it is easy to blame leadership for the difficult state in which the agency finds itself, even when many of the factors that may have led to such conditions are beyond their control. It is important for workers to assess their own behavior and check out when they find themselves reacting more intensely than is typical.

Validating the Feelings of Others

When organizations are in crisis, one of the worst things one can do is deny the crisis. Putting on a happy face when Rome is burning is not useful. This does not mean that leaders should not be positive. Of course, we need to model centeredness and help establish a culture of hope. However, this should come

only after carefully and honestly acknowledging the actual losses and the potential risks. While people rarely want to hear bad news, and often take out their
distress on leaders who share it, organizational health depends on leaders being
transparent about what is occurring within an organization.

Taking Care of Self in Difficult Times

In several places in this book, you will notice that we stress the notion and
importance of self-care. During difficult times, human service workers and
those in various leadership positions are particularly vulnerable to stress. This
stress emanates, often, from the same set of events but manifests differently. For
example, line-level human service workers often are particularly concerned
about their own jobs, while leaders often feel stress over the potential impact
of their actions on the lives of others.

During difficult times, it is important to take stock of your skills and mar-
ketability. Identifying any skill deficits that you have and developing a plan to resolve them can help you move from a sense of vulnerability and defeat to empowerment. For example, one human service worker in a community-based
drug treatment program became extremely worried about losing her job during
the recession. She feared having to search for a new job, in part due to her poor
computer skills. She realized that her computer skill deficiencies would make
searching for a job difficult and also make her less employable. She approached
her supervisor about improving her skills. Her supervisor was more than happy
to allow her to work with one of the secretaries for a half hour a week on computer training. The supervisor also helped her improve her skills during their supervision. While the worker never lost her job, she gained new confidence in
her computer skills; the agency benefited by having a more efficient worker
who became faster and more consistent with her documentation.

Skill growth is not the only thing that human service workers must attend
to. Human service workers must always work at developing a more satisfying
and balanced personal life. Human service workers are the tools of their practice, and tools must be sharp and in good condition.

The Emotional Costs of Leadership

While being in a position of management or leadership can be a wonderful
source of meaning, there are often costs. The following example describes the
types of stresses that leaders often find themselves experiencing during difficult
times. When the director of a community mental health agency was asked to
step down, she was allowed to return to the position of mental health therapist,
which had been her original role in the agency for nearly a decade. After a national search, a new director, Chip, was hired. Chip quickly realized that the
agency was largely divided between those who were very strong supporters of

the former director and those who were not. For the first year, he worked hard at building bridges between the two groups. Things in the agency were going well. Client demand was high, and the agency was able to start a program geared toward serving military families. During Chip's second year, the country slipped into recession. State funding, which constituted nearly 50 percent of the overall budget, was quickly reduced by 20 percent. Chip was forced to come up with a rapid plan for laying off staff. He formed a committee to oversee the process and tried to communicate frequently with all levels of the organization. However, he soon observed the old divisions within the organization coming to the surface. Followers of the previous director soon appeared to be against him. They began leveling criticism toward him as being hierarchical and nonparticipatory, the same attributes that had led to the former director's demotion. As a result, Chip found himself feeling alone and isolated and overwhelmed by the sudden change of sentiment. He became very depressed and began looking for a position elsewhere.

Budgeting

While developing an understanding of the budgetary process is beyond the scope of this book, it is important for social workers to understand the budgets of their agencies. This applies not only to administrators but to agency staff as well. In fact, it is especially important during challenging economic times for administrators to help human service workers understand the nature of the budgetary process. During hard times, administrators often have to make difficult choices about how to spend scarce agency resources. By including workers in the budgetary process, administrators can improve buy-in of staff when organizational changes are required.

Budgets mean different things to different people. Accountant staff and fiscal personnel view budgets from a technical standpoint, while programmatic staff view them as determinants for how money is delivered to serve clients. On a very real level, the budget is a key means by which the values of an agency are actualized.

Moving On

Practitioners must consider and assess their career aspirations and the extent to which organizations provide the practice environment, learning milieu, and opportunities in which such aspirations can be realized. These are individual decisions, but decision making is aided considerably when you learn as much as you can about your organization—what it does, what it offers you, and what you can offer it. Understanding the organization allows you to appreciate the best of what it offers and gives you the ability to identify possibilities for the future (Cooperrider, Sorensen, Whitney, & Yaeger, 2000).

Staff and employing organizations engage in a reciprocal relationship. Some of the dimensions of this reciprocity are illustrated in box 12.4. Human service organizations are people dependent. In order to carry out its work, the organization is dependent on a staff of sufficient size and expertise. Although the organization holds the trump cards, in that it hires, assigns, promotes, rewards, and fires staff, the relationship between staff and the agency is still one of interdependence. The cost to the agency of recruiting and training new staff is high; it is in its best interests to retain good staff and to offer an environment that promotes such retention.

BOX 12.4
The Reciprocal Relationship

The organization offers you:
◆ A setting in which to practice your profession
◆ The sanction to carry out your work
◆ The clients with whom to work
◆ The financial resources necessary to provide services
◆ A salary and fringe benefits
◆ An office
◆ Supervision
◆ Feedback
◆ Staff development and training
◆ Career development opportunities
◆ Collegial relationships
◆ A learning environment
◆ The opportunity to fulfill your career aspirations

In turn, you offer the organization:
◆ Expertise
◆ Commitment
◆ Loyalty
◆ The knowledge and skills necessary to carry out the work of the organization

---

A Final Word

The only constant for human service organizations is change, both externally and internally produced. The world changed suddenly and dramatically on September 11, 2001, when the United States experienced the worst terrorist attack in the country's history. In the immediate aftermath, it was human service organizations that came forward to meet the crisis. The American Red Cross, the Salvation Army, United Way of America, school social workers, and other social workers contributed their services. Family service agencies reached out to their communities to offer crisis intervention and, for those who experienced loss of family or friends, grief counseling. Mental health professionals anticipate an overwhelming public occurrence of post-traumatic stress disorder. Human service organizations are responding throughout the country to what will clearly be a long-term need. What Hollinger-Smith and Ortigara (2004) note about nursing is true for all human services: "In the final analysis, nursing staff retention is about developing and maintaining *relationships, respecting* one another, and *recognizing* quality work" (p. 69). Human service workers, who are trained in developing and nurturing helping relationships, should be particularly skilled at these tasks. Regardless of one's role and function within an organization, human service workers can make a positive contribution to the organizational culture by keeping in mind the values and relational skills of our professions. No matter what the situation, we can show our coworkers, clients, and supervisors appreciation for who they are and what they do. We can play a role in creating organizational change through our actions and by respecting the strengths and worth of everyone we encounter.

Key Points

- ◆ The individual practitioner or group of practitioners should determine which aspects of organizational work they wish to change; not everything can be on the agenda.
- ◆ The appropriate chain of command should be followed in seeking an organizational response to an issue or problem.
- ◆ Informal centers of power and influence can be mobilized to address some workplace issues, particularly those of an interpersonal nature.
- ◆ The need to deal with difficult colleagues is a problem that emerges in all work environments.
- ◆ Collegial relationships can be a positive or negative influence on staff attitudes toward the job and the organization.
- ◆ The expertise of social workers in human relations and problem solving can be applied to the resolution of issues within the workplace.
- ◆ Realistic expectations about work in organizations are important determinants of the degree of personal satisfaction that may be derived.
- ◆ Professional ethics include an obligation to work toward the improvement of the organization.
- ◆ The fulfillment of this obligation involves a broad conception of one's role within the organization rather than a minimalist perspective.
- ◆ Mentoring can have an important influence on one's attitude and career development within the organization.
- ◆ Career mobility within social work tends to be associated with movement from one organization to another.
- ◆ The decision to stay or leave an organization is personal, and depends on the level of satisfaction one derives from the current employment setting and one's overall career aspirations.

Suggested Learning Activities and Discussion Questions

1. Identify a problem or issue related to your organization.
   - Prepare a statement of the issue or problem in concise and clear terms (who, what, where, when).
   - Provide background on the problem or issue.
   - Design a strategy that responds to and addresses the particular problem and the key players who need to be involved to correct the problem.
   - Justify the selection of this strategy over others in terms of such factors as cost, use of people resources, and potential impact. Identify the opposing viewpoints that might arise.
   - Discuss the obstacles/impediments to change that are pertinent to the specific organization and how these obstacles may be overcome.

2. One of your colleagues, Mary, is driving another, Susan, nuts. Mary's idea of teamwork is to drop something on Susan's desk and ask her to take care of it. For example, Mary was given the assignment by the CEO to construct an organizational table to accompany a grant proposal. She came to Susan's office to ask her opinion about how to go about this task. Susan offered a few suggestions. The next morning, Susan found a note on her chair from Mary asking that she go ahead with the construction of the organizational table because she knows so much about these things. Similar incidents have occurred in the past and, reluctantly, Susan has always pitched in. However, now she recognizes the pattern and is resentful. What might Susan do about this situation?

3. You're new to the organization. It's a large place—over 150 professionals on staff. You're used to a smaller, more intimate working environment. You feel lost; you're not sure what you're supposed to be doing first and whether what you have done is right. Your supervisor is not particularly good about giving you feedback. You really want this job; it offers career possibilities in a prestigious setting dedicated to providing family preservation and family reunification services. Consider three strategies you might employ to obtain the guidance and knowledge you need to survive and thrive within your organization.

Recommended Readings

Johnson, H. E. (1997). *Mentoring for exceptional performance*. Torrance, CA: Griffin.

Kadushin. A., & Harkness, D. (2002). *Supervision in social work* (4th ed.).. New York: Columbia University Press.

Peddy, S. (1999). *The art of mentoring: Lead, follow, and get out of the way*. Columbia, SC: Learning Connections.

Shea, G. F. (2001). *Mentoring: How to develop successful mentor behaviors* (3rd ed.). Menlo Park, CA: Crisp Publications.

Zachary, L. J. (2005). *The mentor's guide: Facilitating effective learning relationships* (2nd ed.). San Francisco: Jossey-Bass.

References

Bredemeier, K. (2001, July 9). Difficult decisions for difficult co-workers. *Washington Post*, p. E4.

Cooperrider, D., Sorensen, P. F., Whitney, D., & Yaeger, T. F. (2000). *Appreciative inquiry: Rethinking human organization toward a positive theory of change*. Champaign, IL: Stipes.

Donovan, J. (1990). The concept and role of mentor. *Nurse Education Today, 10*(4), 294–298.

Garthwait, C. (2011). *The social work practicum: A guide and workbook for students* (5th ed.). Boston, MA: Allyn and Bacon.

Gibelman, M., & Schervish, P. (1997). *Who we are: A second look*. Washington, DC: NASW Press.

Hollinger-Smith, L., & Ortigara, A. (2004). Changing culture: Creating a long-term impact for a quality long-term care workforce. *Alzheimer's Care Quarterly, 5*(1), 60–70.

Joyce, A. (1999, October 18). Career track: The right way to approach the boss. *Washington Post*, p. H4.

Joyce, A. (2000, March 20). Career track: Sit. Stay. What a smart worker! *Washington Post*, p. F31.

Jowers, L. T., & Herr, K. (1990). A review of literature on mentor-protégé relationships. *NLN Publications*, no. 15-2339, pp. 49–77.

Murrell, A. J., Crosby, F. J., & Ely, R. J. (1999). *Mentoring dilemmas: Developmental relationships within multicultural organizations*. Mahwah, NJ: Lawrence Erlbaum Associates.

National Association of Social Workers. (2008). *Code of ethics*. Washington, DC: Author.

Schlee, R. P. (2000). Mentoring and the professional development of business students. *Journal of Management Education, 24*(3), 322–337.

Segal, J. A. (2000). Mirror-image mentoring. *HR Magazine, 45*(3), 157–166.

Teixeira, R. (1999). The mentoring process: Beneficial to manager, employee, and organization. *Clinical Lab Management Review, 13*(5), 314–316.

Walsh, A. M., & Borkowski, S. C. (1999). Cross-gender mentoring and career development in the health care industry. *Health Care Management Review, 24*(3), 7–17.

Index

About the Authors

Rich Furman, MSW, PhD, is professor of social work at the University of Washington Tacoma, adjunct professor of women, gender and sexuality studies at the University of Washington Seattle, and adjunct professor of social work at the University of Pennsylvania. He was the 2011 recipient of the University of Washington Tacoma distinguished research award. Professor Furman has published ten books and more than a hundred scholarly articles and book chapters. His most recent books are *Social Work Practice with Men at Risk, Transnational Social Work Practice, Social Work Practice with Latinos: Key Issues and Emerging Themes, An Experiential Approach to Groupwork,* and *Practical Tips for Publishing Scholarly Articles.* His main areas of research are social work practice with transnational populations, men at risk and masculinities, and the use of the arts and humanities in social work practice, research, and education. He has conducted research, practiced, volunteered, and taught throughout Latin America and, recently, in Asia and Germany. His practice background includes ten years experience in direct practice and administration. A qualitative methodologist, he is dedicated to innovations in expressive and creative approaches to research.

Margaret Gibelman, DSW, was professor and director of the doctoral program at the Wurzweiler School of Social Work, Yeshiva University, in New York. Professor Gibelman worked in the human services as a clinician, supervisor, educator, and manager. She was executive director of the Lupus Foundation of America and the National Association of School Psychologists. She was also associate executive director of the Council on Social Work Education, the accrediting body for social work education programs in the United States, and served as a management consultant to the National Association of Social Workers and the Council on Accreditation for Services to Families and Children.